THE COLLECTED WRITINGS
OF MURRAY STEIN

VOLUME 3

GENERAL EDITORS

STEVEN BUSER

LEONARD CRUZ

TRANSFORMATIONS

MURRAY STEIN

CHIRON PUBLICATIONS • ASHEVILLE, NORTH CAROLINA

www.ChironPublications.com

Interior and cover design by Danijela Mijailovic
Printed primarily in the United States of America.

ISBN 9781630519414 paperback
ISBN 9781630519421 hardcover
ISBN 9781630519438 electronic
ISBN 9781630519445 limited edition paperback

Library of Congress Cataloging-in-Publication Data

Names: Stein, Murray, 1943- author.
Title: The collected writings of Murray Stein / Murray Stein ; general editors, Steven Buser, Leonard Cruz.
Description: Asheville : Chiron Publications, 2020- | Includes bibliographical references. | Summary: "Dr. Murray Stein's prolific career has produced a substantial body of writings, lectures, and interviews. His writings, captured in these volumes, span a wide domain of topics that include writings on Christianity, Individuation, Mid-life, the practice of Analytical Psychology, and topics in contemporary society. His deep understanding of Analytical Psychology is much more than an academic discourse, but rather a deeply personal study of Jung that spans nearly half a century. The unifying theme of the papers collected in this volume is the individuation process as outlined by C.G. Jung and adopted and extended by later generations of scholars and psychoanalysts working in the field of analytical psychology. Individuation is a major contribution to developmental psychology and encompasses the entire lifetime no matter its duration. The unique feature of this notion of human development is that it includes spiritual as well as psychosocial features. The essays in this volume explain and expand on Jung's fundamental contributions"— Provided by publisher.
Identifiers: LCCN 2020016256 (print) | LCCN 2020016257 (ebook) | ISBN 9781630517601 (paperback) | ISBN 9781630517618 (hardcover) | ISBN 9781630517625 (ebook)
Subjects: LCSH: Individuation (Psychology) | Jungian psychology.
Classification: LCC BF175.5.I53 S84 2020 (print) | LCC BF175.5.I53 (ebook) | DDC 150.19/54—dc23
LC record available at https://lccn.loc.gov/2020016256
LC ebook record available at https://lccn.loc.gov/2020016257

TABLE OF CONTENTS

TRANSFORMATION: EMERGENCE OF THE SELF[1]

> Even if the world changes as fast
> as the shapes of clouds,
> all perfected things at last
> fall back to the very old.
> Rilke, *The Sonnets to Orpheus* 1, 19

INTRODUCTION

On April 14, 1912, the luxury liner Titanic sank on her maiden voyage across the North Atlantic, signaling the end of an era and the beginning of the Age of Anxiety. Also, in 1912, as the world unknowingly moved toward the abyss of the first worldwide war in history, the term "transformation" forcefully entered European discourse, an oracular cry of things to come. It sounded in the German words *Wandlungen* and *Verwandlung*.

1912 was the year when Carl Gustav Jung finished his book, *Wandlungen und Symbole der Libido* (*Transformations and Symbols of Libido*). This work described the transformational nature of the

---

[1] This work was originally delivered as the Fay Lectures at Texas A & M University in 1998 and published by the Texas A & M University Press. It has been somewhat modified for this edition.

1

human psyche and announced Jung's differences with Freud, thus setting him on his own course of personal transformation that would result in the Red Book, Liber Novus and the founding of analytical psychology. Transformation was a concept that set the young psychologist irrevocably at odds with his erstwhile teacher and guide.

In the same year, Rainer Maria Rilke heard a line of poetry in the wind, and it touched off what would become his most important poetical work, the *Duino Elegies*, a ten-part poem that revolves around transformation as the essential human task, as humankind's most important, sacred duty. It is a poem about endings and new beginnings.

And Franz Kafka, in a brief few weeks at the close of 1912, composed his famous story of transformation, "*Die Verwandlung*" ("Metamorphosis"), a story of degradation in which a human being is changed into a giant insect.

These three authors were all speakers and writers of German, although none of them was a citizen of Germany. One was a genius psychologist and two were brilliant writers (both of whom died at a relatively early age). One was a Protestant, one a Catholic, and one a Jew. All three were psychically gifted and psychologically sensitive to the point of fragility. All struck a common chord that would resound through the coming decades and resonates with us to this day: the theme of transformation. Kafka and Rilke would die before the Second World War broke out; Jung would live long enough to reflect upon its devastation and to create, in that late period of his life, a great work dedicated to the idea of psychological transformation, *Mysterium Coniunctionis*. Today we can see that all three were unintentional prophets and that collectively they provided another name for our times: The Age of Transformation.

The twentieth century was gripped by transformation processes on a global scale. Massive social, cultural, and political upheavals erased many of the most prized and familiar features of traditional cultures throughout the world—in Western Europe, the

Americas, Russia, Asia, Africa—as two world wars, exploding technologies, and competing ideologies swept over humanity in wave upon wave of destabilizing energy. This process of global transformation was represented in the arts, exploited by business enterprises, and studied by the social sciences. Its effect upon individuals and upon groups large and small was to deepen and to expand into every dimension of human life and endeavor. Liminality was the constant theme of the times. Nothing seemed stable and secure. As the poet, William Butler Yeats, foresaw in his famous poem, "The Second Coming," the center did not hold.

As we move through a new and still very much unsettled century, the momentum of change appears to be increasing as we live through the passage from one Platonic Year consisting of twenty centuries - the Age of Pisces - into the beginning of another, the Age of Aquarius. History and myth converge at moments like this, and fears and expectations reach a crescendo. As the rapidity of change accelerates, it becomes evident that no one, not even the people best equipped with the fastest computer networks, can register its myriad details, let alone control them. The times rush ahead like a swollen river, our destination directed by forces beyond our understanding, never mind our control.

This is the social and cultural backdrop against which this present work on psychological transformation has been written. Although I will be focusing primarily on the individual person and on how transformative processes move the individual toward a specific and remarkably precise goal of self-realization, I recognize that there is a profound dynamic interplay between social and political collectives and the individual psyche. Individuals are transforming in large numbers just as (perhaps partly because) large collectives are transforming. I do not want to say, as some sociologists and political thinkers have, that individuals merely mirror collective movements and opinions and are nothing but miniature embodiments of social process and structure. On the other hand, it is also misguided to think that individuals are isolated from the larger social settings in which they live, or that psychologically they are structured only by personal experiences in family and kinship groups and by intrapsychic and genetic factors. At this point in our understanding of the formation of psychic structure, it seems most correct to hold that individuals and their destinies are the complex outcome of many combined forces, some of them genetic, others intrapsychic and interpersonal, and still others cultural and collective.

By collective, I have in mind not only the specific social, political, and cultural influences that press in upon people, but also the world historical and archetypal shapers and movers that create the Zeitgeist of a whole era. The spirit that shapes a historical era also plays a role in shaping the attitudes and visions of individuals. One can argue interminably about Zeitgeist and how to represent it for a specific age. It is particularly difficult to identify and describe when one is speaking of one's own time. It is easier to study fourteenth-century Italy and speak of "the Renaissance" or the eighteenth-century in Europe and name it "the Enlightenment." When it comes to the present, however, things become thickly muddled, not only because this period is so close to us but also because the whole world is implicated in the spirit of this particular age. It is hard to grasp something so large and complex.

For the first time in history, wars have been carried out on a global level. The spirit of Ares has swept over all the inhabited continents and drawn them into heated martial engagement with one another. Out of these conflicts have come deep exchanges on all levels, however. When wars end, enemies may become allies or at least trading partners. In my own lifetime, this has happened first with Germany and Japan, then with Vietnam and with the countries of the former Soviet Union. War brides mix genetic lines in their wombs, and cultures that were opposed on the battlefield end up engaging in commerce and exchanging ideas about religion and the arts. At another stage, conflicts re-emerge as witnessed in the tensions developing among nations and cultures around the world presently. Such processes have had profound effects upon many individuals in all cultures around the world.

The Greek myth makers had a brilliant insight when they saw Ares, the god of warfare, and Aphrodite, the great love goddess, as mates who create the child, Harmonia. What we have witnessed in this dark century of worldwide warfare, ironically, is the birth of a struggling world community. This idea is symbolized in the still highly controversial political idea of a United Nations and International Courts. It has been concretized in multinational corporations. Still in its earliest stages, the notion of a single worldwide human community is showing strong signs of growth and inevitability, even as resistance to it gathers strength and creates disruptions and turmoil. Our era will go down in history, surely, as the period when one-world consciousness on a global collective level was born. However, this new child is also threatened with death by the old cultural orders that are defending their control over populations under their dominance.

In this study, I shall try not to decipher the course of this transformation on the global level but rather concentrate upon the notion of psychological transformation itself and upon the outcomes of transformation for the individual person. For psychotherapists, it is important to understand the nature and purposes of individual psychological transformation. Social scientists may find useful analogies that can be drawn between individual transformation and the collective processes of change. Patterns of development and transformation may be similar on individual and collective levels.

At the outset, it is important to say that personalities that show strong evidence of transformation and the formation of what I will call a self-imago are not always people who elicit our admiration and call for emulation. They are people who are in process and therefore can be looked at as works in progress. They are becoming themselves. Often, though, they are people who have a strong influence on others and on their surrounding cultures. Sometimes this impact is evident and direct as with political leaders, and sometimes it is subtle and interior as with poets and painters.

My guiding idea throughout this work is the notion that transformation leads people to become more deeply and completely who they are essentially. Transformation is realization of potential. The transforming person is someone in whom the inherent self-imago emerges to the greatest extent possible in that individual's life. What that emergent self-imago is cannot be known until the process has reached its culmination. This emergence goes through several stages of transformation, which are often experienced and look upon as existential crises. The final outcome cannot be guaranteed or predicted. Much depends upon personal and cultural circumstances and opportunities. There is always the risk of failure, and the hope of fulfillment.

Evanston 1998 and Goldiwil 2021

Prologue

One day in late November, while I was taking a walk along a well-traveled road in the hills of North Carolina, my eye happened to fall upon a chubby caterpillar busily schrooching along and hurrying down the side of the road. I paused to watch its progress as over the next thirty minutes it pushed along the gravel road for a considerable distance. The sun was still warm in the autumn sky, and it raised some sweat on my skin as I stood and observed and slowly followed the progress of the determined creature.

I had time to wonder what the caterpillar was thinking. I guessed that it was heading for a sheltered place in which it would spin its cocoon and begin pupation. The place must be safe from predators and protected against wind and storms. I wondered if the caterpillar thought about what was going to happen. It was intent on getting somewhere, on doing something and doing it urgently, but did it know what it was in for? Did it have a vision? Can a caterpillar dream of flying?

The questions piled up and went unanswered. After we had traveled about a hundred yards together, the caterpillar crawled into a thicket of brambles and bushes that grew along a low wooden fence, and I lost sight of it. It must have found a place to spin its threads and go into suspended animation for a week or a season. If it was lucky and survived the ordeal, it would become a magical winged creature. It would emerge as a totally different kind of being—a butterfly—no longer bound to the earth but instead hovering above flowers and darting from blossom to blossom, following the flow of air and its own will. It would have freed itself from the confinement of a tomblike cocoon, dried its wings, and discovered its talent to soar.

The Emergence of the Self-Imago
in Adulthood

> "The driving force, so far as it is possible
> for us to grasp it, seems to be in essence
> only an urge towards self-realization."[1]
>
> *C.G. Jung*

A Dream of Transformation

A thirty-five-year-old woman once came to my office to discuss some recent dreams. To my astonishment, and also my everlasting gratitude, she told me a dream of such profound transformation that I have never forgotten it.

> I am walking along a road, feeling depressed. Suddenly I stumble on a gravestone and look down to see my own name on it. At first I am shocked, but then strangely relieved. I find myself trying to get the corpse out of the coffin but realize that I am the corpse. It is becoming more and more difficult to hold myself together because there is nothing left to keep the body together anymore.

---

[1] C.G. Jung, *Two Essays in Analytical Psychology*, par. 291.

I go through the bottom of the coffin and enter a long dark tunnel. I continue until I come to a small, very low door. I knock. An extremely old man appears and says: "So you have finally come." (I notice he is carrying a staff with two snakes entwined around it, facing one another.) Quietly but purposefully he brings out yards and yards of Egyptian linen and wraps me from head to foot in it, so I look like a mummy. Then he hangs me upside down from one of many hooks on the low ceiling and says, "You must be patient, it's going to take a long time."

Inside the cocoon it's dark, and I can't see anything that is happening. At first, my bones hold together, but later I feel them coming apart. Then everything turns liquid. I know that the old man has put one snake in at the top and one at the bottom, and they are moving from top to bottom, and back and forth from side to side, making figure eights.

Meanwhile, I see the old man sitting at a window, looking out on the seasons as they pass. I see winter come and go; then spring, summer, fall, and winter again. Many seasons go by. In the room there is nothing but me in this cocoon with the snakes, the old man, and the window open to the seasons.

Finally the old man unwraps the cocoon. There is a wet butterfly. I ask, "Is it very big or is it small?"

"Both," he answers. "Now we must go to the sun room to dry you out."

We go to a large room with a big circle cut out of the top. I lie on the circle of light under this to dry out, while the old man watches over the process. He tells me that I am not to think of the past or the future but "just be there and be still."

Finally he leads me to the door and says, "When you leave you can go in all four directions, but you are to live in the middle."

Now the butterfly flies up into the air. Then it descends to the earth and comes down on a dirt road. Gradually it takes on the head and body of a woman, and the butterfly is absorbed, and I can feel it inside my chest.

The kind of developmental unfolding imaged in this dream and in its central metaphor, the butterfly's metamorphosis, is what I want to explore in this chapter. This is a transformational epoch that extends over a considerable period of time, over years or even a decade or more, during which people find themselves living in a sort of limbo. I call this *liminality*. The very foundations of a person's world are under construction during this time. Such transformation is life changing. It is a massive reorganization of attitude, behavior, and sense of meaning. While this typically is triggered by a singular encounter with a transformative image - a religious symbol, a dream, an impressive person, an active imagination - or by major life trauma like a divorce, the death of a child, or the loss of a parent or loved one, it will take months and years to become complete. When there is such a major passage, one can think in terms of metamorphosis or transformation, the passing over (meta-, trans-) from one form (morph-, forma) to another. Sometimes the changes and shifts of attitude are subtle while they are happening, and one is hard pressed to know what if anything is going on. In the long run, though, the change turns out to be lasting and profound.

That people change and develop significantly in the course of their whole lives seems to us today a commonplace observation. We take it for granted that there are "stages of life;" "life crises," and "developmental phases." It was not always so, but now these are part of the contemporary vocabulary and its clichés. Twentieth-century psychology has contributed a great deal to this vision of human life. Hundreds of studies have been dedicated to exploring and describing human psychological development, beginning in

11

earliest infancy and proceeding through adolescence and adulthood to old age. Many accounts now exist outlining various emotional, cognitive, moral, and spiritual dimensions of this development. The psychological life of people now is seen as changing and developing almost endlessly.

At the beginning of the century, Freud found only four stages of psychosexual character development worth discussing, and all of these occurred in early childhood. He would have frozen major character development at the end of the oedipal stage (roughly ages four to six), and he considered the rest of life as fundamentally only a repetition of these early patterns. Jung soon disagreed. To begin with, he argued for a pre-sexual stage (with the focus on nourishment), followed by preliminary sexual stages that unfolded in childhood and reached maturity in adolescence.[2] He later expanded this by proposing a full lifespan developmental schema divided into two major parts: the first half of life, which has to do with physical maturation and social adaptation; and the second half, which is governed by spiritual and cultural development and aims. Other theorists, Erik Erikson among them, have argued that people pass through a discrete number of stages. Erikson proposed eight clear-cut and discernible major phases of development that can lead to one of any number of results in the unfolding epigenetic progression.[3] Each phase is loaded with its own specific tasks, hazards, and outcomes. A central question I will be focusing on in this book is: After childhood and youth, what? What happens to people developmentally after they have put childhood behind them? Some, of course, would argue that this never happens. This book is dedicated to the opposite view. I believe that most people

---

[2] In contrasting his position with Freud's, Jung used the metaphor of caterpillar-to-butterfly transformation. He said that a person lives in a caterpillar stage, which is pre-sexual, until adolescence, at which point he or she metamorphoses into a fully sexual being, the "butterfly" (C.G. Jung, "The Theory of Psychoanalysis," in *CW* 4, paras. 237-242).

[3] See Erik Erikson, *The Life Cycle Completed* on the stages of development.

grow up and become more whole and complete than their (demonstrable) repetitions can possibly account for in any significant or interesting way. But my thesis is not, on the other hand, that there is a vast array of options, or changes bordering on the endless, like the image of the "Protean self" that has been proposed by Robert Jay Lifton. There may be a plethora of changes and alterations in personality and character, but following Jung I will argue there are two great developmental eras: a first and a second half of life. The first is a growing and adaptational era, and the second is a consolidating and deepening era. While important psychological developments take place during infancy and child-hood, for me the most interesting and spiritually significant ones happen in adulthood, at midlife and after. I believe that identity forms in deeply significant ways after midlife. This mature identity is rooted in what Jung called the self rather than in the earlier psychosocial structures that have been assumed for the sake of adjustment and adaptation.

I do not mean to imply that we can become whatever we want to be, i.e., an ideal Self. This is a typical illusion of the first half of life, perhaps one important and necessary for installing sufficient ambition and self-confidence in a youth to make the great effort needed for adaptation. But limits are placed on our psyches just as they are on our bodies. Ideals may be no more attainable in psychological life than they are in the physical arena. We may want to be like Michael Jordan physically, but only a few will even begin to approximate his athletic form. In our Western religious traditions, there has been an emphasis on becoming Godlike through an *imitatio Dei* or *imitatio Christi*. This may be no more attainable than becoming small versions of Michael by imitating his moves on the basketball court. When we look at people's lives empirically, we usually see a picture entirely different from what these individuals want to be like or want to appear to others to be. If people live long enough, they become themselves, which is not always reckoned as ideal; they may even be shunned and despised. The self is not something we select; we are selected by it.

What I am interested in exploring is what actually happens to people inwardly when childhood, with its well-known "stages" and its scars and complex formations, is completed and outgrown, not only chronologically but psychologically. What are the instrument and the design that shape our ends, if not childhood patterns and adolescent "outcomes?" Does another kind of psychological development begin in adulthood?

If a person stops looking back to childhood with regrets and secret longings for an ideal paradise, or back to post-adolescence with surges of desire for eternal youth and ever greater expansion of ego and mastery of the world, as well as the physical perfection denied the aging - and must we not all finally do this? - is there then an opportunity for a second birth, another beginning?

I believe there is such an opportunity and this starts around midlife, or sometime in adulthood after its first phase has ended. Sometimes this development begins rather early, in a person's early thirties for instance. Classically it takes place around forty. Occasionally it is delayed until a person has reached the mid-forties or even the early fifties. At some point, though, a second complete era of psychological and spiritual transformation gets under way, similar to what happened in adolescence but showing different psychological contents and meanings. While the new developments build on and make use of the old structures, they also transcend them.

In terms of lifespan development and cycles, I propose the following schema. Childhood (a first caterpillar stage) culminates in a metamorphosis during adolescence, when adult sexuality enters the biological and psychological picture. This leads to a new psychosocial identity (a persona), which Erik Erikson describes very well in his works on adolescence, and to the establishment of an adultlike person whose true self is, however, still latent and hidden by the adaptive structures and requirements of this stage of life.

This is a second caterpillar stage. It culminates in the midlife metamorphosis, which gives birth to what I will call the self-imago,[4] and this personality becomes filled out and actualized in the second half of life. It is possible that there is a third caterpillar stage between midlife and old age, when there is yet another transformation. This final metamorphosis typically gives birth to a sense of self that is highly spiritual and oriented toward the timeless, as a person prepares for the final letting go and what may be a fourth transformation, physical death. In this book I will be discussing primarily the second transformation, midlife, and the period that follows it and reaches to old age, but in the examples I cite in the fourth chapter, there is also consideration of the third transformation in old age.

Before using the butterfly metaphor to extend our thinking about human psychological transformation in adulthood, I want to say a word in defense of analogical thinking. For some people this is a highly dubious intellectual undertaking. Those who prefer abstract and mathematical, or purely logical, thinking often warn about the dangers of using metaphor and analogy. Metaphors can mislead us into making foolish mistakes, they rightly argue. Look at the alchemists, for example, chasing their fantasies of turning base metals into gold. Chemistry could not become a true science until practitioners of this laboratory sport gave up their dungeons and dragons. So the argument goes. Watch those metaphors! This line of thinking certainly is correct in many respects, especially with regard to unconscious metaphors that trap thinking in concrete. Ultimately, this position leads to sterility and spiritual death. Nor does it apply to all areas of knowing. Metaphors can help us to think our way into new territory. They can provoke reflection and suggest new avenues. In fact, it is impossible to think without them. Look at the phrase "new avenues" in the previous sentence. A metaphor is

---

[4] I will use the term self-imago to indicate the personality's mature state. The self-imago is the specific form the archetypal Self takes in the individual psyche.

used there to compare thought processes and streets. It is useful, not misleading. The images of a metaphor can extend our range of thinking and suggest new applications of old learnings and behaviors.

The philosophers Lakoff and Johnson argue that metaphors are essential in concept building. The use of metaphor is woven into the very fabric of the thought process itself and is fundamental to it. Ordinary language is larded with metaphors, and it is impossible to communicate without them. In fact, our notions of reality are made up largely of metaphor. "Our ordinary conceptual system, in terms of which we both think and act, is fundamentally metaphorical in nature,"[5] Lakoff and Johnson assert. This does not mean that metaphors cannot be misleading, but it does mean we cannot get away from them. And as these authors convincingly show, metaphors are necessary if we are to have concepts at all.

The Life of the Butterfly

A butterfly's metamorphosis from larva to pupa to adult is a useful metaphor for the human psychological process of transformation in adulthood. This is an image that I want to press further. How far can it carry our thinking about the process of psychological transformation?

Butterflies undergo what is called a complete metamorphosis. How ever, they also pass through a long series of preliminary moltings before they arrive at the complete metamorphosis. This distinction between large and small transformations will be useful in thinking about psychological transformations in people. Suppose that we undergo many little ones and then, at midlife, a big one. This may suggest a useful perspective on the multitude of changes that occur in the course of a whole lifetime.

---

[5] G. Lakoff and M. Johnson, *Metaphors We Live By*, p. 3.

When larvae hatch from their eggs, they begin immediately to feed, typically on the leaves of the plant where their mothers laid the eggs. From then on they eat without ceasing, and, as they grow to be many times their original size, they shed their skins in a series of moltings. While the moltings are lesser metamorphoses, in themselves they also constitute crises. During each molting, the larva is left vulnerable until a new protective coat grows around it. (Emotional vulnerability and nakedness are characteristic of change periods in a person's life. In fact, this may be the most evident sign of imminent transformation.) When the caterpillar finally is fully grown, its body chemistry changes. What had been a stable balance between the molting hormone and the juvenile hormone suddenly shifts in favor of the former, and this induces pupation, a massive molting rather than just another simple one. The hormone that prevents premature pupation has been termed a youth hormone or a rejuvenation hormone. It is secreted by the *corpora allata*, the "juvenile glands"; it acts as a brake on what otherwise would be a rush to the butterfly stage. It is only when the hormones of the prothoracic gland gain the upper hand, as a result of a process of diminishing levels of the juvenile hormone in the bloodstream, that metamorphosis is triggered. (The promise this hormone holds for eternal youthfulness, not surprisingly, has stimulated efforts to isolate it and use it to realize the common human fantasy of remaining forever young and beautiful. If we could just get enough of this hormone into our systems, perhaps we would never age!)

Think back to the dream of transformation recounted at the beginning of this chapter. The dreamer, who was thirty-five years old at the time of the dream, had reached her full physical and social maturity as a woman. The first half of her life was coming to an end. Until then she had lived on schedule, so to speak, accepting tasks and roles laid down by culture and nature. The various steps of maturation, physical and psychological, had been traversed. She had made good use of her native talents and advantages in life to adapt to the social setting into which she had been born. She had developed a highly effective social persona and had achieved a suitable psychosocial identity; she had realized her female biological potential for childbearing; she was in a favorable position educationally and economically. She had lived the first half of life well enough, and she had accomplished its primary objective-adaptation to the physical and cultural world into which she was born. Ego development, while not ideal, at least was more than adequate. Now, at the midpoint of her life, she was experiencing a "hormonal shift" (metaphorically speaking - she was not yet in menopause), and it registered as depression: "I am walking down a road, feeling depressed." Her actual life in fact was no longer satisfying, and indeed she was threatened with a major depression. The stage of adult caterpillar life was about to end, and unconsciously another phase was in preparation.

Today a depressed person can take medication to correct the mood. But imagine what would happen if the caterpillar went to an insect psychiatrist and asked for a prescription of antidepressants to fend off emotional pain: "Moltings have become so hard lately. I'm just beside myself during those painful periods! Help me!" If the doctor were not aware of the bigger picture - of the nature of the life cycle and the importance of bearing the suffering at this particular juncture - the big crisis might be postponed by drugs. Medication, as useful as it sometimes may be for reducing psychic pain, is by no means always the answer. Pupation is terrifying, but without it there is no transformation, no butterfly. A shift in chemistry is needed for the next stage to begin. The juvenile hormone puts off pupation until the larva is able to take on a full metamorphosis. Delay is a necessary defense against too early onset of maturational processes. One can look at maturation as an increasing ability to bear what at times is the overwhelming challenge of major transformation, with its extreme anxiety and depression. Earlier crises are practice for the later ones which inaugurate the second half of life and later end that life.

Some budding adolescents resist the normal physical developments that accompany another critical stage of development. Anorexia nervosa in adolescent girls, for instance, often is rooted in the wish to remain pre-sexual, to cling to childhood. The same dynamic holds in midlife. Resistance to transformation is strong. If one extends the reasonable wish to be youthful too long and continues to get pumped up with juvenile hormones beyond the appropriate time, however, one will become nothing more than a slowly aging caterpillar, struggling ever harder to put off the final day of reckoning. The mature personality and the deeper, archetypally based identity will not form. After a certain point in life, the puer aeternus ("eternal adolescent") and his sister, the puella aeterna, cut rather sorry figures, precisely because they lack this quality. It is a quality of depth and integrity, rooted in layers of the psyche beyond the superficial levels of social adjustment (persona formation) based upon a need to please, to join in, and to get along. Cosmetic surgery may prop up the illusion of never aging, while the real benefit of aging-transformation into one's full identity as an adult person- is lost in the cuttings on the floor. The shift in body image and chemistry is part of the whole life plan, not an increasing deficiency to be remedied artificially so as to feel young a while longer.

When the caterpillar hears the call, it begins preparing for pupation. The change that now transforms the caterpillar into a pupa is of far greater magnitude than any other molts it has undergone previously. This is the big one. Entirely new structures will emerge and become dominant as a result of this metamorphosis. Complete metamorphosis is a dramatic transformation, out of which a creature emerges that bears no resemblance to the one that existed before. Who would guess, just by looking at it, that a swiftly darting butterfly once was a thick worm lumbering heavily along the ground? How does this happen?

First of all, this actually is the same creature. Only in appearance is it utterly different. At a deeper level, it carries what were formerly latent structures, now made vibrantly manifest, along into this new stage of life. The form has changed, but it is not a different being, not a changed soul. Scientific observers have determined that the rudiments of both pupal and adult structures already are present in the mature caterpillar. Indeed, some of these rudimentary structures are present at the cellular level during early embryonic development in the egg. They are primal and always have been part of the organism, but before this phase of life they remained latent. In their latent form, they are called "imaginal disks;"[6] a name that indicates their status as faint images or pre-figurations rather than as substantial organic structures. It seems that these disks simply bide their time until conditions are ready to support their advancement into mature form in the adult. The adult insect must develop in its own time, and when it does, its form is called the imago.[7] The butterfly is the imago of the insect that previously was incarnated as a caterpillar. The passage from imaginal disks to imago is, as we shall see, a difficult and some times hazardous process.

In passing from one form to another, the butterfly draws upon the latent structures that have been present all along but were undeveloped, hidden from view, or disguised by other features. The change from caterpillar to butterfly is a transformation in which underlying latent structures come to the surface and assume leading positions, while other features that were prominent change radically or disappear. In this, we recognize an important feature of psychological transformation in human adults. If one looks carefully into an adult person's early life, into infancy and childhood traits and fantasies and early dreams-that is, into the substructures latent and unconscious in earlier stages of life-one usually can find rudimentary and partially formed images of things to come. The child is father to the man, the old expression goes. In childhood and adolescence,

---

[6] A. Portmann, "Metamorphosis in Animals," p. 299.
[7] *Ibid.*

attitudes take form which later will undergo change and development, but which will, for all that, express themselves as variations on the same theme.

Character structure, psychological typology, interests like sports or music, sexual orientation, vocational inclination, vocal cadences, sense of humor-all of these may take shape early in life and be recognizable in the adult who grows out of the adolescent, even if they are subtly altered and readjusted in light of later experience. Sometimes the later features that become so prominent in the adult are, like imaginal disks, tucked away behind more obvious features and gross behaviors. In the lives I will be considering later in this work those of Rilke, Jung, Rembrandt, and Picasso - we shall see that some qualities that are largely hidden earlier in life become the most prominent and outstanding features of the second half of life. This can be, and indeed has been, conceived of as the difference between the "false self" of persona adaptation in childhood and early adulthood and the "true self" that emerges after midlife. The socially adapted personality often hides in the shadows personality elements that are the "stone that the builder rejected" and later become the cornerstone of the adult personality. These might be prefigured in the youthful personality but are hard to identify except in a careful retrospective analysis.

The early indications of these later structures, before the full structures show themselves more clearly later in life, could be subject to a variety of interpretations. In the early stages of development, one could imagine a thousand possible outcomes. Only in retrospect can one see the full imago that previously was hidden in shadow. The future is prepared in the womb of the past and the present. For some people, there seem to be huge discontinuities in life - almost several different lifetimes - but this is only a surface phenomenon. At a deeper level, there is a single process of becoming. Major but perhaps hidden continuities exist between latent structures from the past and prominent structures of the present. Children sometimes will dream or imagine or play-act their future imagos with surprising intuitive accuracy. One may be bold enough to think that a psychological ground plan for life is present all along and that, if occasionally we contact it in dream or intuition or vision, we can foresee the future of our lives.

The stunning transformation of caterpillars into butterflies through the virtual death of pupation historically has given rise to much speculation about analogies to human fate and destiny. Perhaps, it has been proposed countless times, our entire earthly life is analogous to the caterpillar stage. Our physical body is a larva. At death, when the body begins to decay and dissolve into its basic chemical elements, a soul emerges from it, like the butterfly from a pupa, and soars into a life beyond the material world. The butterfly, so this thought goes, symbolizes our immortal soul, which is released by death from the larval body and freed into its new life in the spirit. The physical experience of dying is really only a kind of pupation. This analogy between the immortal soul and the butterfly is ancient and widespread. The Homeric Greeks saw the soul leaving the dead body as a butterfly, and the Aztecs considered the butterflies fluttering in the meadows of Mexico to be the reborn souls of fallen warriors. The Balubas and Luluas of Kasai in Central Zaire speak of the grave as a cocoon from which a person's soul emerges as a butterfly. Turkic tribes in Central Asia believe that the dead return in the form of moths.[8]

In our skeptical scientific culture, we are inclined to doubt the possibility of an afterlife, so we look for transformation on this side of the grave. It is this skeptical attitude, I believe, that has opened the way to observing (and expecting!) developmental changes in humans during their earthly life. Only since the end of the Middle Ages has there been a general awareness of such "stages of life" as childhood, adolescence, adulthood, and old age. And it has only been in the twentieth century that these stages have been observed

---

[8] J. Chevalier and A. Gheerbrant, *A Dictionary of Symbols*, pp. 140-41.

carefully from physical, psychological, and spiritual viewpoints. We prefer to locate transformation on this side of the grave.

As depicted in the dream, the central act of the transformation drama takes place during the pupa stage. This is when the larva disintegrates and gradually assumes the form of a butterfly. The onset of pupation, which is the name of the process by which a caterpillar enters its dark night of the soul, is triggered by a shift in hormonal balances. This change in body chemistry stirs the larva to begin preparing for its virtual death and rebirth. The caterpillar stops feeding for the first time and sets out to find a safe place to pupate. This does not always mean that it will spin a cocoon. Some types of caterpillars do not.

There are three main methods of pupation. In one, the pupa hangs head downward, attached by an organ called a cremaster that is deeply embedded in a mat of silk fibers secured to a stable surface such as a fence post. The vulnerable pupa is protected by a hardened surrounding shell, and together they constitute the chrysalis. In a second group of insects, the pupa hangs by its tail in the open air, held in place by a silk girdle that raises and supports its head. In a third group, we find the true cocoon, which the larva creates by spinning silk and constructing a sac, often adding other materials to make a firmer structure.

While not all larvae create cocoons, all go through a state of radical disintegration, so it is of paramount importance for them to find a safe place with adequate shelter. The quest for a suitable site may take considerable time and effort. Sometimes hours pass in a patient search for a place to settle. Once there, the larva goes to work spinning threads of sticky silk and anchoring them to a secure surface. A final expulsion of excreta frees the larva to begin building a cocoon; in the pupa there is no more excretion of waste. Transformation of the larva into the mushy disintegrated pupa does not always occur immediately after entering into the cocoon. The larva can live intact inside the cocoon in a state of profound introversion for weeks or months, in what is called diapause. The duration of diapause is determined by the interplay of hormones secreted by glandular tissue in the head and prothorax. These hormones are carried by the blood to various parts of the body, where they trigger or inhibit specific activities. The pupal diapause ends, it is supposed, when the prothoracic glands, stimulated by a secretion of neurosecretory cells in the brain, release a triggering hormone into the bloodstream. These brain cells secrete their substances when certain environmental stimuli reach them. The necessary stimulus to set this chain of events in motion, for some species, is the increasing warmth of spring; for others, it is the moisture that indicates the end of a dry season. It is this combination of external stimuli and internal hormone release that determines the specific timing of pupation.

The endocrine mechanism of the insect has been compared by biologists to the function of the pituitary gland in vertebrates. There are organic tissue similarities, and both function as master timers of bodily activities. Adolf Portmann concluded in the early 1950's that the discovery of insects' brain chemistry and of the hormones that regulate the stages of an insect's life had been "one of the most significant achievements of zoology in the last fifteen to twenty years."[9]

This discovery further cemented the analogy between insect metamorphoses and human aging and transformation processes. Human transformation is certainly also biologically conditioned, and its timing has close links to sequences of physical growth and change.

The turning point from first half to second half of life is timed by an internal biological clock, and the subtle physiological changes in hormonal balance and equilibrium that occur in humans at this stage of life may well be the key also to the timing of that profound shift in attitude, perception, valuing, and attribution of meaning at the psychological level that we call midlife transformation.

---

[9] A. Portmann, "Metamorphosis in Animals," p. 301.

Hormones, in short, may be a trigger of the midlife crisis. This means that the point of the life cycle that we call midlife is not only, or even primarily, a sociological phenomenon found only in Western postindustrial societies, as is sometimes supposed. It should be evident wherever and whenever people live long enough in a relatively healthy condition to experience this phase of life. When lifespans regularly and normally reach the seventies and eighties, the phenomena of midlife transition can reasonably be predicted.

Adolf Portmann, the Swiss biologist and for many years a leading figure in the Eranos Conferences in Ascona, stressed the important insight that, while the hormones secreted by the larva are triggers for a process, they are in no way to be taken as creators of the content or the structures that come about through the processes they set off. They are stimulants that constellate a process which allows inherent potential to be realized. The innate potentials themselves "result from hereditary reaction patterns in the tissues."[10] They are created by genetic programs. In the case of human psychological transformation, similarly, it needs to be recognized that the hormonal changes at midlife do not account for the essential features of the new attitudes and for the content of the psychological and spiritual developments that come about. They do not create the images that transform consciousness (see chapter 2 for a discussion of these images), but they well may control the biological conditions under which the unconscious is stimulated to release these images into consciousness. Hormones can be the triggers of the psychic processes. What happens when pupation finally comes into full play is a massive breakdown of larval tissue, called histolysis. ("At first, my bones held together, but later I felt them coming apart" - the dream cited above.) While the disintegration of larval structures in the pupa is not total, there is a considerable amount of it (the most radical disintegration takes place in the muscular system). Histolysis is combined with another

---

[10] Ibid.

process that moves the now emergent imaginal disks into place and substitutes them for former structures. The most specialized larval structures give way to new specialized structures of the imago. Meanwhile the pupa exists in an impermeable, sealed integument ("he brings yards and yards of Egyptian linen and wraps me from head to foot" - the dream). The pupa has been described as "a complete introvert."[11] There is almost no exchange of substances with the environment and only minimal respiration by diffusion through the spiracles. There is no food intake and no discharge of waste.

This prolonged period of incubation and restructuring has captured the imagination of psychotherapists and other helping professionals who are often faced with the task of accompanying people through periods of transformation. In my book *In MidLife*, I write about three phases of this process and refer to this one - the middle one - as liminality. It transpires "betwixt and between" the more fixed structures of normal life (the larva and imago stages). In liminality, a person feels at a loss for steady points of reference. When the established hierarchies of the past have dissolved and before new images and attitudes have emerged fully, and while those that have appeared are not yet solid and reliable, everything seems to be in flux. Dreams during this psychological meta-morphosis tend to show themes both of breakdown (images of buildings being torn down, of changing houses, sometimes of actual dismemberment and physical disintegration) and of emergence (images of construction, giving birth, marriage, the divine child). Angst is the mood of liminality. A person is ambivalent and depressed, and this is punctuated by periods of enthusiasm, adventure, and experimentation. People go on living, but not quite in this world. The analyst feels like the old man in the dream quoted above watching a process unfold, observing the seasons passing, waiting patiently for new structures to emerge and solidify. It is an

---

[11]A. B. Klots, *The World of Butterflies and Moths*, p. 44.

article of faith that what is under way is "a system 'developing itself,' a process embodying the whole specific nature of the living creature"[12] - faith that a butterfly will emerge from the cocoon where liminality reigns.

Does the caterpillar know that it will emerge as a butterfly when it enters the cocoon, becomes a pupa, and dissolves? There must be an act of instinctual faith on the insect's part. "Instinct" is our bland name for a remarkable act of spontaneous courage. For the larva must not resist the process that grips it with such urgency, but must cooperate with all its energy and ingenuity. Some larvae, when they enter the stage of pupation, must perform amazing feats of gymnastics, "as though a man hanging by the grip of one gloved hand had to withdraw the hand from the glove and catch hold and hang from it, without using the other hand or anything else to hold on by during the withdrawal."[13] Surely the insect's resolve is accompanied by a guiding image, a sort of vision. As Portmann puts it, these "systems of action [the hormones] and reaction [the tissues] . . . are parts of a larger system, which already in the germ cell is attuned to transformation in time."[14] The insect has been waiting for this moment all its life. In metamorphosis, it is fulfilling its destiny by obeying the guidelines inherent in this "larger system." In analytical psychology, we refer to this master system as the Self. The self-imago is programmed into the developmental agenda of the self. It is the fullest approximation of the Self a person will ever manifest.

Once the imago has taken shape within the pupal shell, the adult insect can emerge. At this stage it has a double task: first, to break out of the pupal encasement; and second, to free itself from the surrounding cocoon. For extricating itself from its protective covering, it either possesses cutters or is able to secrete a caustic

---

[12] A. Portmann, "Metamorphosis in Animals," 299-300.

[13] A.B. Klots, *The World of Butterflies and Moths*, p. 35.

[14] A. Portmann, *"Metamorphosis in Animals,"* p. 306.

substance that dissolves the cocoon. In one way or another, it is able to force separation from the protective shell. At a certain moment, the body forces a burst of fluid into the head and thorax, which puts enough pressure on the pupal shell to crack it open. Thrusting upward, the insect pushes its legs forward and then pulls its abdomen through the opening. Freed of encasement, it maneuvers itself to a place where it perches, wings downward, and begins to expand its body parts by swallowing large amounts of air into its stomach, or crop, and its tracheal sacs. At first it is a delicate and fragile creature with pliable structures. But muscular contractions force blood into the wing pads, which expand to their full size and begin hardening in place. The drying membranes of the body stiffen and hold the wings steady. They are now spread to their full extent. Other body parts also harden. Next the proboscis is formed by uniting the two jaws of the ancestral chewing mouth, forming a tube through which the butterfly can later draw liquids. Once formed, the tube is pushed neatly into place underneath the face. This is a rapid sequence of unfolding structures.

Compared to the lengthy period of pupation, which may have extended over weeks or months, or in some cases even years, the final emergence of the adult is lightning fast. It may take only fifteen minutes. Within so brief a time, the insect becomes ready to take up its adult life as a butterfly. The dream depicts the same process: there are intense periods of activity at the outset and at the conclusion, and a long spell of slow transformation in between. At the beginning is the sudden entry into pupation, as the hormonal balance shifts and depression sets in and an intense preparation is begun for what is to come. At the end there is the emergence of the new form, a butterfly, which, in the dream, after drying out and trying its wings, becomes the dreamer-as-human again, while the butterfly is absorbed into her center as a soul image. The butterfly is a symbol of her new nature. She now has her imago, her adult form. Through this transformation she indeed has become a new being, but a being whom she always fundamentally has been. For the imaginal disks the latent form-have been resident in her psyche since the beginning of life. The soul is fundamental, and the imago is its incarnated form. It is absorbed, as it were, into her earlier body form and character structure, a new psychic constellation that will guide and orient her through the course of her future life.

Living the process of transformation yields a new form of life, something different from what has preceded it. At the end of the process, we look for a new self-definition and identity distinct from that of the first half of life. This new imago rests upon, or surrounds, the former character structure and gives it new meaning. It is not that the personality is changed such that old friends would not recognize the person anymore. But there is a new inner center of value and direction. There is a new consciousness of soul. This appearance of the inner life in the midst of adulthood is what in traditional terms is called the creation of the spiritual person.

The actual person who dreamed of transformation into a butterfly lived her midlife transformation in part by returning to school and assuming a professional identity, in part by establishing some new personal relationships and changing old ones, but in greatest part by learning to trust her unconscious and live her deeply spiritual nature. She could connect to what Jung called "the transcendent function;" the link between conscious and unconscious process. A new form of life emerges from this dynamic exchange, which includes some pieces of the past, discards others, draws out latent images and structures from the primal sea of potentials in the unconscious, and assembles the parts into a new imago for adulthood. This is the form that then is lived, deepened, and enriched throughout the remainder of the individual's life. I believe the dream states this process better than any sort of conceptual language could.

On the Emergence of the Self-Imago in the Poet Rainer Maria Rilke

What actually happens concretely to people as a result of passing through midlife transformations, of course, varies greatly, as we shall see in the following chapters. Basically, each becomes the unique individual personality he or she always potentially was. As we shall see in the next chapter, Carl Gustav Jung became the "Jung" we know as the psychological sage of Zurich. The midlife transformation of an exact contemporary of Jung's, the poet Rainer Maria Rilke, is the story of the full emergence of a major poet, for it was during this time in his life that he wrote the *Duino Elegies*, his most important work. Although he was a poet of considerable fame and high repute before he composed the *Duino Elegies*, it was through this labor that he evolved into the truly mature poet we honor today. In this series of poems, the earlier pieces of Rilke's work all came together and formed a coherent unity. In many obvious ways, his journey was different from that of Jung (which I shall describe in the following chapters), just as his life as an itinerant artist bears little resemblance to that of the Swiss psychologist Jung, yet the two men's paths exhibit surprisingly numerous parallels and similarities. Both truly were episodes of profound transformation, fulfilling archetypal patterns.

I view Rilke's life between the ages of thirty-six and forty-six as an example of psychological transformation at midlife, and I use the analogy of the butterfly's metamorphosis as a model to help understand what was going on in Rilke's deeply introverted personality during this time. Before examining Rilke's midlife metamorphosis, however, I would like to draw attention to some surprising and instructive points of contact between his life as a whole and that of Jung, to begin establishing a platform upon which to build the argument of the following chapters. I compare Rilke to Jung because the latter's life and work constitute the major theoretical backbone of this essay on transformation and on the full emergence of the self-imago in adulthood.

René Karl Wilhelm Johann Josef Maria Rilke (a name later shortened to Rainer Maria Rilke) was born in Prague, the capital of Bohemia (now the Czech Republic), shortly after midnight on December 4, 1875. In the same year, on July 26, Karl Gustav Jung (later changed to Carl Gustav Jung) was born a few hundred miles away in Kesswil, a small village near Romanshorn on Lake Constance, where Switzerland borders on Germany. Geographically and temporally, their lives lie close together. Culturally this is also the case. They shared German as a mother tongue, and both were born and lived just outside the borders of Germany itself, in areas that were dominated by German culture. Both also became fluent in other languages (Rilke remarkably so in French, Jung in English and French). In their early years, they shared a cultural milieu, that of Middle Europe in the fourth quarter of the 19th century.

Both also had difficult childhoods because of marital problems between their parents. Rilke's parents, whose marriage already was in decline when René was born, separated during his childhood and lived apart for the remainder of their lives. Jung's parents stayed together but were not well suited to each other temperamentally, and this friction generated an atmosphere of tension and unhappiness in the home. In both cases, too, the boys' births occurred after the death of former siblings: Jung's brother Paul died two years before his birth, and Rilke's birth was preceded by the death of a first-born sister. Their mothers understandably were affected by these losses, and Jung's mother suffered a major depression in his early years. René was an only child, Carl an only child until his sister was born nine years later. Both had conflictual relationships with their mothers; the fathers in both cases were more positive figures, if somewhat distant and unsuitable for idealization and identification. Both boys hated school and suffered the torments of abuse from teachers and bullying from fellow students.

A profound sense of vocation also was common to both men. Rilke found his vocation as poet and writer while still a youth, perhaps as early as middle school; Jung discovered his future career toward the end of medical school as he was preparing for exams in psychiatry. Both certainly were blessed with a keen sensitivity to spiritual settings and objects, to the sacred or the numinous. Both were tightly connected to conventional Christian religiosity through their families, although neither practiced it denominationally in adulthood. Rilke's mother, a fervently pious Roman Catholic, added the name Maria to the long list of rather pretentious names given her newborn son because he was born near midnight, the time when tradition says Jesus was born, and on a Saturday, which was considered the Virgin Mary's Day.[15] Jung was born into a Swiss Protestant parsonage, and in addition to his father he had six uncles and a grandfather who were ministers in that denomination. Religion dominated the early years of both men. Both later sought out older men of genius to idolize, learn from, and apprentice themselves to: Rilke to Rodin, Jung to Freud. Each man, moreover, was destined for greatness and had an instinctual faith in his inner daimon.

In 1912, the thirty-seventh year in each man's life, both began a journey - a katabasis and a metamorphosis - that would lead to transformation and to the emergence of a full adult self-imago. For each, the years between ages thirty-seven and forty-seven were crucial, years of pupation and incubation, out of which would hatch a magnificent imago. This transformation at midlife would forge a stable adult identity as well as bring into reality the creative work each man was born to actualize.

To be exact, it was on the stormy morning of January 20, 1912, that Rilke, while taking a walk outside the Duino Castle near Trieste and studying a letter from his lawyer that pertained to his impending divorce, suddenly stopped in his tracks when "it seemed that from

---

[15] W. Leppmann, *Rilke: A Life*, p. 3.

the raging storm a voice had called to him."[16] What he heard, according to Princess Marie von Thurn und Taxis-Hohenlohe, the owner of Duino Castle, was the line that would become the opening of the First Elegy: "Wer, wenn ich schriee, horte mich denn aus der Engel Ordnungen?" (in Steven Mitchel's translation: "Who, if I cried out, would hear me among the angels' hierarchies?"). The Princess continues and writes that Rilke stood listening for a moment: "Wer kam?... Er wusste es jetzt: der Gott" ("Who came? . . . He knew it now: (the) God"). Then he took the notebook he always carried and wrote down the words he had heard. Putting aside the notebook, he finished his business with the letter, and later in the day returned to the beginning of this new poem. By evening he had completed the First Elegy, which he transcribed and immediately sent to Princess Marie, his friend and patron, who was spending those days in Vienna.

In the weeks following, he completed another poem, the Second Elegy, plus fragments of what later would become the Third, the Sixth, the Ninth, and the Tenth Elegies. From the first moment of inspiration, it seems, Rilke knew that this was to be his major work. Intuitively realizing that the process of incubation and birthing would be long and hard, he complained in a letter to Lou Andreas Salome: "I am affected almost as badly by conception as I was before by sterility."[17] Yet he had a first glimmering vision of what might lie ahead, and this would give him the courage and faith to hold out.

The emergence of the *Duino Elegies* is an artistic expression of what was taking place in Rilke's psyche during his midlife crisis. In other words, it is a psychological document as well a work of art. This poem corresponds to Rilke's soul because it so profoundly embodies the contents, the dynamics, and the structures of his

---

[16] Stephen Mitchell quotes this sentence from Princess Marie von Thurn und Taxis-Hohenlohe's *Erinnerungen an Rainer Maria Rilke*. (S. Mitchell, *The Selected Poetry of Rainer Maria Rilke*, p. 315).

[17] Donald Prater, *A Ringing Glass: The Life of Rainer Maria Rilke*, p. 207.

inner life. It reveals the essence of the man and, most importantly, conveys his deep identification with the poet as self-imago. For in Rilke's case, we must recognize emphatically, the poet as self-imago was not only a social persona - a psychosocial structure, such as is described by Erik Erikson in his discussions of adolescence and youth - but the realization of an archetypal human form of being. The self-imago is grounded in the self-archetype. It is psychic bedrock.

Rilke's pupation began on January 20, 1912, and it continued until a second period of intense creativity shook the poet to his psychic foundations in early 1922, when the self-imago suddenly became complete. During this period, Rilke actually refers to himself as a pupa in a letter to Hans Reinhart dated Nov. 29, 1920: "As soon ask the pupa in the chrysalis to take an occasional walk, as expect me to make the slightest movement."[18] In January, 1922, almost exactly ten years after the first announcement in the wind at Duino castle, Rilke entered into a period of nearly sleepless poetic creation that extended into February and left behind, as a monument to artistic enterprise and visionary exaltation, the completion of all ten *Duino Elegies*, as well as, remarkably, *The Sonnets to Orpheus*, a somewhat lesser companion work. After this intense labor, the butterfly was born and soared to meet the world.

Between two distant winters - January 1912 and January 1922 - and through a period that included the First World War, Rilke endured the liminality of pupation. This was an inauspicious time, collectively, for poets. World conditions such as World War I did not favor the completion of Rilke's inner process. Following the first outburst of inspiration, there was silence, with only occasional murmuring of things yet to come -completion of the Third Elegy in 1913 and the appearance of the Fourth in 1915. Mostly it was a time of anxious waiting, of searching for the right external conditions regarding living space, of preparatory work in voluminous letter writing, of several love affairs, of many moves. Some of this long

---

[18] Ibid., 324.

delay could be placed at the feet of Rilke's neurotic ego, or attributed to outer circumstances. The war interrupted his creative life traumatically. He was required to join the ranks of the Austrian army for some six months until highly placed friends could spring him free to pass the remainder of the war as a civilian in Munich. He was also hurt emotionally by the war, because it revealed a dimension of evil and stupidity in human affairs that cultured people of the time were unprepared to assimilate. The times were depressing. In addition, the old social order, on which Rilke relied for his livelihood and patronage, was passing, as European culture itself entered a period of massive structural change. It seemed that everything was awry during these years.

After the conclusion of the war, Rilke reluctantly accepted an invitation to give readings in Zurich. On June 11, 1919, intending to return shortly to Munich, he crossed the border by train into Switzerland near Romanshorn, very close to Jung's birthplace. Rilke had never found Switzerland much to his liking, He felt that the mountains were too dramatic, the country too much like a calendar photograph to be real, and the people lacking in refinement and cultural sophistication. When he finally managed to bring himself to cross the border, however, he discovered a land that would become home to him for the rest of his life. The audiences were grateful and enthusiastic. Most importantly, some wealthy Swiss admirers offered him financial and social support, as well as, in several cases, abiding and committed friendship. Most notable among these were Nanny Wunderly-Volkart of Zurich and her brother Werner Reinhart of Winterthur. Not unaware of the importance of their generous offers of support, Rilke accepted the proffered beneficence and found ways of extending his visa privileges - at some cost and difficulty, as is usual in Switzerland. With the help of his friends, he managed to continue living in various Swiss locales until his death in 1926. His preferred area was the French-speaking part of the country around Geneva and the Valais.

If one views January 20, 1912, as the onset of pupation and the period following as an extended diapause, when his creative spirit lay mostly quiescent, wrapped in a cocoon and encased in an impervious pupal shell, the diapause terminated shortly after Rilke found his final and by far his most preferred home, the simple tower named Chateau de Muzot, near Sierre in the Valais. Structurally, the Chateau de Muzot is not unlike Jung's famous tower at Bollingen. (Coincidentally, Jung and Rilke found their towers' locations within a few months of each other.) By the end of July, 1921, Rilke was able to move into Muzot, and he passed the fall in his typical ways of preparing for a poetic visitation - letter writing, arranging furniture, and waiting for the voice to speak of things more profound than ego consciousness could manufacture. By January, the passages of his poetic mind were open wide. What erupted in the week of February 7-14, 1922, was a veritable gale-force wind of energy and inspiration. Never before and never again afterwards would the poet be so thoroughly possessed by the Muse as when the text of the remaining Elegies poured from his pen. It was a furious culmination after ten years of waiting, a feverish burst into consciousness of images and words and of a vision that had been waiting for release.

I cannot hope to give a complete account of the contents of the *Duino Elegies* here. Many books, dissertations, and entire conferences have been devoted to this subject without exhausting their seeming infinite complexity and depth. I will only select some themes and images that seem central in this work and that also pertain to the theme of psychological transformation. I will discuss, if only briefly, the images of the Laments, the Angel, and the Open, together with the themes of transformation and death. In the *Elegies*, these are woven together and deeply interconnected and, I believe, constitute the major thematic fabric of the work.

Why call one's major life work *Elegies*? This I asked myself when I first began to study Rilke's masterpiece. Of course, there are formal traditional reasons for this, as literary commentators have argued. Goethe wrote some famous elegies, so perhaps this was the literary reason for Rilke's choice. But I was looking for a psychological reason. Then I discovered that a mood of elegiac nostalgia and mourning dominates Rilke's entire artistic life. Perhaps because he was born to a mother who recently had experienced the death of her only child, a little girl, Rilke had a lifelong sensitivity to what he called the "youthful dead." A tone of mourning that lost potential, of intense grief giving way sometimes to intimations of immortality but often simply of loss, characterizes much of the poetry throughout his career. In the *Duino Elegies*, we find the deepest and most complete expression of this tone. Rilke had an ability to mourn almost without ceasing. It is as though the elegy - not as a technical poetic form, but as a fundamental structure of feeling - were an imaginal disk carried in Rilke's unconscious from the moment of birth. In the *Duino Elegies*, he sets the elegiac mood squarely in the foreground. It occupies the central position; it is a privileged structure in his adult self-imago. It seems, too, that the act of mourning was the essential catalyst - the stimulating or triggering psychological "hormone" - for Rilke's poetic creativity. His entire poetic oeuvre is, in a sense, one immense monumental lament.

But lament is not the telos or ultimate aim of this poetry. That is reserved for the theme of transformation. Lament is the occasion, the necessary condition, for transformation. The awareness of the "youthful dead," the poet realizes in the First Elegy, often is needed by the living to make spiritual progress. Grief also stimulates the birth of music and is the generative force behind poetry:

Finally, they no longer need us, the early departed,
one weans oneself gently from earthliness, as one mildly
outgrows the breasts of the mother. But we, who need such
great mysteries, for whom out of mourning so often
blissful progress arises-: would we be able, without them,
to be?
Is the legend of no avail, how in the lament about Linos
daring first music once pierced through parched numbness;

> how it was only in startled space, which an almost divine
>   youth
> had suddenly stepped from forever, where emptiness first
>   entered
> that motion that sweeps us away now and comforts and
>   helps us.[19]

(1:86-95)

Tragedy is regarded as generative and spiritually fertile.

Rilke mentions the Greek figure Linus in this passage. According to tradition, Linus was a young singer who dared to compete with Apollo and was killed by the jealous god. Another story has it that Linus was abandoned by his mother in Argos, raised by shepherds, and later torn to pieces by dogs. This time Apollo was outraged by the injustice and sent a plague upon the people. To appease him, the Argives invented dirges, called *lini*, and sang them in honor of the fallen youth. From the anguish of grief and guilt, dirge music – "daring first music" - arose. There are also obvious associations between Linus and Orpheus, another famous singer who was known for his elegiac grief work and who also was torn to pieces.

What Rilke is emphasizing here is the transformative power of mourning. From it, music and poetry arise, which in turn convey the presence of the soul. For Rilke, this doubtless was the case. Mourning had its early roots in his childhood, in the family emotions surrounding his infant sister's death and in what must have been a heavy burden borne by mother and eventually also by the replacement child, René. In his first years, the boy was dressed by his mother as a girl. Named René, which is frequently a girl's name, the young boy stood as a replacement for his lost sister. (Rilke himself later changed his name to the more unambiguously masculine Rainer.[20]) Lamentation and grieving are central to the

---

[19] Unless otherwise noted, all translations of passages from *The Duino Elegies* are by David Oswald.

[20] "René, which stems from the Roman name Renatur, was originally a man's name – only, over time did it become a woman's name in France with a different spelling

poem, as they are to the poet and to his creativity. Rilke personifies lamentation in the Tenth Elegy, which concludes the cycle. Here we are introduced to the mythic territory and the history of the Laments. This is entirely an inner landscape of feeling. Like Dante being guided through the inferno by Virgil, the reader is led through this territory by the poet.

First there is a gaudy carnival in the City of Pain, which is noted and passed by, and then we are escorted past the outskirts of town where reality begins to set in and where lovers are seen to embrace. We follow the progress of a young man who walks into the fields beyond the city's boundaries. This figure, it turns out, has fallen in love with a young Lament and is following her into her territory, the Land of the Laments. At one point the youth turns to leave but then is captivated by the words of an older Lament who tells him about their clan and its declining history: "We were rich at one time," she says. She then guides him further into what we must now assume is Rilke's most essential inner landscape, the hills and valleys of his soul:

> And she leads him with ease through the broad landscape of
>   the laments,
> shows him the pillars of temples or the debris
> from those castles where lament-princes once wisely
> ruled the land. Shows him the tall
> tear trees and fields of blossoming sorrow,
> (the living know of these only as gentle foliage);
> shows him sadness's animals, pasturing, - and sometimes
> a bird startles and, flying low through their lifted gaze, traces
> into the distance the image that letters its lonesome cry.

> (10: 61-69)

---

but the same pronunciation. Rainer, also spelled Reiner, has always been a man's name. It stems from Reginher: *ragin* = advice, decision; and *hari* = army, troop." Ruth Ilg, personal communication.

Nostalgia and sadness fill the air here. They advance to the graves of the elders, "the sibyls and warning-lords," and arrive at a tomb that resembles the famous Egyptian Sphinx. They have entered the realm of death. This is the classic *katábasis*, a descent to the underworld. In this land, one is required to grow accustomed to "the new death-sense of hearing" and to the new constellations of stars, "Stars of the grief-land." The Lament names them: Rider, Staff, Garland of Fruit, Cradle, Road, the Burning Bush, Doll, and Window. And then looking even further:

> ... in the southern sky, pure as inside
> a blessed hand, the resplendently clear "M"
> that means mothers. . . .-

(10 93-95)

Invoking the Mothers, the guiding Lament shows the poet the ultimate source of his inner cosmos. At this point in the poem (and in life), Rilke has completed his psychological journey inward, and there he can see and name the major constellations that have orchestrated his conscious life. Most of these stellar configurations are familiar to readers of his earlier works. They are the symbolic reference points that have oriented his imagination for decades, and now they are drawn together under a single celestial dome and anchored in their ultimate source, the Mothers. Here we witness a moment of extraordinary integrative vision, as though imaginal disks are snapping into place and forming the wings that will carry the poet onward in this life and the next.

The old Lament reveals another mystery when she points to the source of human energy itself, the "well-spring of joy." She informs the poet that "Among mankind it's a sustaining stream" (10:102). Both the indomitable will that takes humans by force and "wrings them, bends them, twists them and swings them, flings them and catches them back" (5:4-6), and the power that discharges a "seething chaos" (3:30) and arouses "that hidden guilty river-god of the blood . . . the Lord of Desire" (3:2-4) have their source here in the mythical land of the Laments. In this land of death, paradoxically, also lies the origin and well-spring of life.

The Land of the Laments is this poet's own native land. It is the source of his joy and energy, and it is the landscape of his soul. To arrive here, he had to leave the distractions available in the City of Pain (represented graphically by Rilke in his only novel, *The Notebook of Malte Laurids Brigge*, which, published in 1910, was based on his years in Paris as a young man) and undertake the journey inward. The poet had to forego the joys and consolations of love and enter the land of the dead. There he could find the deepest constellations and the music born in the emptiness of this egoless state. In these passages, Rilke displays the most intimate workings of his soul, as well as his experience of contacting the poetic Muse.

Rilke realized his full adult imago in the form of the poet, but this self-imago was carefully guided to its fulfillment by the numinous presence of the Angel. The figure of the Angel in the *Duino Elegies* is equivalent to the old Master in the dream quoted earlier, each being a transcendent and catalytic figure who presides over the process of transformation. The Angel is implicitly present in the opening line of the First Elegy —"Who, if I cried out, would hear me then, out of the orders of angels?" This is the line that arrived in Rilke's ear fully realized above Duino Castle. Throughout the poem, he speaks his lament to the Angel, whom he simultaneously fears and approaches, as holy ones are both drawn to and fear the numinous presence of God. Angels, Rilke tells us, transcend the dichotomy of life and death; indeed, they "often go about without knowing if they're with the living or dead" (1:82-83). The Angel is a "stronger existence" (1:3) who terrifies. "Every angel strikes terror" (2:1), Rilke cries out in a famous line. Angels are beings who are utterly self-possessed and resist all attempts by humans to appropriate them. They elude humans by "re-creating their own streamed-forth beauty, drawing it back into their own faces again" (2:16-17). Rilke reacts to the Angel with ambivalence, on the one hand directing to the Angel his notes of lamentation and his prayers for comfort, while on the other confessing that "my call's always full of Away; you can't stride against current so strong" (1:88- 89). He is cautious about entertaining, in his mere humanity, the numinous presence of the Angel. People have been wounded by inviting angels too freely.

Yet, the Angel also is the ideal and the goal of transformation. The angelic realm is the symbolic achieved and realized. As the poet reflects upon the human condition, he places humanity between the animals, who are at home in the concrete world of objects and live at one with their instincts, and the angels, who exist in a realm of pure transcendence. We humans, he writes, live in an "interpreted world"(1:13), partly concrete and partly symbolic. Being neither altogether animal nor fully transcendent angel, humans are in transit, passing from the one state to the other. This is their trajectory – to become angels. And it is the task of humans, he says, to transform the concrete object world into the angelic order of symbolic reality:

> Earth, isn't this what you want: to arise
> Invisible within us? – Isn't your dream
> to be invisible once? - Earth! invisible!
> What, if not transformation, is your pressing
> assignment?
>
> (9:67-70)

Transformation, that signal word, appears urgently in this crucial passage. This is the poet's meaning, which Rilke fully accepts: "Earth, my love, I will"[21] (9:71). To me, this cry of the heart is the entire work's most critical moment. Here Rilke fully accepts his destiny and his self-imago as a poet, which means he embraces the profound work of transformation of body to soul. He fulfills this vocation by transforming objects into language, by naming things – "house, bridge, fountain, gate, pitcher, fruit tree, window- at best:

---

[21] Translation by A. Poulin.

pillar, tower" (9:33-36) and then presenting them to the angelic orders with the utmost intensity of feeling. This is the poet's mission. This vocation is the Angel's gift to Rilke.

Transformation is Rilke's continuous meditation. He not only observes and intuits the angelic orders, but he addresses them with poetic offerings from the mundane world of ego consciousness. Such naming toward the realm of the archetypes, which is a kind of communion, transforms concrete objects into words, sounds, and images, ultimately placing them into a matrix of transcendent meaning. This process has a remarkable parallel in the Roman Catholic rite of transubstantiation. The most common mundane objects of the creature world in the Mass is bread and wine, while in Rilke's poetry it is house, pitcher, window, etc.- are transformed into sacred symbols with transcendent referents and properties. The poet is a priest who mediates between earthly concrete existence and heavenly transcendent Being. "There is in the first place a bringing to life of substances which are in themselves lifeless, and, in the second, a substantial alteration of them, a spiritualization, in accordance with the ancient conception of pneuma as a subtle material entity (the *corpus glorificationis*),"[22] Jung writes in his essay "Transformation Symbolism in the Mass." The same can be said for Rilke's poetic opus. He changes the mundane and inert into the transcendent and spiritual. A window is not only a window after the poet has named it with intensity. It is a *Window* with all the symbolic meanings that image suggests. He has induced a transformation from profane to sacred, from concrete object to symbol. And this is what he does also with his own life. He lives the life of the Poet, an archetypal identity.

In order to produce this magnificent opus, the *Duino Elegies*, Rilke had to suffer through the actual experience of his own transformation. In the end, he was able to break into the Open, which for him is a term implying full realization of the self-imago. In

---

[22] C.G. Jung, "Transformation Symbolism in the Mass," in *CW* 11, par. 338.

the Open, butterflies can spread their wings and fly. It is the realm of complete freedom to be oneself in the deepest and most symbolic sense. To arrive at the Open fully, Rilke tells us, he had to journey through the land of the Laments and go on alone. It is only through such radical isolation that this poet - a veritable pupa encased in a shell and enclosed in an impermeable cocoon - comes to his ultimate self-realization. He "climbs away, into the mountains of primeval grief" (10:104), alone. In this movement, he stimulates and awakens further images - in himself and in his readers - of empty cocoons and "rain that falls on dark soil in the spring" (10:109). The poem ends with these words. The self-imago is now complete, and the butterfly leaves its encasement. It is a time for freedom, the birth of the soul.

What we find at the conclusion of lengthy transformative experiences such as those of Rilke and Jung, who was undergoing his famous "confrontation with the unconscious" in precisely the same years, is a manifestation of the adult self-imago, the image of self that a specific individual is destined to realize in maturity. In one sense, as Jung repeats in his writings many times, the process of individuation is never finished or completed, because there is always more unconscious potential to bring into the personality's full integration. Yet we must also conclude that the self-imago, once filled out after midlife has been traversed, shows the indelible outlines of the "whole person." What remains to be done in the second half of life is to deepen, to ripen, to add detail and substance to the self-imago that has emerged from its cocoon. The life of the butterfly may be short or long, but from now on it will remain true to its achieved imago.

Rilke's life was cut short by illness. He died at the age of fifty one, some four years after completing the *Duino Elegies*, his masterpiece. By the age of forty-seven, he had assumed fully the self-imago of the Poet, an Orpheus, and he had become an archetypal lyric poet for the twentieth century. Had Rilke lived another thirty years, as Jung did, he well might have written the equivalent of *Faust* Pt. II and become a second Goethe. Goethe is the archetypal poet for the Germans, as Orpheus is for the Greeks. As it was, with the creative energy remaining during his years of physical decline, Rilke wrote masterful, playful, much lighter, but delightfully provocative poems in his newly adopted language, French. He passed his last years in his beloved Chateau de Muzot, tending roses and receiving occasional visitors. It can be said that he completed his life, although he died at a relatively early age.

The Transformative Image

> Many fathomless transformations of personality, like sudden conversions and other far-reaching changes of mind, originate in the attractive power of a collective image.[1]
>
> C.G. Jung

"Listen to me," she said leaning forward. "I want to change. This is not the person I want to be. This is not the person I AM!" She spoke in a voice filled with passion and urgency, the words bitten off in a clipped and clearly enunciated accent.

"Can a person enter a second time into her mother's womb and be born?" I asked. "How can I possibly help you? You are looking for a miracle."

This conversation never took place in reality, but it has occurred in my private thoughts many times during psychotherapy sessions. I can see the urgent desire in the eyes, the need, the driving force behind the wish for transformation, and it is awesome. People want desperately to change. Can they do it? And "change" in what sense? Many people try with New Year's resolutions, but

---

[1] C.G. Jung, CW 7, par. 232.

most fail. What makes significant psychological and spiritual change possible?

On August 5, 1989, the New York Times carried an obituary of William Larimar Mellon, Jr. (1910-1989) that caught my attention.[2] Two half-columns of print were juxtaposed with a picture that showed Mellon dressed casually in an open-necked shirt, his hair a bit disheveled, squinting through thick glasses, smiling slightly. A good-looking man, he appeared to be in his sixties when the picture was taken. The article stated that Mr. Mellon had died at his home in Deschapelles, Haiti, at the age of seventy-nine. The writer made the point that William Mellon was a member of one of America's wealthiest families. Born in Pittsburgh, he had attended some fine schools and gone on to marry, divorce, and remarry. In the mid-1930s, he bought a ranch in Arizona and settled down to become a working rancher. When World War II broke out, he served in the OSS (the predecessor of the CIA) and was sent on missions to Portugal, Spain, and Switzerland.

The obituary does not say that Mellon met Jung in Switzerland, but it is likely that he did. Jung was a close friend of Paul and Mary Mellon, relatives of William's, and Jung too was in contact with the OSS's network of spies operating under the direction of Allan Dulles, who was stationed in Switzerland during the war.

In 1947, William Mellon happened to read an article in Life magazine about Albert Schweitzer, the German medical missionary, philosopher and renowned musician whose hospital at Lambarene, Gabon had become world famous. Mellon became fascinated with Schweitzer's mission and wrote the doctor a letter asking how to set up such a hospital. Schweitzer sent back a handwritten letter advising Mellon about the need for medical training and addressing the practical problems involved in setting up a hospital under Third World conditions. From this letter, Mellon's life took its future

---

[2] Glenn Fowler, "W. L. Mellon, Humanitarian, Is Dead at 79," New York Times, Feb. 24, 1991, p. 15.

direction. He enrolled in medical school and four years later became a physician. At the same time, his wife studied laboratory science. After graduation, they searched for a suitable country in which to build a hospital on the model of Schweitzer's at Lambarene. They settled on a site in Haiti that had been abandoned by the Standard Fruit Company, and in 1956 the Albert Schweitzer Hospital of Deschapelles opened its doors. Here Mellon and his wife spent the rest of their lives, working in the hospital and engaged in local community activities.

If one asks how major life changes like this come about in a person's adulthood and looks for the means of such transformation, one quickly discovers the role of what I will be calling transformative images. For William Mellon, Albert Schweitzer was a transformative image. The image of Schweitzer's life and mission suggested and shaped the direction of Mellon's maturity. In this chapter, I want to discuss how these images work upon the psyche. The stories of William Mellon and his wife, Gwen Grant Mellon - both healthy, affluent, socially successful adults - offer evidence that such transformations actually do take place in the middle of life.

Transformative images are engaging and unusually arresting metaphors. To live through the transformational process they often engender is a special experience. From the moment these images appear, they take possession of consciousness and, at least temporarily, change it, sometimes dramatically. Dream images, for example, sometimes will haunt a person for days and continue to draw out emotions and memories, incite desires, and even stimulate concrete plans for the future. Occasionally a poem, a painting, a film, or a concert has the same effect. The major symbolic experiences of this kind we call numinous or religious. For a moment, one almost becomes another person; in the long run, one sometimes actually does. If these powerful archetypal images are strong and impressive enough, the whole pattern of a person's life can be transformed. Their effects are not only momentary. Over time they become irreversible. This is because these images reflect a new and potentially dominant pattern that is emerging in a person's psyche and give it shape. They are metaphors with profound underlying structural support and meaning.

If we look back at a life from its endpoint, rather than moving forward from its beginning in infancy and early childhood, we usually can find major eras and turning points laid out in bold relief. For those who cannot read a newspaper without studying the obituaries, this is a familiar perspective. Obituaries look back over a whole lifetime. They mark the end of a life and, if well done, they indicate the most significant moments of transformation in the lives of their subjects. Written with little detail and from an objective viewpoint, obituaries condense a life into a few features that define it and show its major turning points, the crises and resolutions. They offer snapshot portraits and tell readers who these people were, at least in the eyes of the public. A short obituary can sum up an entire life in a few lines of spare prose. If the obituary is subtle, it also hints at the kind of spirit the individual embodied, the color and feeling tones of the person, the meaning this life had for others. It gives the reader a bird's-eye view of what perhaps had been a gradual process of unfolding development and achievement over the course of a lifetime, along with the sudden twists and turns that ended up defining its ultimate course.

An obituary, however, can only provide the merest hint of the complicated process involved in personal transformation. If we look more deeply into adult development through the encounter with powerful and compelling transformative images, what do we find? Perhaps more than any other psychologist before or since, Jung studied the phenomenon of transformation from the inside. Unlike the obituary writer, who must accept severe limitations in describing a person's life being limited mostly to a view from the outside and from a public angle, Jung's vision focused on studying the inner world of the psyche. Jung viewed transformation as a profound process of change that takes place in the depths of the psyche. Sometimes it manifests itself only dimly in the outer features of a person's known life, however, and would not even show up in an obituary. It is a complex process with many possible outcomes, some of them judged as positive and some as negative.

In a key letter to Freud dated February 25, 1912, Jung wrote: "I have ventured to tackle the mother. So what is keeping me hidden is the *katabasis* [Greek: 'descent,' i.e., to the underworld] to the realm of the Mothers, where, as we know, Theseus and Peirithoos remained stuck, grown fast to the rocks."[3] At that moment, Jung was composing Part 2 of his self-defining work, *Wandlungen und Symbole der Libido* [*Transformations and Symbols of the Libido*], which would crystallize his distance from Freud into a permanent and irrevocable break and catapult him into his own midlife crisis. In 1912, Jung was thirty-seven. At the same age, William Mellon read about Albert Schweitzer in Life magazine. Jung was at the beginning of a personal crisis that would not be completely resolved until he was nearly fifty years old. The transformation that resulted from this crisis would set him on a course that like Mellon he would pursue to the end of his life. He would write about this profound shift theoretically and autobiographically for the rest of his days.

Jung broke with Freud for many reasons. Among them, there was a conviction that Freud overemphasized the role of sexual problems in the etiology of neurosis. As he got to know Freud closely during their years of collaboration through many exchanges of letters, several visits to each other's homes, and traveling together by ship to America, Jung was struck by the older man's peculiar and intense reactions whenever they touched on the subject of sexuality. It was as if a god were summoned, Jung says in his late memoir. Freud's thought was dominated by this issue, and emotionally he was fixated on it. To some this may have seemed like a magnificent obsession, but to Jung it did not make for good science. Jung was not uninterested in sex as a personal matter, but he really was not a devotee in the sense Freud was. For him, libido

---

[3] W. McGuire, *The Freud-Jung Letters*, p. 487.

could flow in the paths of sexuality rather freely and powerfully, as many writers have noted and even dwelt upon, but his fundamental personality constellation was organized by other images of the numinous. Nevertheless, at the time Freud was his most important teacher, also a father figure and mentor, and when Jung broke with him his emotional life entered a period of severe crisis. The latter coincided with his midlife years.

In a Seminar given to his students in 1925,[4] Jung spoke about his transformation experiences some 10 years earlier and presented an account of his thinking and personal development following the publication of his book *Wandlungen und Symbole der Libido*, in 1911-12. Here he spoke publicly for the first time on record about his inner experiences during the crucial period between 1912 and 1918, which in his autobiography he calls "Confrontation with the Unconscious." Much of what he said in the seminar also is reported in the memoir, but not of one experience in active imagination that was especially dramatic and transformative. Jung used this personal confession to illustrate the psychological transformation process. He spoke of it objectively, and he related that it had been transformative for him. It included an image that remained fixed in memory and which had become a central reference point in his individuation process. Jung was speaking as a psychologist and reflecting on the inner side of psychological transformation. This is a different level than a biographer or obituary writer usually has access to in the subject unless there is a personal diary or account available. It is the view from the inside.[5]

Jung told his audience how he first began using a practice that he would call active imagination in order to contact his unconscious fantasies. The first efforts were not successful, but then he broke through and came upon a group of figures: an old man who named

---

[4] C.G. Jung, Analytical Psychology: Notes of the Seminar Given in 1925, pp. 92-99.
[5] This entire process is recorded in Jung's personal diary, *Liber Novus*, which was published in 2009 with the title *The Red Book*.

himself Elijah, a blind young woman companion named Salome, and a black snake. This much also is recounted in the autobiography. What is not described there is the subsequent active imagination. Several days later, he said in the Seminar, he tried again to contact these figures, but a conflict blocked the way. Two serpents, one white and the other dark, were fighting each other. Finally, the black snake was defeated and left the scene. Jung now could go on. He next encountered the woman and the old man again, and eventually he entered a space that he identified as the underworld: "Elijah smiled and said, 'Why, it is just the same, above or below!'" It was the house of Salome and Elijah. Then comes the decisive event:

> A most disagreeable thing happened. Salome became very interested in me, and she assumed that I could cure her blindness. She began to worship me. I said, "Why do you worship me?" She replied, "You are Christ." In spite of my objections she maintained this. I said, "This is madness;" and became filled with skeptical resistance. Then I saw the snake approach me. She came close and began to encircle me and press me in her coils. The coils reached up to my heart. I realized as I struggled, that I had assumed the attitude of the Crucifixion. In the agony of the struggle, I sweated so profusely that the water flowed down on all sides of me. Then Salome rose, and she could see. While the snake was pressing me, I felt that my face had taken on the face of an animal of prey, a lion or a tiger.[6]

In the commentary that follows, Jung interprets these images by placing them in a symbolic context: "When the images come to you and are not understood, you are in the society of the gods or, if you will, the lunatic society; you are no longer in human society."[7] At its core, he said, this experience in active imagination is equivalent to

---

[6] C.G. Jung, *Analytical Psychology*, p. 96.
[7] *Ibid.*, 99.

an ancient deification mystery such as was practiced in religious circles such as the one at Eleusis. *The Golden Ass of Apuleius*, which contains an account of such a mystery, was well known to Jung. If a person's sanity is not sufficiently grounded in an ego that recognizes the difference between fantasy and reality, however, such a transformation of consciousness easily can result in delusions of grandeur, or what Jung calls a "mana personality." As a young psychiatrist at the Burghölzli Klinik in Zurich, where he trained and worked for ten years, Jung probably saw his share of such patients. He himself was not given to such delusions, fortunately, and was able to understand and assimilate the images on a symbolic level.

What Jung was demonstrating by drawing on his own personal experience was the transforming effect of active imagination. The images that appeared drew consciousness powerfully to themselves and had a transforming effect. In this instance, Jung changed form and became first a Christlike figure and then Aion, who, he explained, derives from the Persian deity Zrwanakarana, whose name means "the infinitely long duration."[8] Jung noted in his seminar that this process of deification was a regular part of ancient mystery religions. As F.M. Cornford writes in a passage about the Greek mysteries at Eleusis, "So man becomes immortal in the divine sense."[9] In the presence of immortal archetypal images, a person takes on their qualities and features and is spiritually molded by them into a similarly immortal figure. This is a symbolic happening, but it shapes one's sense of identity and value. Aion is a god who rules over time, controls the astrological sequences, and presides over the calendar. "The animal face which I felt mine transformed into was the famous [Deus] Leontocephalus of the Mithraic Mysteries, the figure which is represented with a snake coiled around the man, the snake's head resting on the man's hand, and

---

[8] *Ibid.*, 98.
[9] F. M. Cornford, *The Unwritten Philosophy and Other Essays*, p. 77.

the face of the man that ofalion."[10] At this moment of trans-formation, Carl Jung became a classical image of deity. The experience would change him profoundly.

From the brief obituary of William Mellon, we cannot know what kinds of effect the image of Albert Schweitzer had on his inner life. Did he dream about Schweitzer, or have the equivalent of an active imagination with his image? He must have had fantasies about him, and at a deep level he identified with the image. From the evidence, it is clear that Schweitzer became a compelling image for Mellon, one that changed his life permanently. One can only guess that, deep in the subterranean levels of Mellon's unconscious fantasy life, Schweitzer corresponded to a godlike figure, an archetypal image, whom he wished to emulate and with whom he identified. What Jung did through his method of active imagination was to unearth the unconscious fantasies and lift them up into the light of day, where they became the subject of his science. In *The Red Book*, he shows us the inner side of the transformation process.

It seems clear from Jung's autobiography that active imagination became a kind of personal mystery religion for him. It is a method that offers a quasi-sacred space in which a modern person can encounter religious images and experience the spiritual effects that the mysteries provided for the ancients. The great discovery of this twentieth-century psychologist was that modern people, although thoroughly secular and alienated from traditional customs and beliefs, nevertheless have access to the riches of all the great cultural and religious traditions. They can have a personal encounter with the archetypal images of the collective unconscious. Such images, if deeply engaged and regularly related to over a sufficient period of time, have the power to transform conscious-ness in the same way that traditional images and mysteries have transformed humans identity for millennia.

---

[10] Jung, Analytical Psychology, 98.

The Mithraic god Aion. Courtesy Biblioteca Apostolica Vaticana Museo profano 7899.

It is important, however, to point out a major difference between Jung's approach to these sacred archetypal images and traditional religious approaches. Jung strongly recommended letting oneself become affected by the images, even to the point of temporary identification with them. So far, he and traditional practices agree. However, Jung did not advocate remaining identified, whereas they do advocate this. Traditions want people to become as closely identified and united with the dogmatic images as possible, to practice *imitatio Dei*. Jung, on the other hand, disidentified from the image and consciously reflected back upon the experience. He maintained a psychological distance from the archetypal images. It is this move that maintains identity as individual. Otherwise the archetypal images simply create replicas of themselves and individuality disappears. Jung's notion of individuation is based upon a twofold movement: temporary identification with the unconscious images in order to make them conscious, then disidentification and reflection upon them as an individual. An individual is affected by the contact but does not become totally controlled or possessed by the images.

In his second active imagination, which Jung carefully noted as taking place in December 1913, his consciousness clearly was transformed – "deified," as he says - by the images. The woman worships him and calls him Christ, the serpent twines around him, and his head becomes leonine. The images, too, change dramatically, particularly the image of Salome. Addressing him as Christ, she asks for healing. She is blind and would see. Jung declines the inflated status of Christ-the-healer, but he notes in passing that Salome is healed nonetheless. She receives her sight. Thus, the archetypal image also is transformed - but only after Jung did sweat until water flowed down on all sides of him, he declares. He became the Crucified for a moment, and a miracle of inner healing took place.

Who is the blind Salome, and why is she blind? Jung himself identified her as "the inferior function which is surrounded by evil."[11] In *Memories, Dreams, Reflections*, he interprets her as a symbol of Eros and feeling.[12] It is well known that he considered himself to be an introverted thinking intuitive type, and therefore his inferior function was extroverted feeling. This is the function of relationship. There lies his blindness, and this is what prays to him for healing. Taken in this light, the conscious Carl Jung is the only one who can heal Salome, and she is correct to look to him to give her the miracle of sight. He must sweat it out on the cross of transformation in order to sacrifice his superior function thinking - to give life and light to his undeveloped, inferior, blind feeling function in order to obtain awareness of connection and attachment to others. Before he is deified as Aion, he is crucified, and his feeling function gains sight.

Although I am focusing this discussion of transformative images on mature adulthood and the second half of life, I do not want to give the impression that archetypal images do not also shape and affect the young. On the contrary, they have extraordinary impact on the plastic psychic structures of young people. They are present *in potentia* from the beginning of life and may be constellated well before midlife arrives.

An example of how such an archetypal image can perform its coordinating and directive function in a young person appeared on my doorstep one summer evening. The doorbell rang shortly after dinner, and when I answered, a young man about twenty years old explained that he was collecting donations for a group dedicated to saving the planet from ecological catastrophe. Its mission is to save the earth, he told me. I stepped outside and asked him to tell me about his organization and his involvement in it. I usually am not an easy touch for money, and I pressed this young man to explain his mission. Why was he concerned about the planet? What did his

---

[11] *Ibid.*, 97.
[12] C.G. Jung, *Memories, Dreams, Reflections*, p. 182.

organization realistically expect to accomplish? Where would my donation end up? He was patient and answered my somewhat rude questions politely. He seemed clearly to be college material, intelligent, of good family. He was doing this, he said, out of conviction. He received little pay and no power or fame, and he was working strictly for the cause. And then his voice broke a little; his hands pointed outward and swept across the landscape as he exclaimed, almost in tears, "Don't you see? Mother Earth needs our help! She is suffering!"

Now I understood. He was moved by an image of the Great Mother, and he was offering his energies in service to Her. A glimpse into the primordial world of archetypal images had galvanized his psyche and sent him on a mission. His psychic energy was being shaped and organized by this archetypal image and its implications. He was moved by an age-old image of the Great Mother that has shaped and stirred human psyches from time immemorial. It is an image of Beauty (Plato), of the Mother archetype (Jung); and its effect is to transform consciousness. Every human psyche, if it is developed and realized above the base level of sheer survival and instinct gratification, is shaped by such images that orient life and give it meaning.

The defining theoretical issue between Jung and Freud was precisely the issue of transformation. Freud was immovable on the subject. Adamant that psychological life was largely reducible to sexuality and that the sex drive supplies all the energy at the disposal of the psyche, Freud reduced all forms of human culture and every kind of pleasure ultimately to the sexual realm. Moreover, he attributed all forms of neurosis and even psychotic disorders to causes that were rooted in distorted sexuality. This would mean, as Jung pointed out incredulously, that art, philosophy, religion, and commerce were but pale substitutes for the real goal of human desire, namely sexual pleasure. All ideals would be mere disguises for frustrated sexual wishes, and all psychopathology would be laid at the feet of disturbed sexual functioning. Freud stubbornly held this to be true, arguing that, in fact, human culture was the disguised product of a complicated network of sexual compromises. Sublimation was his term for the process that fed the sex drive into the cultural act.

Jung could not believe that Beethoven's symphonies and the cathedral at Chartres could be explained as a sublimation of their creators' sexual instincts. Nor would he reduce Albert Schweitzer's thought, vision, energy, and missionary zeal to sublimated sexuality. Jung would take the position that, if human beings do not manage to integrate their various instincts and drives through a trans-formative image, they will tend to drift into multiplicity, a mere collection of complexes without a center. People who fail to coalesce in this way remain partial, in pieces, unintegrated. It is indeed a psychological tragedy if a person's psyche will not allow for integration around a transformative image. Borderline personality disorder an example. Such an individual's deep conflicts and splitting defenses are so severe and entrenched that they destroy every attempt on the part of the psyche at integration. They smash potentially transformative images with the destructive force of intemperate rage and anxiety that often borders on panic.

The question was how to account for the rich cultural and spiritual interests and diverse passions of human beings. The effort to answer this question led Jung to formulate his own theory as a counterproposal to Freud's. The term Jung chose to speak about the deployment of psychic energy and its redistribution from one form to another in the course of development was transformation. In German the word is *Wandlung*. Hence the title of his book, *Wandlungen und Symbole der Libido*. *Wandlung* means "change," typically change of form. Psychic energy, Jung argued in this early work, can assume many forms, just as energy does in the physical world. It is an expression of the life force - the Will, following Schopenhauer - that animates human bodies and moves them in all the complicated ways humans behave. In itself, libido is not attached to any specific drive or motivation. So the real question becomes how to account for the variety of motivations and behaviors human beings display. For Freud, all could be reduced to sexuality and its sublimation; for Jung it could not. Jung was searching for a mechanism that could transfer and dispense energy from one channel to another. This mechanism, he thought, would be internal to the psyche, part of a growing, balancing, self-adjusting process. The psyche initiates its own transformations, Jung concluded, and these have many aims and purposes, sexual fulfillment being only one of them. Other forms of human activity have their own goals and their own pleasures.

It would take Jung some years to work out the details of his argument, but for our purposes I can pass over them and offer the final conclusion with a brief quotation from *Symbols of Transformation*. Jung inserted this passage when he revised the original text in 1952: "Except when motivated by external necessity, the will to suppress or repress the natural instincts, or rather to overcome their predominance (*superbia*) and lack of coordination (*concupiscentia*), derives from a spiritual source; in other words, the determining factor is the numinous primordial images."[13]

The argument is that archetypal images direct the drives and harness and coordinate them. These primordial images grip a person's consciousness, and the biologically based drives are enlisted to supply the energy. The symbolic images emerge within the psyche and take the form of archetypal projections (such as perhaps happened in the case of Mellon's projection onto the figure of Albert Schweitzer) and numinous experiences, which traditionally have been formulated as myths or religious doctrines and rituals. These images, then, have the effect of redirecting psychic energy into corresponding pathways. Each of the patterns of behavior, fantasy, and thought that originate in archetypal images has a will and an aim of its own. It is these images, which behave like instincts,

---

[13] C.G. Jung, *Symbols of Transformation*, par. 223.

that account for the creations of culture such as art and literature, for social and economic structures such as constitutions and other legal systems, and for the content of religious doctrines and values. In other words, Jung saw human nature as fundamentally invested with psycho/spiritual and not biological direction.

The etymology of the word transformation is instructive.It is made up of two Latin words, *trans* and *forma*. In Latin, *trans* means "across, over, on the other side." Think of the banks of a river: To carry something across, one "trans-ports" it. In turn, the Latin word *trans* grows out of the stem *tra-*, which has cognates in Sanskrit, Celtic, and German. *Tra* is a basic word, a primal utterance: A word like this is necessary for human consciousness and therefore must be included in every language. The English word "through" is rooted in this stem. In general, then, *trans* communicates the sense of coming through or being moved "from one place, person, thing, or state to another."[1] In the psychoanalytic term "transference," we refer to a projection that carries a psychic image over from an intrapsychic context to an interpersonal one. But *trans* can also be stretched to signify "beyond," as in the words "transcendence" and "transpersonal." This locates something as being on "the other side," "over there" or "above." When t*rans* is linked to "form" - a word descended from the Latin *forma*, meaning "form, figure, shape, image, mold, stamp" - it indicates a movement of change from one figure or image to another. Probably this meaning at first was rather concrete. At one time, the word *forma* meant the shape of a shoe. If one wanted to give shoes a different shape in order to change or improve their style, one's imagination could be employed to bring another shape over from across the river of possibility and apply it to the shoes already in the workshop. This would have "transform" them.

This term was found to be extremely useful for thinking about change in many areas. In theater, for instance, transformation refers

---

[14] *Shorter Oxford English Dictionary*, p. 2344.

to a change in character; in zoology, it denotes a change of form in animal life; in mathematics, it means a change of form without alteration in quality or value; in physics, it can refer to a change in form from liquid to gas, for instance, or to a change in energy from one form to another; and in reference to the domain of electricity it means the change in current due to a transformer. The word has many applications. Small wonder that it was taken up by psychology, too.

Jung was drawn to analogies between psychology and various sciences. For him, the word transformation referred to a change of psychic energy from one form to another, much as physicists use it to describe changes in energy from mechanical to electrical, etc. Common to all particular forms of energy in psychology, as in physics, is the underlying fact of energy itself, which Jung considered, again as in physics, to be subject to the law of conservation. Energy cannot simply disappear from the psychic system. If it is lost to consciousness, it is to be found in the unconscious.

What Jung had uncovered by excavating the deeper layers of the psyche was a level of psychic object and process that underlay Freud's concept of the id. While analyzing psychotic patients at the Burghölzli Klinik and comparing their seemingly bizarre fantasies and ritualistic behaviors with anthropological accounts of ancient traditional customs and behavior, he found that he was exploring a layer of psyche that is archaic, or as he would later say "archetypal." Movements like rhythmic swaying, gesturing, scratching, and sucking are irreducible to any specific instinctual activity - nourishment, sexuality, etc.- but rather are tied into all of them. Musical performance and sexual behavior, for example, have many things in common - rhythm, movements of the body, feelings - but this does not mean that the former is a substitute or replacement of the latter. Rather, both draw on the same reservoir of human behavioral patterns and energies.

This breakthrough to the truly primordial level of the psyche was decisive for Jung. Now he could say that processes of transformation are primary and not secondary (not mere sub-stitution), and that transformation is driven by a force that has a will and a goal, which is what I am speaking of as the emergence of the self-imago. What we see in the lives of people like William Mellon is how a symbolic figure (for him the famous medical missionary, Albert Schweitzer), i.e., a numinous archetypal image of the self, gathers energy to itself like a magnet, transforms this energy into a new set of ambitions and motivation, and gives a human life its final direction and meaning.

As an interlude, I want to acknowledge that what Jung created in his theory of the psyche was a psychologically based version of Plato's philosophical vision of human nature and the transcendent Forms. In the Republic, Plato teaches that there are three types of people among the citizenry of the polis: those who are mostly motivated by economic gain and the sensual pleasures that money can buy; those who are intent on gaining power and enjoying fame and celebrity; and those who prefer to observe life at a distance, to reflect on experience, and to pursue wisdom - the philosophers. However, everybody is partly motivated by each of these desires for pleasure, power, and wisdom. The person who does best is the one who manages to keep all three in balance and is able to satisfy each without succumbing to the tyranny of any one of them. This is not easy, because each is powerful and compelling. Sensuality easily can come to dominate life and become one's chief end. (Jung felt this had happened to Freud, at least in his theory of human nature. His mind had been captivated by the divinity of sensuality, by the pleasure principle.) Similarly, power and celebrity can take over and become the prime motivation in all human relationships and dealings. (Adler, the theorist of power, in a sense worshipped this god.) The love of wisdom, too, can become one-sided and can distort life to the point of denying one's normal desires for some sensual pleasure and a bit of power. (Religious fanatics and ideologues, as well as some academic philosophers, fall into this group.) Jung would agree with Plato that the goal is to achieve balance among the instincts, to offer each its due in appropriate measure, and to strive for wholeness rather than perfection.

But what can harness these three powerful drives and temper them? How can wholeness be achieved? For Plato, it was clear that the philosopher should be in charge of the "republic," inner and outer. This is because the philosopher is a person who truly has followed the path indicated by Diotima (through Socrates) in the Symposium and has experienced the reality of the Forms. According to Socrates, Diotima taught that the medium by which a person is drawn to the ultimate Form, the Beautiful, is Eros. After being drawn first to many beautiful objects in the sensate world, the reflective person will realize that what is desired above all is not this or that object, which may embody the Form of beauty for a while, but rather Beauty itself. Thus, in being led from concrete object to abstract realization, the philosopher comes to love Beauty itself and even to recognize the identity between Truth and Beauty. For Plato, the vision of Beauty is the transformative experience that allows the philosopher (famously Socrates) to strike a harmonious balance among the desires for pleasure, power, and wisdom. The transformative image of Beauty has the capacity to hold the warring factions together and to elicit unity of aim among them. It transforms disunity and competitive striving, moving them toward harmony and unity of purpose. The transformative image pulls the various disparate energies together and gives them an overall direction.

While Jung's depth psychology is fed by sources other than Plato and philosophical reflection - most importantly, by personal and clinical experiences and observation - it has many points of contact with Plato. Not the least of these is a common appreciation for the transforming power of that which Jung would call archetypal images and Plato, the Forms. Where Jung and Plato part company I shall indicate later.

A transformative image, then, is an image that has the capacity to redirect the flow of psychic energy and to change its specific form of manifestation. The way in which this image relates to the instinctual needs of the individual is critical, for this will determine whether the constellation supports balance and wholeness or represses aspects of human nature and results in one-sidedness and distortion. This brings us to the question of the role of culture and society, and especially religion, in the psychological life of the individual. All individuals live in large and small collective groups and organizations. These provide opportunities for accessing transformative images, but they also create hazards for individuals who are striving to live their wholeness.

Cultures and religions are repositories of transformative images from the past. This is evident to all sensitive students of human culture and history. From time immemorial, the cultures of humankind have housed and treasured the primordial images of the collective unconscious and made them available to people in their religious mysteries, sacred rites, and rituals. When a person experiences one of these images deeply, it has a profound effect upon consciousness.

F. M. Cornford, a preeminent interpreter of Greek philosophy and especially of Plato, summarizes Plato's doctrine of transformation as follows:

The final object - beyond physical, moral, and intellectual beauty - is the Beautiful itself. This is revealed to intuition "suddenly." The language here recalls the culminating revelation of the Eleusinian mysteries - the disclosure of sacred symbols or figures as the divinities in a sudden blaze of light. This object is eternal, exempt from change and relativity, no longer manifested in anything else, in any living thing, or in earth or heaven, but always "by itself," entirely unaffected by the becoming or perishing of anything that may partake of its character. The act of acquaintance with it is the vision of a spectacle, whereby the soul has contact with the ultimate object of Eros and enters into possession of it. So man becomes immortal in the divine sense. As in the Republic, the union of the soul with Beauty is called a marriage - the sacred marriage of the Eleusinia - of which the offspring are, not phantoms like those images of goodness that first inspired love of the beautiful person, but true virtue, the virtue which is wisdom. For Plato believed that the goal of philosophy was that man should become a god, knowing good from evil with such clearness and certainty as could not fail to determine the will infallibly.[15]

In this passage of his brilliant work on what had not been recorded in the ancient texts, Cornford describes the well-kept secrets of the ancient Greek mystery religion at Eleusis, which was dedicated to the Mother Goddess, Demeter. In the mysteries, we can clearly see the central role played by religious ritual in constellating the transformative archetypal image for the participants. A person is ritually prepared for exposure to the sacred symbols and images, and if this preparation is propitious a visionary "marriage" takes place between the soul and the numinous symbolic object. From this union a profound transformation of self-identity results. It is the same, Cornford writes, for the individual philosopher who contemplates the Beautiful. The soul and the object of contemplation become united, and the soul is transformed.

Because religious traditions possess and employ such powerful symbols for transformation in their rituals and images, they can channel psychic energy on a massive collective level. They also collect a surplus of archetypal energy from the projections of their adherents, and this typically is used to build up and enrich the institutional organizations. This surplus can be used well, as for good works, for healing, for initiation and transformation; or corruptly for selfish, sexual, or power-abusive ends.

---

[15] Cornford, *Unwritten Philosophy*, p. 77.

As Plato and Jung knew only too well, cultures and organizations can distort human nature as well as help to fulfill it. But what is the criterion for deciding whether the transformative images of traditional cultures and religions, ancient or modern, foster health or illness? For both Jung and Plato, the test would be pragmatic: do the transformative images that are being held up and promoted by a specific culture support or thwart the individual psyche's urge toward wholeness? Do they coordinate and balance the various "faculties" (Plato) or "instinct groups" (Jung) and direct them in a manner that allows for optimal fulfillment under the aegis of an overarching symbol of meaning and purpose? Plato witnessed directly the intolerance of advocates of traditional religion in the trial and death of his hero, Socrates. Jung analyzed the central transformative images of his own religious tradition, Christianity and found the images lacking something essential.

While Jung recognized the image of Christ as a transformative archetypal image of great power and persuasiveness, he also judged it to be incomplete because it did not sufficiently attain the balance between the opposites and symbolize wholeness. It lacked shadow, in his judgment. Jung's argument, made repeatedly in his later writings, is that the Christian God image, the Trinity, lacks shadow integration. It is wholly "good," and evil is defined as mere *privatio boni*, the absence of good. For Jung, as for Plato, a transformative image that represses, neglects, or denies important features of human nature will not do the job of integrating the whole person and balancing all the aspects and forces of the personality.

To be fair, one must admit that Jung was right about the dogmatic Christ image, the image of a perfect man in whom there was no sin; but he was off the mark with respect to the image of Jesus in the Gospels. In the Synoptic Gospels (Matthew, Mark, and Luke), Jesus is depicted as the Son of Man, as a person who mingles with common people, who eats and drinks freely with publicans and prostitutes, whose first miracle is to turn water into wine for the added merriment of a wedding party, who breaks the rigid religious rules regarding the Sabbath, and who can display anger to the point of being intemperate. He also treats the body, healing the physically sick, the blind, the diseased. In short, he is shown to be fully embodied, living a human life and suffering the common human experience of death. He breathes, he sweats, he laughs and cries. This is not an image of abstract and inhuman perfection. If anything, the Gospel writers went out of their way to create an image of a flesh-and-blood individual. Jesus is a man of action, engaged with issues of his day, involved in the human condition at all levels. With regard to the portrait of Jesus in the three Synoptic Gospels, Jung plainly errs in his judgment that it lacks shadow.

Where Jung correctly identifies a problem is in the dogmatic version of Christ, as this image was elaborated in New Testament times by Paul and his early followers and by later church authorities, theologians, and Councils. The focus shifted away from the human Jesus of Nazareth to theological problems such as redemption from sin and atonement (Christ had to be the perfect sacrifice, otherwise God's justice would not have been satisfied). The puzzles concerning Christ's two natures, one human and one divine, and his relations within the Godhead (a Trinity) gave rise to a host of careful philosophical and theological distinctions but obscured the Jesus image of the Synoptic Gospels. Moreover, the early church's insistence on creating a biblical canon that would include so many disparate writings - the Pentateuch, words of the prophets, and the Psalms, along with the Synoptic Gospels, the Fourth Gospel, the writings of Paul, other epistles, and even the bizarre Book of Revelation - ended by placing Jesus in a "complexed" context. The transformative image of Jesus of Nazareth was compromised by its setting. Jesus had to become the answer to Old Testament prophesies, the fulfillment of ancient Messianic promises, and the Son of God rather than the Son of Man. All of this had the effect of at once elevating the image and distorting it, taking away its uniqueness and pumping it up with theological and philosophical helium. The human Jesus got lost in the interpretation, and the quest for the historical Jesus so far has been unsuccessful in recovering him.

Nevertheless, what was made available by the Christian tradition as it grew and eventually became dominant in the Roman world was an image of transformative power that profoundly altered the West's values and basic assumptions about life. It is beyond dispute that Christianity transformed classical culture importantly. Dante's *Commedia* is a vivid textbook of this definitive transformation of cultural attitude. The Christian myth redefined the terms of good and evil, drew a veil over the body, and clothed the naked pagan statue. Christianity offered an myth of history that taught the fall of humanity in the Garden of Eden and the dire consequences of original sin. In turn, it offered hope for salvation and a promise of eternal life beyond the grave. It transformed the vision of the nature and destiny of humankind, and it defined the means of grace. Nothing in Western culture was left untouched. But the transformative image at the center of Christianity - Jesus of Nazareth – was moved to the periphery in the march toward social and cultural hegemony. By the time the famous image of the Renaissance Pope Leo X, who in all his magisterial earthy sensuality and secular splendor and power, was painted brilliantly by the Italian master Raphael (ca. 1517), Christianity had little in common with the figure of Jesus of Nazareth. The transformative image of Jesus itself had been transformed into a self-satisfied and well-fed Italian prince, and the time was ripe for reformation, a transformation back to the original.

Both the Reformation and the Renaissance, more or less coinciding historically, were efforts to reach back to origins. The Reformation of Christianity attempted to recapture the spirit of the early church as represented in the original images of the New Testament. The Renaissance, on the other hand, looked back to the ancient Greeks and Romans for inspiration and sought to recapture the image of the human in with all its beauty and corporeal sensuality. While both sides were blessed with genius aplenty and an outpouring of inspiration and energy, their joint existence signaled a major crisis in Western culture. A dead end had been reached, and to go forward Western ·culture reached far back into the past for transformative images.

What the transformative image offers is a pattern for channeling psychic energy along specific lines of thought and action. For the Reformation, the Bible served this purpose. New translations in local languages proliferated and preaching from the Bible and rigorous Bible study became the guides by which life in Protestant communities was shaped. A new interpretation of the biblical text often would result in a new denomination, yet common to all sects was the transformative image itself, the Bible. As long as one could locate a viewpoint or a doctrine in the sacred text, one was on firm ground. This would establish and justify a lifestyle, a set of rules and laws of conduct, a behavioral norm. Some of these were relatively generous and life-enhancing, but many were repressive, life-denying, and punitive. The Counter-Reformation followed suit, also moving toward intolerance and rigidity. Human nature chafed under these burdens. In seeking relief, people created the famous sub-terfuges of eighteenth- and nineteenth century European culture. It was into this world that Freud and Jung were born, and both were famously unaccepting of hypocrisy.

Jung's critique of the Christ image - that it lacks shadow - derives in part from his personal experience in the Swiss Reformed Church. His opinion of this religious denomination, in which he grew up and in which his father and six of his uncles and one grandfather were pastors, was that it was without life. The mainsprings of psychic energy no longer were organized by or contained within it. It did not move the emotions or touch the heart. It was a dead letter, a mere convention. What this church, and Swiss culture generally, supported was Respectability - a new god of the age, Jung called it- while the radical message of biblical Christianity had little commanding influence on individuals or on society as a whole. Who wanted to hear the biting words of Jesus, or pick up a cross and follow him? Nor did the church's image of Jesus become an important figure in Jung's inner life. For him, the Swiss Protestant church's image of Jesus had an unreal quality; it was too abstract and one-dimensional to move him. The religious tradition of his family and his culture no longer could persuade him or contain his psychic energy. He was a modern man, and he spoke as one who was in search of his soul. Yet, as we saw in Jung's transforming active imagination, the image of Christ crucified played a key role in his midlife transformation and helped him gain access to his inferior feeling function.

It was Jung's opinion that in modernity the religious traditions generally were losing their power to move the psyche and to provide transformative images. He shared the view of many intellectuals and scientists of his generation that Religion had become culturally passé. While many people continued to adhere to them, many did so simply out of habit and for the sake of respectability. It is like going to the opera - one goes in order to be seen by others who are there. Some people, of course, are genuinely contained by and find resources in the images provided, but in modern industrialized and technological societies these are ever fewer in number. The loss of religious feeling and conviction was considered by many to be a central problem of modernity. Where, then, could one possibly look for symbols of transformation? European modernity had become a time not unlike that of Socrates: The old religion had become a mere formality. So where was one to turn for the transformative image needed to harmonize the disparate parts of the psyche and impart a sense of direction and meaning? Jung gave up on organized religion and looked to private inner psychological experience. The individual psyche became the temple where the god images could be found.

The "way of the dream" is one approach to the problem of discovering effective transformative images for the modern individual. To those not schooled in this way, it may seem improbable that dream images could function as transformative images in the same way that traditional religious symbols do. Dreams are ephemeral, constantly changing, a symptom of the flux of psychic process in the state of sleeping rather than stable forms that can organize conscious attitudes and behavior. And yet, to the careful catcher of dreams it will happen that occasionally a symbolic dream occurs that stands out from all the rest, like the one I discussed in the previous chapter. Jung distinguished between little dreams and big dreams. A big dream is one that has the potential to become a transformative image.

A transformative image, I remind the reader, is one that channels will and desire will into specific attitudes, activities, and goals. In order to have this potential, an image must have deep roots in the archetypal level of the psyche. A transforming dream image is one that manages to capture an important aspect of the Self and lend it to consciousness, which uses it for meaning and direction.

Jung himself was gifted with many big dreams that guided his inner development in essential ways, but he is not alone. Many people who pay close attention to their dreams for an extended period of time find that they have big dreams, and it is not an uncommon happening in analysis. For example, I had a dream while I was in training analysis that has never left me. I have used it as a meditation many times since then. In the dream,

> I am in a large assembly hall. The room is packed, and the audience is waiting for the speaker to appear on stage. At the appointed time, a gentleman who looks like the Indian teacher, Krishnamurti, walks to the center. He is holding a canvas about six feet wide and three feet high with a simple drawing on it. The drawing is a single unbroken line that depicts a house, a rock, and a tree. The distinguished speaker asks the audience to volunteer interpretations of this picture. A few people do so but without much success, and so the lecturer himself says: "You can see that the drawing depicts several objects, but

it is made with one unbroken line. This means that all things are connected." Pause. "And what connects them is - love."

The dream ended with this lesson. It is a teaching that is not especially novel or surprising, given the speaker, and if this incident had occurred in waking life I might have forgotten it soon enough. But because it came to me in a dream - specifically to me alone - it made a strong impression.

This dream needs no specialized psychological interpretation. It speaks for itself. If one penetrates into its message and fully integrates it, it can be transformative. A whole world view is embedded in this dream. It is an image that expresses the universal connections beneath the multiplicity of the phenomenal world of appearances. In the numinal world, everything is linked by love, even if, in appearance, objects and people are seen as separate and distinct. Both levels are true. A house is not a tree is not a stone. You are not me, I am not my brother, he is not his neighbor. . .This is true. Distinctions are important, even essential, for consciousness. Good fences make good neighbors. And yet, this teaching holds that at a less obvious level we are all made of the same stuff - same atoms, same molecules, same energy systems - and that the whole is held together by a glue that is called "love." Eros is the substance that holds everything in place and connected. Obviously what is meant is not romantic love, erotic energy, or sexual libido, even if romantic love and sexual libido also draw us together and often lead to a feeling of oneness and a recognition of the unity of all things. But sexual libido is only one kind of love energy. It is the general energy of love libido itself - that is the bond, the glue of the universe of objects, inanimate and animate. Sexual love is one instance of love, kinship libido another, agape yet another. The dream teaches that love is not only a personal emotion; it is an impersonal bond, a force that works within the heart of the cosmos toward maintaining unity and connection.

I share this dream as an example of a potentially trans-formative image. It implies a vision of life and has practical implications. In another dream about the same time, I was given the chance to witness the original creation of matter. At the bottom of a deep hole in the ground, two elements – gases - were brought into contact with one another, and they created what in the dream was called "original matter." This was a scientific experiment. Again, the notion of union is expressed in this dream image. I puzzled about these dreams for years, remembering always that Heraclitus said that war is the mother of all things. How to square conflict with unifying energy, hate with love? It is an ancient problem. Some philosophers, like Empedocles, wanted to say that both are necessary. One force unites and draws things together; the other separates and differentiates them. My own conclusion, following Jung's suggestions and my dreams, is that there are two levels. At the level of consciousness, differentiation is a crucial value; but at the level of the deeper psyche, within the self, love and unity predominate. We actually live in two worlds simultaneously.

Dreams offer potentially transformative images to conscious-ness, but the outcome depends on what a person does with them. One reason religious images have such a profound effect on individuals and on whole collectives is that they are repeated regularly over long periods of time. The sheer repetition of the Mass, day after day, Sunday after Sunday, year after year, in exactly the same form creates patterns in the conscious and unconscious psychic energy systems that become indelible. Compared to this institutionalized round of rite and ritual, the single, once-only, unique experience of a dream image appears to be highly evanescent. But if the dream image is taken up by consciousness, retained, worked with (not necessarily compulsively, but regularly) over a period of time, it has the potential to transform conscious attitudes and, following that, behavior and motivation. The psyche has the capacity to regulate itself and to provoke its own development.

It is my argument, throughout this book, that a person's destiny which is made from the qualities and markings that end up establishing themselves as the deepest etchings of character, mission, and meaning in life, the features that define a particular life as unique - is importantly, perhaps most essentially, constituted by a group of transformative images and experiences. What happens is that a person's integrity and potential as a unique human being become realized through these transformations. One becomes the person one most essentially and uniquely is by means of the images that draw one's psychic energy into a specific configuration of attitude, behavior, and motivation. The configuration is archetypal, and therefore collective (such as Poet, Physician, Mother, etc.), but the individual is a unique instance of it.

How individual lives turn out in the end depends upon how transformative images are received and developed. The images embody complexity and the potential for further development. The notion that archetypal images themselves also need development and conscious intervention would occupy Jung's interest for the rest of his life. In his late work, *Answer to Job*, he wrestled with this question in reference to the biblical God image. According to Jung's view, Yahweh was blind to his anima and had an inferior feeling function, just as Jung did. Like Jung, too, Yahweh put himself through death by crucifixion in order to redeem his Eros and his emotional connection to humankind. Finally, as in Jung's psyche, the blind anima of biblical tradition, having regained her place in the patriarchal pantheon of Father, Son, and Holy Spirit as the deified and elevated Virgin Mother, is transforming consciousness in our time. Jung must have felt he was assisting this development in collective consciousness by suffering through the experience of writing this text, which came to him in a burst of inspiration during a brief period of time while he was recovering from an illness. He was recapitulating his own inner development and trying to use it to heal his ailing religious tradition and to move it forward into a new stage of development around the transformative image of quaternity.[16] For Jung, his personal transformation and the collective transformation of Christianity became intertwined.

The key point is that, while transformative images mold and shape our attitudes, values, horizons of meaning, and purposes, they themselves also are in need of, and subject to, a process of transformation. Immemorial and timeless as the images are, when they are drawn into encounters with us and we with them, they too will change. Here Jung parts company with Plato and anticipates the thinking of modern process philosophers and theologians. The alchemy of the interaction between archetypal images and individual consciousness produces what we call individuation, a process of mutual evolution toward wholeness.

---

[16] See my book, *Jung's Treatment of Christianity*, for an extended discussion of this topic.

Transformative Relationships

> "Wholeness is a combination of I and You, and these show themselves to be parts of a transcendent unity whose nature can only be grasped symbolically."[1]
>
> C.G. Jung

She is dreaming.

A doorbell rings, and she walks through the house to answer it. Friends have arrived for a visit. She greets them enthusiastically and leads them to the guest rooms in the basement, which until then she had not realized existed. The basement is a discovery. It is much larger than the house itself - six times as big! -and beautifully laid out with wide corridors and elegant guest suites. (In actuality, her house has no such basement.) As she escorts her friends into this space, she warns them of the water at the entrance. Boots are required to pass over the threshold.

"Where shall we stay?" her friend inquires.

---

[1] C.G. Jung, *Two Essays in Analytical Psychology*, para. 233.

"I would recommend the suite on the far end, to the left. It has such beautiful views of the ocean and the terraced gardens. On the other side, of course, you can see the mountains, but I think this view is nicer."

Odd, it seems to her, the "basement" is above ground. As they enter, they find many friends and colleagues of her husband's wandering through the halls, seeming to be busy with various matters. Her husband has been building this space for some time and is moving forward toward the front of the house as he proceeds. His work is nearly complete. He greets their friends, hammer and saw in hand, and helps them with their luggage.

The dream ends here. The next day she marvels at the large space beneath their home.

The woman's husband had been busy with some projects that he had not had time to tell her about in the few days before the dream. In their mutual unconscious, which is the large basement under their home, this was noted. The views from the basement, surprisingly, look out on a world that the house above ground in actuality does not share. The psyche is an open space, and the farther inward you go, the more you find yourself outside.

Relationships have many levels and aspects, and not all of them are easily accessible to consciousness. When a relationship begins, one may worry about the role of projection and "transference" - that is, effects carried over from past relationships. Also, images of an ideal are created by the psyche, using the hair, eyes, and other personal qualities of a person one has just met. After forming a relationship and living in it for a time, one expects less projection, less idealization, and resolution of transference or its flight to another person. But, even then, there are levels of unconsciousness, and elusive interactions continue. People, it turns out, are connected in many surprising and enduring ways, and they continue to discover new facets endlessly.

Before embarking on what is for me the difficult task of exploring the transformative effects of personal relationships - difficult because so much material lies in the territory of intimacy, which must remain unspoken and shrouded in confidentiality and in personal and professional discretion - let me restate my general viewpoint. Psychological transformation is the "passing over" (Latin, *trans*) from one "organized pattern" (Latin, *forma*) of psychic content to another. Although this can happen at many times in life, my focus is on psychological transformation in adulthood. In the first two chapters, I argued that the means by which this transfer of pattern is accomplished is the psychic image – dream, vision, voice, projection. Images arise from the archetypal collective unconscious - whether "inner" or "outer" is immaterial - like activated imaginal disks in the pupa of a butterfly, and they create the bridge between the old psychological constellation of attitude and self-identity and a new one. The formation of the mature adult self-imago installs a new or significantly altered and augmented sense of identity. A new vocation may be born from this, or an earlier one may be confirmed at a deeper and more convincing level. The former path we see in the life of William Mellon, who experienced the transforming image of Albert Schweitzer who became a model for his new vocation as a doctor in Haiti. The latter option is evident in the biography of Carl Jung, who experienced the image of Aion and at midlife became a new kind of teacher and healer, and in the story of Rainer Maria Rilke, who heard a voice in the wind speaking about angelic orders and became a deeper poet and a modern Orpheus. Jung speaks of this transformation as a modern version of an ancient "mystery" known as "deification." This is because the transformative images are archetypal and transcend the ego's former sense of identity. Through this process of transformation, an individual assumes their destined specific self-imago, which will shape their journey throughout the rest of their adult lives. To have its full effect, the transformation process may extend over a longer period of time, but typically it begins with a powerful symbolic experience that is triggered by physical and psychological factors which become active during adulthood and behave like change hormones. One of the most powerful of these factors is the experience of intimate relationship.

The full adult welf-imago that emerges is a pattern of attitudes, self assessments, and motivations; it consists of aspects of the psyche that previously have lain partially or completely dormant and undeveloped in the unconscious. The self-imago that develops out of the transformative process will draw forth, contain, and channel psychic energy into what potentially is a person's realized whole-ness. It is typical of this transformational era that it begins dramatically with an announcement of endings and glimpses of things to come, then passes through an extended period of liminality, and concludes with the rapid configuration and emergence of the newly formed self-imago. Think of the trans-formation of the caterpillar into a butterfly.

The account of psychological transformation in adulthood so far has ignored the important factor of an inter-personal context. What is the relational context in which the transforming person lives? In the introduction, I acknowledged that other factors must be taken into account besides seemingly spontaneous happenings such as dreams, intuitions, visions, and archetypal projections. Biologists have ascertained that in the timing of the termination of diapause in the pupa of the butterfly environmental factors such as light, warmth, and the amount of moisture available play key roles in triggering the hormones that set off the final burst of imago formation. So, too, with psychological transformation. In the period before and during the early stages of adolescence, for example, social and familial factors play a critical role in triggering and shaping the adolescent experience of transformation. Social expectations and family lifestyle, economic situation, physical and medical conditions, political events, and personal relationships play a large role in the timing and outcome of the transformation process both in adolescence and later at midlife. These constitute the environment within which the transforming images arise and the context in which the transformation process takes place. This chapter focuses specifically on personal relationships in adulthood as the context of transformation. The power of Eros to constellate the psyche and to change human lives has been acknowledged from time immemorial in imaginative literature and biographies. Intimate relationships are perhaps the richest environments for psychological transformation throughout human life, including adulthood.

The analytic relationship is the context in which depth psychology has examined transformation most closely. To approach this subject, therefore, I shall turn to a consideration of the practice of psychotherapy, in which the relationship between therapist and patient generally is recognized as being a critical factor in thera-peutic change. Consideration of the therapy context supplies an occasion for reflecting, albeit somewhat indirectly and discretely, upon the transformational energy involved in all intimate relation-ships.

Whenever I have asked professional psychotherapists, "What heals in therapy?" the most frequent answer has been "the relation-ship." The personal relationship between therapist and patient typically is seen as the essential factor upon which change and psychological growth depend. It is as if this is what releases the hormones that stimulate transformation in therapy.

While this seems to be the consensus today, it was not always so. In the early days of psychoanalysis, it was supposed that the analyst's insightful interpretations, which uncovered repressed thoughts and memories of early trauma and made them conscious again, played the critical role in producing a cure. Transference was regarded as essential, not because it offered a "corrective emotional experience," as was later held, but rather because it offered the opportunity for repeating the past and thereby raising the repressed conflicts to the surface of consciousness and allowing them to be interpreted. Interpretation was the way to make the unconscious conscious and to follow Freud's dictum: "Where id was, there ego shall be." More light in the dark would release people from their neurotic conflicts. Enlightenment and ego mastery over psychic life were the aims of early psychoanalysis.

Jung's relationship with Freud got off on the right foot when he passed Freud's test question in their first meeting in 1907. Freud asked him what he thought was the most important factor in psychoanalysis, and he responded without hesitation, "the transference." Freud assured him that he had grasped the main point. The focus of analytic treatment was to be on the fantasy relationship the patient spun around the quiet, reflective and mostly invisible presence of the analyst. All the love and hate the patient had experienced in childhood with parents would be repeated in the analytic relationship, suffered all over again, and regurgitated as wish-fulfilling dreams, slips of the tongue, emotional resistance, incestuous longings and memories, and acting-out behaviors. This material would be gathered by the attentive analyst, assembled into a pattern for interpretation, and offered as an explanation for why the patient was suffering from such specific symptoms as hysterical blindness, compulsive acts, obsessive thoughts, etc. The cure was measured by increased rationality, greater ego control, and better insight into chronic behavioral and emotional patterns.

Jung at first also practiced this sort of transference analysis on his less pathological patients at the Klinik. With chronically psychotic patients, however, it proved not useful to interpret transference, and Jung became convinced early on that schizophrenia was an organically based mental disorder that would not yield to transference analysis. Nonetheless, in his private practice and with his healthier and more intellectually gifted patients, he performed what then was considered correct psychoanalysis. But it became apparent to him that there was more to the relationship in therapy than a one-sided transference. Two psyches are involved in the therapeutic encounter, both are subject to emotional reactions, and both are given to projecting unconscious contents into the other. A new term had to be invented to cover the analyst's involvement in the relationship. Between them, Freud and Jung came up with the infelicitous term countertransference (in German it sounds even worse than in English: *Gegenübertragung*). This would become a way of saying, "She made me do it!" The analyst's emotional response was seen simply as a reaction to the patient's transference. Eve offered the apple; Adam responded to the invitation.

It now is known that Jung was caught up in a troublesome countertransference at the time he met Freud.[2] He was treating a (to him) fascinating young Russian Jewish woman named Sabina Spielrein. She had been sent as an adolescent by her parents to the worldfamous Burgholzli Klinik in Zurich and there became a patient of Jung's, who was chief resident at the time. Spielrein, though not named, appears as an item of concern early in Jung's correspondence with Freud. On October 23, 1906, he wrote, "I am currently treating an hysteric with your method. Difficult case, a 20-year-old Russian girl student, ill for 6 years."[3] Freud showed interest in the symptoms and replied with a detailed analysis of them on October 27. About a year later, Jung again wrote to Freud about a problem he was having with an obsessional patient who had made him the object of her sexual fantasies (October 10, 1907): "Should I continue the treatment, which on her own admission gives her voluptuous pleasure, or should I discharge her?"[4] It is supposed that this is another reference to Spielrein. Freud's letter in response is lost, but Jung's reply indicates that Freud gave him advice, which he took (October 28).

What Freud and his followers eventually developed as the ideal treatment model was what the American psychoanalyst Merton Gill has called the "one person situation." It is a viewpoint that considers only one psyche in the consulting room. The patient's psyche enters

---

[2] For detailed documentation of the relationship between Jung and Spielrein, see John Kerr, *A Most Dangerous Method.*

[3] W. McGuire, *The Freud-Jung Letters,* p. 7.

[4] *Ibid.,* p. 93.

the analytic space and occupies it exclusively, generating free associations, offering dream reports for analysis, presenting resistances, and acting out. The invisible analyst, on the other hand, maintains emotional calm and neutrality ("evenly hovering attention") and offers occasional summarizing interpretations. Anything else contributed by the analyst in the way of interpersonal interaction - whether verbal, enacted, or even simply silently felt - is regarded as "contamination" of this ideal analytic space and should be viewed as a countertransference reaction and analyzed away because it is interference in the analysis.

In Jung's analysis of Sabina Spielrein, there clearly was a lot of such contamination. In fact, according to the correspondence published and discussed by Aldo Carotenuto, he eventually engaged with her in a highly erotic (it is still debated how far they went) relationship. This took place after years of analytic treatment. It is evident that during this time Spielrein had changed from a severely disturbed, mentally ill adolescent patient at the beginning of Jung's treatment into a highly gifted, competent medical doctor and nascent psychoanalyst at the conclusion of her time in Zurich. Their relationship passed through several phases in the course of the ten years or so that they worked together, evolving from a psychiatric patient-doctor relationship to a romanticized younger woman-older man constellation, and then to a mentorship configuration in which Jung was Spielrein's dissertation advisor and helped her to publish her first professional paper. Eventually the relationship evolved into a more distant but still mutually respectful collegial one after Spielrein left Zurich and joined Freud's circle in Vienna. It was this kind of therapeutic relationship - so unorthodox in Freudian terms, so difficult to manage in a professional context, so challenging to the psychoanalyst - that stimulated Jung to rethink his position on the nature and transformative potential of the analytic process. Eventually he came to regard transformation in analysis as dependent upon psychic interaction rather than on detached interpretation. Something must happen in a person's affective psychological life, and not only in their cognition, in order to produce transformation. The relationship takes it deeper.

By 1929, when Jung wrote "Problems of Modern Psychotherapy" for the Swiss Medical Yearbook, he had behind him over twenty-five years of clinical experience with a wide variety of analytical cases and interpersonal constellations. In this article, he offered a summary of his experiences as an analyst and as supervisor and teacher of a new generation of younger analysts. He describes four "stages of analysis": confession, elucidation, education, and transformation. I will consider the first three just briefly here before moving on to more crucial one of transformation.

In Jung's mind, psychotherapy is historically a descendant of a religious practice traditionally found in the Roman Catholic church, the sacrament of Confession or what is today often called Reconciliation: "The first beginnings of all analytical treatment of the soul are to be found in its prototype, the confessional."[5] Suggested by the term confession, too, is the confidential nature of the psychotherapeutic interaction and communication and the opportunity in therapy to speak openly about otherwise carefully guarded and often shameful secrets, both acts and thoughts. To one degree or another, all schools of psychotherapy have this stage in common, although behavioral and cognitive modes tend to downplay it.

Elucidation is the term Jung preferred to use for the second stage, by which he means interpretation. By this term he refers to the act of understanding and explaining the patient's symptoms as referring to past traumas, unconscious conflicts, and childhood carry-overs into the present. One such "carry-over" is the transference, images and feelings from the childhood relationship to the parents to the present relationship to the analyst. In this stage, the analyst explains the present psychological situation of the patient reductively by referring to formative persons and scenes from

---

[5] C.G. Jung, "Problems of Modern Psychotherapy," in *CW* 16, par. 124.

childhood. Elucidation becomes necessary in therapy when, he writes, after a person confesses and transference begins to emerge. The analyst is now experienced with deep feeling as an intimate confidante with moral and psychological authority. The early analysts discovered rather quickly that catharsis arising from confession was not enough to produce permanent healing. It might alleviate symptoms temporarily, but it did not lastingly cure the patient. In order to go further, the transference now had to be raised to consciousness and analyzed. Jung writes: "The patient falls into a sort of childish dependence from which he cannot defend himself even by rational insight . . . Obviously we are dealing with a neurotic formation, a new symptom directly induced by the treatment."[6] This bond with the analyst is based upon unconscious fantasies, and it is to Freud's credit, Jung acknowledges, that he uncovered this. Jung himself had experienced this with Freud, who had assumed the image of a father figure. Elucidation serves to return the authority vested in the analyst back to the patient's ego, thereby strengthening it and making it more autonomous. This stage of analysis helps a person grow out of childish dependency and assume the power and responsibility of adulthood. The stage of elucidation also uncovers and brings into consciousness the shadow side of the psyche: "It is the most effective antidote imaginable to all the idealistic illusions about the nature of man."[7] Elucidation has a corrosive effect upon unrealistic and inflated conscious attitudes and grounds the ego in a more realistic perception of self and others. It is a powerful tool for change, and Jung continued to believe in using it vigorously in the treatment of neurotic (and especially, of young) patients.

Following elucidation, the patient is left with the task of making new adaptations to life. The old habits of idealization and childish wishful thinking have been unmasked and seen through, and now a

---

[6] *Ibid.*, par. 139.
[7] *Ibid.*, par. 145.

new approach to the tasks of living is required. Analysis enters a third stage at this point: education. Education is the Adlerian stage, Jung says, and it is an almost inevitable consequence of elucidation. Elucidation, the Freudian stage, frees energies that were tied up in neurotic childishness and dependency on external authorities, and the question now becomes where to invest this free energy and how to use it. Adler recognized the need for social education beyond the understanding of the unconscious and insight into its primitive workings. He was fundamentally an educator who sought to help his patients make a better adaptation in their everyday lives through, first, achieving high self-esteem and, second, investing it in broad social interest. Here the analyst becomes an educator and helps to shape behavior and adaptation to social ideals and realities.

Transformation is the fourth stage of analysis. In it, the therapist is prepared to lead the patient one step further, beyond the issues of ego-building and adaptation to the collective and social dimensions of life. This stage is not suitable for everyone, and generally it is reserved for patients in the second half of life who already have made an adequate adaptation and contribution to society and who are not pathologically impaired. It focuses on individuation and on releasing the person's unique personality from its bondage to conscious and unconscious restrictions. Here Jung brings out his views on the dialectical interaction that takes place between analyst and analysand: "In any effective psychological treatment the doctor is bound to influence the patient; but this influence can only take place if the patient has a reciprocal influence on the doctor. You can exert no influence if you are not susceptible to influence. It is futile for the doctor to shield himself from the influence of the patient."[8] Transformation is a two-way process, Jung explains. Both the doctor and the patient are affected by the profound engagement that takes place between them when this stage of treatment is entered.

---

[8] *Ibid.*, par. 163.

There are challenges in this stage beyond the ones usually encountered in psychotherapy. Sometimes a power question arises in this relationship, and it becomes a contest of whose personality will prevail. Occasionally, Jung hints darkly, the patient's psyche assimilates the doctor's, and more than one therapist's professional and personal life has been ruined by falling victim to the psychological impact of a patient's unconscious. It is not that either party in this interaction necessarily wishes consciously to overpower or destroy the other, but, since the engagement between them takes place at unconscious as well as conscious levels, the forces at work in it are not under the control of the ego. A genie escapes from the bottle and is let loose in the analytic space. What Jung speaks of in this article, but only in the most general terms, is the interactive alchemy that takes place between two people as their psyches become deeply enmeshed. The outcome of this interaction, which he calls transformation, is unpredictable, but he hopes by these means to generate a new realization (on both sides of the therapeutic equation) of the Self and the reorganization of psychic energy around this new constellation. The analytic process itself now becomes the pupation stage of psychological metamorphosis, and its end result is a self-imago.

Some seventeen years later, in 1946, Jung published "The Psychology of the Transference," his definitive statement on the transformative potential of the analytic relationship. In this major essay, he focuses specifically and at length on the fourth stage of analysis transformation - and offers a far-reaching theory of what takes place psychologically in a transformative relationship. "The Psychology of the Transference" is divided into two parts, the first a general theoretical section and the second an interpretation of a series of alchemical pictures from the *Rosarium Philosophorum*, a medieval text, which Jung uses to illustrate and develop his thesis. The most essential point to grasp is his observation that four actors in the two-person relationship: the conscious egos of the two people involved (A and B), and the respective unconscious of each

(A' and B'). Relational dynamics are active among all four factors. In other words, there are six couples in a two-person relationship: A/B; A'/B'; A/A'; B/B'; A'/B; B'/A.

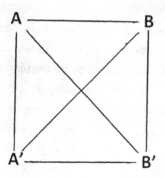

In the classic psychoanalytic setup of "only one psyche in the room," the situation appears to be much simpler. The analytically trained ego of the doctor observes the patient's associations and collects observations about the patient's defenses and repressed unconscious material. These are offered back to the patient in an interpretation of the B/B' couple. There also are interpretations of the relation between the patient's unconscious and the analyst, the classic transference relation (the B'/A couple). Privately the analyst will consider as well the countertransference couple (A'/B). But where this view of the relationship falls short is in failing to recognize the mutual unconscious relationship that becomes operative between doctor and patient (the A'/B' couple). In Jung's version of analysis, this relationship between the unconscious couple A'/B' not only is acknowledged but is regarded as the most critical for transformation.

At the outset of therapy, the full dimensions of the complexity of the relationship that will develop between analysand and analyst cannot be known. There is the official professional relationship, the conscious couple, which is established at the beginning of treatment and maintained throughout (the A/B couple). This is regarded as a mutual agreement, and each partner takes on certain specific obligations: the analyst will follow the rules and ethics of the profession and to use all available training and skill for the benefit of the patient; the patient will cooperate with treatment by being as open as possible with the analyst and offering unconscious material as it becomes available in fantasies, dreams and associations. Meeting time, fees, boundaries, and professionalism set the terms for this contract, and the ensuing relationship is thus contained within this secure framework. It is the first and simplest (if not always the easiest) obligation of the analyst to maintain this relationship and keep it firmly in place at all times during treatment (and perhaps also even after treatment officially has ended). Confidentiality is a rule required by ethics and the law. The conscious relationship is the container of analysis, and it is required in order to create trust and safety.

The classic transference relationship, which takes place between the patient's unconscious and the doctor's persona presentation (the B'/A couple), also was recognized by Jung. This is a partially unconscious couple. The analysand's unconscious reacts to the analyst's professional attitude and words, the office space and persona presentation in a particular way, based upon earlier history and life experience, and from the unconscious arise associations to somewhat similar figures from the past. There may be a response of immediate and unwarranted trust, even love; conversely, there may be an irrational reaction of fear and suspicion. These are based upon previous experiences with authority figures such as parents, guardians, and teachers. Freud was a master at eliciting and elucidating this relationship, and he made this the centerpiece of, and indeed the necessary condition for, psycho-analysis. No "transference neurosis," as it was called, no analysis. Jung supplemented the understanding of this relationship by introducing the idea of archetypal transference: the figure of the analyst may be embellished not so much by one's personal father imago (the inner image of one's own father) but rather by a larger-than-life and much more powerful figure like the hero, the lover, the sage, the magician, or even God.

A similar hybrid couple is constituted in a corresponding dimension between the analyst's unconscious and the analysand's conscious presentation (the A'/B couple). Jung's early analytic experience with Spielrein developed into an unruly relationship between his own unconscious and the fascinating presence of his young female patient. Something foreign and mysterious about her stirred his poetic soul and entranced him. The psychic factor responsible for this response derived from his own unconscious psyche and was projected onto the patient, young Sabina. This psychological factor was what he would come to call the anima, the soul image of the eternal feminine embedded in a man's unconscious.

With this undeniable realization that the doctor could be hooked psychologically by the personality of some patients, not in the parental complexes but in other unconscious centers of desire and archetypal activation, the conception of the analytic interaction began to take a new turn. It was not especially surprising that a young doctor could become sexually stimulated and excited by an attractive young female patient, nor was it a cause for wonder that this was considered contamination of the process and something to be rejected before it could interfere with professional treatment. Such would have been the view of Freud, with whom Jung certainly would have agreed on this point. But the deep tenacity of Jung's emotional response, and its meaning for his own psychological development and for his life, called for some rethinking of theory and technique. Perhaps the doctor was in analysis, too; and perhaps this was more of a two-way business than at first had been realized. Jung no longer was just a neutral listener. He was being drawn by his patients into a mutual play and interaction of psyches. And perhaps it was foolhardy and the result of youthful naiveté that he let himself enter into the relationship with Spielrein and others (not only with women but also with men) and allowed himself to be affected by these professional relationships to the extent that he did. The term countertransference, as it then was defined and understood as a reaction to the transference, did not explain the phenomenon in these cases. Jung not only was reacting to his patients' projections and transferences; he actively was projecting his own unconscious material into them as well. In other words, there was a kind of mutual transference going on. From such experiences, Jung would learn a great deal and would vastly change his therapeutic technique and his understanding of the analytic pair.

A fourth couple exists in the relationship between the doctor's conscious ego and unconscious matrix (the A/A' couple). As it is usually described in standard textbooks, countertransference is a result of arousal in this relationship. If the analyst in a particular session becomes unaccountably anxious or emotionally reactive, it usually is taken to be due to some stimulation of a complex in association to something the patient has presented, said, or done. Perhaps a gesture or a phrase of the patient triggers a complex in the analyst's unconscious by association with a parental figure or a scene from childhood. The analyst is trained to monitor this type of reaction and silently analyze it, all the while maintaining composure and facilitating the process under way in the session. Michael Fordham, a leading English Jungian psychoanalyst of his day, named this "illusory countertransference."[9] This type of emotional reaction on the therapist's part is widely recognized by many schools of psychotherapy and was what Freud and Jung had in mind when they invented the term countertransference.

While this is going on in the analyst's psyche, a similar process is occurring in the analysand's in the B/B' couple. Disturbing reactions in response to the doctor's words, office, or physical appearance may arise in the patient's consciousness during a specific session. The rule of analysis is to verbalize these reactions so that they can be examined for their unconscious content.

---

[9] M. Fordham, *Explorations into the Self*, pp. 142-43.

But what had not been recognized at first by the psycho-analysts and was later much emphasized by Jung is the sixth couple, the A'/B' couple. Since Jung formulated his final contribution to the discussion in "The Psychology of the Transference," this relationship has become the center of much interest and attention in the field of analytical psychology. To explain the intractability of some transferences and countertransferences and of the relationship that comes into being in the course of long-term therapeutic encounters, Jung reflected upon the subterranean relationship of unconscious to unconscious (A'/B'). This is an aspect of the relationship that is experienced long before it is, or even can be, analyzed - if indeed it ever is made fully conscious. It is here that we look for images and dynamics that lead to what he designates as transformation.

As the analytic relationship begins to form at this level of mutual unconsciousness, Jung says, a distinct uncanny feeling of "kinship libido"[10] develops. He speaks of a "peculiar atmosphere of family incest."[11] The experienced analyst can detect this mutual affinity and the natural resistances to its recognition and may find evidence of its existence in dreams, mutual associations, and synchronistic events. What is in the making is the psychic glue that will bond the two persons in this analytic undertaking and hold them in place throughout its duration and after. This energy of kinship libido attracts and repels the two people in the analytic relationship, and eventually it feeds into the creation of an image based upon a combination of the two psyches involved in this alchemy. This is the transformative image that will contain and guide the pair. It may be brother and sister, father and daughter, mother and son, brother and brother, sister and sister, cousin and cousin, etc., something with the flavor of a close kinship bond. An irrational union takes place here between the two unconscious systems.

---

[10] C.G. Jung, "Psychology of Transference," in *CW* 16, par. 431.
[11] *Ibid.*, par. 368.

The *Rosarium* pictures, which Jung uses to depict the development of this mutual image in the unconscious, show a process that begins with a formal meeting, enters a middle phase of intimacy, union, and death, and concludes with the emergence of the self-imago. It runs its course along the lines of the model I proposed in chapter one. In the transformative relationship, a caterpillar (larval) stage of becoming acquainted and forming an intimate union is followed by a cocoon (pupa) stage of dormancy, introversion, and seeming death; finally, a butterfly (adult self-mago) stage completes and solidifies the union and gives it permanence.

Both partners in the relationship participate in this transformation, and both enjoy (or suffer) its outcome. Somewhat difficult to grasp and to remember in Jung's written account is the unconsciousness of this process: the entire drama unfolds and plays itself out in the psyche's inner parts, where everything is obscure and where male may be female and female male. This is not to say that effects of this drama cannot be detected in consciousness, but they are fleeting and subtle. Equally so is the transformation that slowly takes place in each personality of the therapeutic dyad as the two partners in it encounter one another steadily over an extended period of time.

As Jung describes this transforming interaction, using the *Rosarium* pictures as a guiding thread, the story opens with an image of a sacred space, a fountain (*Rosarium* Series no. 1). This is an image of wholeness that announces the underlying nature and quality of the psychic process to come. It symbolizes a magical space that will contain and nourish the psychic process with its ever-vivifying waters. This is the psychological precondition for a transformative relationship. Such a pregnant moment of maximum opportunity must be constellated, but it also must be recognized that this is beyond the ego's control. Analysis offers a space, formally structured by its ethical rules and boundaries and nourished by the attitudes and values that guide its procedures, but there can be no guarantee that the transformative Mercurial fountain always will be present.

The fountain, and indeed the whole ensuing process, is presided over and encircled by autonomous archetypal forces and powers - sun, moon, stars - which enclose both analyst and analysand in this mutual undertaking: "The unconscious spiritus rector will take over and lead the mind back to the unchangeable, underlying archetypes, which are then forced into projection by this regression."[12] The unconscious is the creator of the relationship that is about to begin; it is present at the beginning, the middle, and the end of the process. And the unconscious is unpredictable by the ego.

The transformative relationship itself, which begins in the second picture of the *Rosarium*, starts with a left-handed handshake (*Rosarium* Series no. 2). The meeting of the left hands indicates that the two unconscious players (A' and B') of the drama are coming into contact. This signals a pregnant moment of irrational recognition, each of the other, felt as an unusual and surprising sort of openness to a stranger, trust being granted without need of evidence or proof, easy familiarity, confidence. It is a moment of pure projection, suffused with archetypal fantasies and a profound longing for union. This moment also is graced by a sign of transcendence. In the *Rosarium* picture, a dove joins in blessing the relationship that is forming between a King and a Queen as they shake hands. In therapy, this sign may be an impressively symbolic initial dream or a synchronistic event. This marks the beginning of a timeless relationship that will endure. The paths of two lives have crossed, and the meeting is momentous.

The images of the *Rosarium* that follow upon this initial meeting depict the gradual development of a relationship between the King and Queen. There is the moment of full self-disclosure when they face one another naked (*Rosarium* Series no. 3), followed by their entry into a bath (no. 4). They enjoy coitus (no. 5), and from

---

[12] *Ibid.*, para. 407.

that moment onward they are shown as united in one body (no. 6). A profound merger of unconscious psyches has taken place, and the two have become one. From this new conjoint body, a tiny infant, their mutual soul, emerges (*Rosarium* Series no. 7) and flies away into the sky. The mutual body now lies lifeless and inert, as though laid out in a tomb. This is the period of pupation. The relationship, having passed through the phases of self-disclosure, intense bonding, blissful union in a warm bath of mutual unconsciousness, and fertilization, enters a period of quiet.

Rosarium Series no. 1

Analyses go through this sort of quiet and seemingly dead period, and so do non-analytic relationships. After an initial period of regression, archetypal projections occur that create symbols of transformation and lead to the giving and receiving of inspiration and energy. A union takes place, hope surges, there is a birth of new life, and the unconscious responds with magical assistance and fertile imagination. Then, all is quiet for a time. On the surface, life may go on as before, with routines in place, conventional exchanges, even the important daily therapeutic work of elucidation and education continuing unhampered. But the deeper energies are quiescent. For especially sensitive people, this may cause panic and lead to withdrawal. The work seems to lack "presence" and "soul."

Rosarium Series no. 2

While this is a well-known phase in transformative relationships, it is always a stressful one. In the conscious relationship of ego to ego, there can be talk about the felt deadness in the relationship, but this will not resolve it. The best approach is patience and faith.[13] The eighth illustration in the *Rosarium* Series shows a sign of hope: it is raining.

Rosarium Series no. 3

---

[13] See M. Stein, "Faith and the Practicing Analyst."

Rosarium Series no. 4

Rosarium Series no. 5

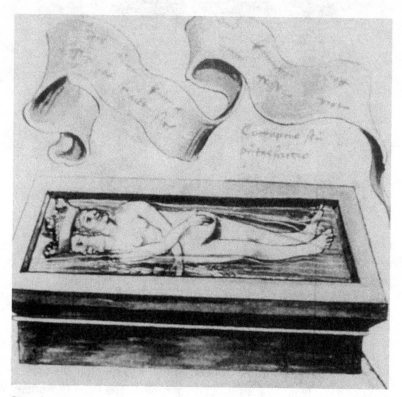

Rosarium Series no.6

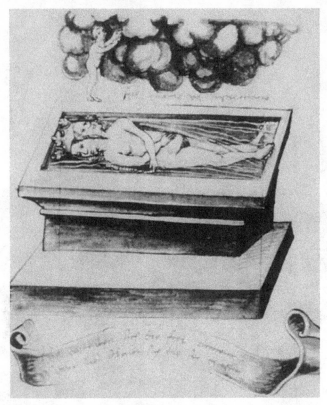

Rosarium Series no. 7

What we have seen up to this point in the *Rosarium* pictures is preparation for what is to come namely, the *Rebis*. In the ninth illustration, the soul returns from up yonder and reenters the united body, and this leads to a resurrection or rebirth. The *Rebis* (*Rosarium* Series no. 10) is an image of the King and Queen united and alive. When the conjoint body rises from the tomb, it reassumes some of the paraphernalia of royalty - a crown, a pair of scepters which had been put aside during the bath. Still naked, it bestrides the moon and bears the wings of an angel. This is an image of culmination in the alchemical opus. All of alchemy is about transformation - of lead into gold, *prima materia* into the *lapis philosophorum*, the conflicted instinctual body into the whole body.

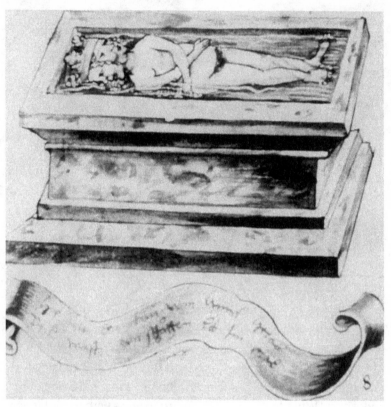

Rosarium Series no. 8

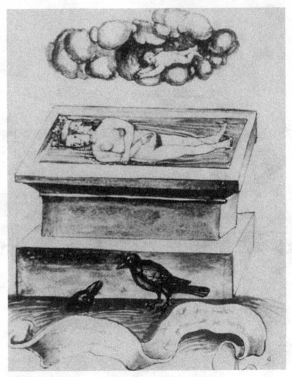

Rosarium Series no. 9

In the *Rosarium*, the transformation of two separate objects into one complete unity is depicted by the *Rebis* (see no. 10). When the King and Queen unite and become one, they create a child, who at first separates from them and then returns and is reabsorbed. Now the *Rebis* appears. The *Rebis* symbolizes a realized union of the opposites: "What the alchemist tried to express with his *Rebis* and his squaring of the circle, and what the modern man also tries to express when he draws patterns of circles and quaternities, is wholeness - a wholeness that resolves all opposition and puts an end to conflict, or at least draws its sting. The symbol of this is a *coincidentia oppositorum* which, as we know, Nicholas of Cusa identified with God."[14]

---

[14] C.G. Jung, "Psychology of the Transference;" in *CW* 16, par. 537.

Rosarium Series no. 10

In a transformative relationship, an experience of the archetypal self becomes available to both partners through the symbolic object that forms between them. This is their permanent bond. It seems that human nature is such that the activation of transformative images often occurs between two people (or more) who are joined intimately at deep unconscious levels. Out of this common psychic matrix arises the imagination that generates symbols which not only bind the pair together for life and through generations, but also offer them access to the archetypal basis of psychological life, the Self. The fountain of living water from picture number one returns as a wellspring of imagination that fertilizes the union and transforms both people in it.

While such symbols of the archetypal self arise spontaneously between people engaged in a transformative relationship, they belong to neither one of them. Actually, they belong to no one. They are archetypal images that dwell in the collective unconscious of humankind. As such they are universal and generally available to everyone, everywhere, anytime.

How is the kinship bond affected by termination of formal analysis? Not at all, because the *Rebis* is archetypal and belongs in a sense to eternity. "On many occasions I have observed," Jung writes in his commentary on the *Rebis* image, "that the spontaneous manifestations of the self . . . bring with them something of the timelessness of the unconscious which expresses itself in a feeling of eternity or immortality."[15] Time and space categories do not apply to this level of the relationship, which continues to exist as a symbolic center available to both partners at any time they choose to renew contact with it.

I have used the analytic relationship with its six "couples" - or, rather, six vertices of one highly complex couple - to discuss transformative relationships. The same model prevails in all emotionally charged relationships. But in other contexts they usually are not so consciously reflected upon. Instead, the vertices tend to fuse explosively in the tempestuous dramas of the relationships between people who are alternately attracted to and repelled by each other. Attracted, they seek merger and oneness; repelled, they desire a great degree of separation and individuality. Love and hate thus combine in a dance that creates marriages, business partnerships,

---

[15] *Ibid.,* par. 531.

and relations of many sorts, and then either destroys them or fosters some measure of individual development. If one could analyze these emotionally charged relationships psychologically, one most likely would find that they are the triggers and the contexts for adult transformation, for the formation of a self-imago.

It is noteworthy that Jung dedicated his essay on transference to his wife. Whatever his difficulties in marriage may have been, he must have found in retrospect that his relationship with his wife, Emma, was transformative. In fact, the marriage was a deeply bonded, enduring relationship for both of them. For many people, marriage is a highly complex and at least potentially transformative relationship. It changes many aspects of people's lives. It rearranges their perceptions of past, present, and future, and it channels energy into directions that typically include home, family, and social networks. It changes a person's self-definition from "single" to "coupled." Wedding rings signal this new state of affairs.

A marriage does not become transformative automatically, however, and simply by verbalizing the wedding vows, trading rings, cutting the wedding cake, and enjoying a honeymoon together. Marriages pass through many phases and crises, and only if an irrational bond grows up between the partners and holds firm as the relationship develops and deepens can one speak of marriage as a transformative relationship. To be transformative, a union must take place not only in the conscious relationship but also in the subterranean levels of both partners. In marriage, there is an ego level of relating, which is hard enough to manage and is what marriage counselors tend to focus on when trying to improve communication skills and tolerance. But there is also the level of the deep unconscious. It is frequently the case that a tacit agreement is reached between marriage partners to work out issues on a persona level and ignore ignoring the other dimensions. This is what Guggenbühl-Craig has called a "marriage of well-being" rather a "marriage of individuation." This can be a good enough arrangement at a social level, but it will not be a transformative relationship.

Marriages that are transformative have the effect of generating symbolic images of wholeness and unity, which both partners can relate to as meaningful. These are not images of an ideal couple, but images of integration that embody the opposites. The images may be grotesque from a naturalistic viewpoint, as in fact the *Rebis* is. The mutual image of a particular couple - in itself an impersonal archetypal image of the collective unconscious - is uniquely expressive of the pair's specific relational alchemy. At this level, there are no rights or wrongs. The *Rebis* may consist of a brother-sister pair, a mother-son pair, or a father-daughter pair. It simply is what it is and what it has to be. Nor are the partners at this level any longer two separate individuals; they are one, like Siamese twins. They share a single heart. In their egos and conscious adaptations to the world, and in their personas and complex structures - their heads, their upper stories, their personal history - they may be (indeed, they usually are and should be) two unique, very different individuals with separate interests, hobbies, careers, passions. But at the level of the *Rebis*, they are one in a way that they probably cannot articulate. An irrational bond exists. Here there is a winged being, a *Rebis*, who is neither of them and yet both of them.

In a transformative relationship, the *Rebis* is not a static image or an object, like an idol, to worship and propitiate. It is a vital presence, the spirit of the union, the irrational foundation of the joint enterprise. It can be seen in the aura that surrounds a pair. It is the source of their joint energy and vitality as a couple. What has transpired through the relationship is that the spiritus rector, who brought the couple together in the first place-through an improbable accident, a synchronistic event, a chance encounter-and blessed them with the gift of instant recognition and a flow of kinship libido, now is absorbed into the ongoing relationship. The *Rebis* is winged, a spirited background presence, the particular atmosphere and aroma of a couple. It is the source of the intuitive foreknowledge which allows one to anticipate the words and thoughts of the other, the psychological factor which sends one of them dreams which pertain to the other as well, the unconscious link connecting the couple's timing even when they are far apart. The *Rebis* is bound by neither time nor space. And it survives the absence or even the death of a partner, maintaining the relationship beyond the seemingly final limit of the grave.

In his late-life memoir, *Memories, Dreams, Reflections,* Jung reports two dreams that illustrate this permanence of the marriage bond. The first is somewhat humorous. He tells of a dream he had in 1922 when he was in his mid-forties, some twenty-five years after his father's death. In it, his father comes to him for marriage counseling. Paul Jung had been informed that his son was a knowledgeable psychologist, and he wanted to consult him about marital psychology. As Carl began to prepare a lecture on the complexities of marriage, he suddenly awoke and was surprised to have had this unusual dream. Shortly thereafter, his mother died unexpectedly. "My dream was a forecast of my mother's death, for here was my father who, after an absence of twenty-six years, wished to ask a psychologist about the newest insights and information on marital problems, since he would soon have to resume this relationship again."[16] In Carl's unconscious, at least, the marriage bond between his father and mother was permanent and still intact after twenty-six years of separation by death. The synchronistic connection between his dream and his mother's death bears a mysterious witness to the enduring tie.

Similarly, Jung had a dream of his wife, Emma, after her death. At that point, he was in his late seventies and had been married to her for fifty-three years. By all accounts, his marriage, like his father's, had been a difficult one, yet it had been a vital and deeply meaningful relationship throughout his adult life. Certainly, it had been a transformative relationship, as well as a containing one, for both partners. Jung writes that his wife appeared to him as in a

---

[16] C.G. Jung, *Memories, Dreams, Reflections,* p. 315.

portrait, dressed in her beautiful original wedding gown, which was designed and created by Jung's cousin, Helene Preiswerk. Emma faced him squarely, and her expression indicated the wisdom of acceptance and objectivity. She was beyond emotion. The portrait, he says, summed up their whole relationship. "Face to face with such wholeness one remains speechless, for it can scarcely be comprehended,"[17] he writes about this image of Emma. This dream exemplifies the timeless transcendence of the bond, a *Rebis* that joins the partners in symbolic unity.

The Rebis bond in a transformative relationship continues to work its effects over a long course of time. It is what creates the underground spaces in a relationship, as depicted in the dream I quoted at the beginning of this chapter. While it is the ground and basis for the relationship, it is also the channel by which the dynamic power of the unconscious continuously recreates the relationship and the partners in it. Relationships often are seen as containers for people- the "container" and the "contained" is how Jung describes the two partners in a marriage[18] - but they are equally transformers if they constellate the *Rebis* factor. The relationship becomes the dynamic factor that changes both people in the direction of a mutual image of integration and wholeness. It is an image that holds conscious and unconscious, masculine and feminine, good and bad, in a frame of joined polarities. It is not a matter of one partner becoming inclined to be more like the other, but rather of both coming to approximate a shared image of wholeness.

The reason old married partners sometimes look so much alike and share so many values, attitudes, and behavior patterns is that they have been unconsciously guided in the same direction by a joint imago. This has not been imposed on one by the other, unless one of them has an exceptionally dominant personality. Rather, it has grown up in both of them from below, from the Rebis that has

---

[17] *Ibid.*, 296.
[18] C.G. Jung, "Marriage as a Psychological Relationship;" in *CW* 17, paras. 332 ff.

formed out of the union of their unconscious psyches. It is this factor that transforms them over the course of a long span of life together, often until it becomes difficult to tell one from the other, so close do both now approximate their common self-imago.

This sort of transformative process also underlies and guides whole kinship groups, communities, and collective movements. Communities of nuns who live together for years under the spiritual presence and direction of a powerful founder unite through an imago that unites their personalities through unconscious mergers and identifications. The founder may be the magnet drawing them into this communal imago, although her individual character and personality may remain unique and distinct from those of her followers. But as they take on similar features of attitude and behavior, even of physical appearance, a common *Rebis* image constellates and can be detected beneath the surface. As a unit, they portray an imago of the collective unconscious. The Amish people, whose personalities are immersed from birth to death in collectively shared values and attitudes, achieve adult forms (self-imagos) that are nearly identical. The transformation process that shapes an individual life from birth and youth into its adult imago depends upon the constellation of a symbol from out of the depths of the collective unconscious. In the case of tightly woven communities, this constellation is anything but unique and individual. It is collective and strictly defined by the group consciousness, precisely with the aim: of producing adults who in their mature adult self-imagos match established markings and colors to the greatest extent possible. An individual has to struggle to separate from these magnetic communities, and even when this is done, the adult self-imago often still resembles the traditional one.

What I have argued in this chapter is that self-imago formation may take place within the context of a two-person relationship if it goes deep enough to constellate a *Rebis*. When that happens, the couple supplants the community as a decisive influence in shaping the mature adult self-imago. In modern times, with the general breakdown of large communities, families, and marriages, the relationship developed in psychotherapy sometimes becomes the most significant transformative relationship in an adult's life. The *Rebis* constellated by the analytic pair has helped to shape contemporary notions of maturity and adulthood. Analysis has been a relational context in which the spirit of transformation has been invoked and welcomed.

Three Portraits of Transformation: Rembrandt, Picasso, Jung

> The secret of alchemy was . . . the transformation of personality through the blending and fusion of the noble with the base components, of the differentiated with the inferior functions, of the conscious with the unconscious.[1]
>
> C.G. Jung

Listening to a Beethoven symphony or string quartet, it is hard to refrain from believing that the composer was born specifically to give the world this music. Is there a Master's hand at work in such manifestations of spirit in human life? The beauty and astonishing variety of butterflies is matched by the splendor and generous abundance of forms taken by the human self-imago. God must be an artist of the spirit as well as in nature.

By studying people's lives, we can observe that there are some who hear when angels call as Rilke did, and who engage creatively when transformative images and opportunities fall unannounced into their lives. Through this response and interaction, they not only

---

[1] C.G. Jung, *Two Essays in Analytical Psychology*, in CW 7, par. 404.

produce works of significant cultural value but also transform themselves and constellate their adult psychological self-imagos. No more than caterpillars ask for metamorphosis do people consciously invite these moments of transformation into their lives. Nor do they choose the final form of the self-imago that will come into being in their personalities. Often periods of deepest transformation are lived as dark nights of the soul when there is no sign of things to come. This is the pupation phase in the evolution of a self-imago, whose ultimate design is beyond conscious intention.

Having discussed (in Chapter 1) the process of transformation in the middle of life, argued (in Chapter 2) that transformation takes place by means of transformative images, and discussed intimate relationship (in Chapter 3) as a context in which adult trans-formation may occur, I wish in this chapter to explore how people symbolize and express the self-imago when it is constellated.

The following is a reflection on the biographies of three supremely gifted individuals whose lives exemplify transformation and a self-imago formation realized in their life and work. My hope is that these capsule portraits will suggest how the innate imaginal disks buried within the personality are drawn forward and knit together to achieve full capacity in the adult individual's conscious attitudes and activities, and how the resultant self-imago then reflects and guides a person's destiny in the second half of life.

When the psychological self-imago is constituted and fully realized, a person acquires with it the freedom to expand and deploy the expression of psychic energy in a distinctive and unique way. The self-imago opens vistas for the free expression of personality, while it also defines the individual's unique voice and style. It brings this freedom because it draws together the most important opposites in the individual psyche - the high and the low, the sacred and the profane, the conscious and the unconscious - into a singular pattern and allows them room for expression. The self-imago is an internal structure made up of psychic polarities, and therefore it often is represented as something grotesque and unrefined from a naturalistic point of view, like the *Rebis*. But this very lack of conscious polish and perfection gives it the ability to embrace the psyche's vitality and to function as a guiding, releasing, and orienting channel for psychic energies. The formation of the self-imago is the precondition for full adult freedom to be oneself and to become the person one most deeply longs to be. Constraints imposed by an earlier persona formation, by arbitrary social and psychological restrictions placed upon the individual by a psychosocial identity, are largely surmounted through the active presence of the self-imago. With this formation, a personality becomes free to experience and to express a much greater degree of inherent wholeness than was possible previously. I see this kind of expanded freedom to imagine and to exercise innate gifts within the frame-work of a distinctive style in the three figures under consideration in this chapter.

I have chosen three people whose biographies, I believe, demonstrate a well-formed self-imago: Rembrandt van Rijn, Pablo Picasso, and Carl Jung. These three men certainly do not qualify as saints or unblemished heroes, but in each case, while problematical character structures remain evident throughout the second half of life, the adult self-imago functions to express and orient the manifestations of psychic energy. While the self-imago transcends character, it does not abolish it or change its fundamental features. It adds another dimension to the psyche that guides the disposition of surplus psychic energy.

I have chosen these figures as exemplars not because I believe they represent high moral or spiritual ideals but because each undeniably achieved a sharply distinctive self-imago. All three lived remarkably creative and fairly long lives and left behind concrete evidence of the transformation process and its net result in their works. The painters Rembrandt and Picasso deposited a detailed record of their transformation processes in their works of art and especially in their selfportraits, and Jung left a written account of personal transformation and a physical monument to his wholeness in the stone tower he built at Bollingen on the upper Lake of Zurich. Because their processes were externalized in artistic images and written works that are publicly available, they lend themselves to analysis. While their lives obviously differed in many ways, these men have in common vividly limned adult self-imagos that defined them and freed them to express their psychic potential to a large degree.

I chose these three figures, too, because, among other things, they offer sufficient contrast and differences to avoid the presumption that all transformation processes must culminate in the same type of self-imago. Human self-imagos are as varied as butterflies. One could multiply examples almost endlessly, but limitations of time and space force me severely to limit my selection. I considered including a woman - Eleanor Roosevelt came to mind as a prime candidate for study, as did Georgia O'Keefe and Frieda Kahlo - but I decided instead to use the historical contrast between a more traditional self-imago in the case of Rembrandt and the more modern ones in the cases of Picasso and Jung.

These biographical vignettes are intended as illustrations and not as ideals. Each man can be seen as limited by his own character structure, historical period, and culture, but each also grew beyond these limitations and embodied a self-imago of archetypal dimensions. These are three examples of individuation process, yet they are radically different from one another. Different gods yield different imagos. While we can affirm that all gods ultimately are One, the concrete manifestations are many, and plurality is what confronts us when we look at the world empirically.

Rembrandt van Rijn was born in Leiden on July 15, 1606, and lived his entire life of sixty-three years in seventeenth-century Holland. His father, Harmon Gerritszoon van Rijn, was a miller who had converted to Calvinism, while his mother, Cornelia Willems-dochter van Suyttbroeck, remained Roman Catholic. Rembrandt was the eighth of nine children in a traditional middle-class Dutch family.

He was the only one of his siblings to take up an artistic career, which was an individual decision on his part. His father sent him to the University of Leiden at the age of fourteen to study law, but after a few months he left and apprenticed himself to a Leiden painter named Van Swenenburgh. While Rembrandt must have been at least somewhat literate, no written records or texts from his hand are available. What is known about him is contained in several early biographies and in records of his professional and financial dealings. More important is that we can read the development of his inner life from his masterful paintings. Already in the paintings of his youth, he shows a vital, lively, adventurous personality. He had astonishing natural talent. Quickly he outstripped his masters, demonstrating the brilliant flair for dramatic gesture and expression that would characterize his work throughout his life.

Many books have been written about Rembrandt's life and paintings. I will draw on some of them but do not propose here to review them or to duplicate their efforts. What I am interested in is looking at his work - particularly at his self-portraits - for evidence of psychological transformation and self-imago formation. The general stages of his psychological development can be read in his self-portraits. They reveal what Rembrandt saw when he looked in the mirror, what he wanted his audience to see in the way of a maturing and mature European painter of his day, and, to the psychologically trained eye, what was transpiring in his psyche as he grew and then metamorphosed into the self-imago he was to become. Certainly, he was an accomplished painter and artist before he became himself in his maturity, but the late works are a revelation of what his self-imago looked like and a testament to his range of experience and freedom of expression.

In the course of his life, Rembrandt drew, etched, or painted his self-portrait approximately one hundred times. He began creating images of himself early on. Using himself as a model, he experimented with expression, light and dark contrast, and clothing.

There are many images of him as a young man. In some of these he is scowling, or frowning, or snarling; in others he is dressed as a dandy, a nobleman, a blade about town. Occasionally he paints himself in historical costume as a distinguished noble or exotic prince. Although Rembrandt never traveled physically outside of his native Holland, his imagination roamed far and wide, and he tried on many imagined personae. He was showing the many sides of his emerging young personality as well as his formidable skill as a portrait painter.

Meanwhile, he enjoyed early success as a fast-rising star in the world of art. Holland's economy was booming, its freedom from Spain recently having been won, and wealthy middle-class merchants and their families were generating a strong demand for paintings of all kinds to decorate their well-stocked Amsterdam houses. After Rembrandt moved from Leiden to Amsterdam in 1630 at the age of twenty-four (the same year his father died), his career took off, and by 1632 he was numbered among the famous in his newly adopted city. His grand historical and biblical paintings were popular among the prosperous burghers of Amsterdam, and his portraits of citizens and their wives and children commanded good prices. As a painter, he had arrived, and this was crowned with a very successful first half of life development when he married Saskia Uylenburgh, an intelligent and literate young woman who, though an orphan, brought into the marriage a substantial dowry of forty thousand guilders, a handsome fortune at the time. With this money, the couple bought a large house in Sint Anthoniesdijk, a respectable area of the city, and there Rembrandt set up his studio and with Saskia lived the life of a proper middle-class citizen. A famous painting from this period entitled "Self-Portrait with Saskia" (1636), shows the painter holding Saskia on his lap, both of them dressed in gorgeous finery and the husband wearing a boldly feathered hat and a prominent sheathed sword. According to commentators, he is proposing an audacious toast to his audience in rebuttal to charges that he was wasting Saskia's money. At this stage of his life Rembrandt was rather full of himself and more than a little inflated with his own powers and importance. His considerable worldly success gave him grounds for feeling self-confident. He was established.

Unexpectedly and tragically, after giving birth to Titus (the only one of their three children to live beyond infancy), Saskia died in 1641, and a new chapter opened in Rembrandt's life. At thirty-five, he had arrived at midlife.He was at the peak of his public celebrity and recognition, but things soon were to change. Though still surrounded by students, commissions began to dry up because other younger artists were pursuing new styles and genres that were gaining in popularity. Never one to adjust his artistic preferences to current fashion, Rembrandt saw his income decline. His remarkable genius, though still recognized, diminished in commercial value, and his character turned troublesome and stubborn. Clients complained of his tendency to please himself rather than adapt his work to their desires, and Calvinist Amsterdam frowned hard when it became known that he had begun an intimate relationship with his attractive young housemaid, twenty years younger than himself, named Hendrickje Stoffels.

Gorgeous portraits of Hendrickje - as a woman in elegant furs, smiling subtly like Mona Lisa; as Bathsheba at her bath; as a voluptuous young woman lifting her dress and bathing in a stream; as a dark and richly dressed femme fatale peering out of a window with a totally black room behind her - mark this period of Rembrandt's artistic output and indicate his profound grasp of her meaning for him as an image of the eternal feminine, the anima. There is to my knowledge a no more moving testimony to a man's intense anima preoccupation at midlife than that found in Rembrandt's paintings of Hendrickje. In the portraits of Saskia, he depicted a lively and attractive wife who showered wealth and love and support on her heroic young spouse; in those of Hendrickje, he shows the transformative anima image, the woman who takes a man into dark, unexplored waters of the psyche. Rembrandt followed her with characteristic abandon. This was his midlife transformation period, and it lasted for some fifteen years.

By 1656, Rembrandt was bankrupt financially. He was fifty years old. Most of his belongings were sold off to pay debts, and ownership of his house had to be transferred to his son, Titus. Students of Rembrandt's self-portraits comment on the irony of his great painting of 1658, in which the artist depicts himself seated in regal splendor, a Jovian image with scepter held lightly in his left hand, presenting to the world an image of golden success and middle-aged prosperity. Materially, nothing could have been further from the truth. Psychologically, however, he was not faking. He was painting the portrait of his self-imago as the fully realized artist he had inwardly become. This is a representation not of a worldly persona, but of an inner figure as constituted by his life experience in the preceding years of transformation. Rembrandt had arrived at the height of his powers as an artist and as a man, and he had the inner conviction and identity to match. His brilliant dark eyes look out at the viewer with piercing intensity. He challenges anyone to question his authority. The firm mouth and set jaw reveal none of his worldly troubles or financial circumstances. Not defiant, he simply carries his years with authority and supreme dignity. It is the image of a man in the prime of his adult life, for all the world a master and a king. This is the culmination of his development as a distinguished public painter of his times, and he recognizes himself as a man of great worth and stature. In this self-portrait, Rembrandt represents himself as a fully realized artist with the personal authority and freedom to execute his will absolutely and to spend his capital of psychic energy as he sees fit. No one else will dictate style or content to such a master of his own house.

After this, however, Rembrandt's self-portraits change dramatically in style and tone. He has entered another phase of inner development, which we can conceptualize as further deepening and enriching the self-imago we see in the self-portrait just described. In addition, it represents a dramatic extension of

Rembrandt, Self-Portrait, 1658. Courtesy The Frick Collection, New York.

certain features of that self-imago, as the artist grows into what will be for him old age. As he takes up this last phase of his life - he will live to be only sixty three - the trappings and aura of pomp disappear, and another distinctive image begins to come forward. It is this archetypal imago that will carry him to the end and give his late paintings their spiritual quality.

Throughout his career, Rembrandt was a painter of impressive religious images. Biblical scenes were one of his stocks in trade. He became famous for them. In some, he included himself as one of the characters in the scene. In late life, though, a shift occurs, and his work becomes more personal and highly realistic. The self-portraits begin to depict his face and hands with graphic realism. Wrinkles, jowls, a bulbous nose, gray hair become apparent. The age of idealized persona presentation and self-promotion now is behind him. He no longer emphasizes the ego. The dramatic costume no longer is his prop. In these late paintings, we find a simple, rather unattractive old man, but light, signaling inner illumination, begins to emanate from his forehead, in striking contrast to the evidence of creeping physical decay and decrepitude. He is extending his imago into the spiritual dimension while recognizing the physical ravages of age.

In the Self-Portrait, c. 1661-62, Rembrandt once again depicts himself as an artist. He is wearing a simple white hat and holds his palette and brushes in one hand as he stares soberly ahead. The point of most intense illumination falls on the right side of his forehead. It is as if light were emanating from his head. Obviously, he now is a fully mature, even somewhat elderly man (the painting was made in his fifty-seventh year). If anything, he exaggerates his age. There is little trace of narcissistic self-flattery here. The left side of his face is in shadow, while the hat and his upper forehead are bathed in in tensely bright light. The bottom of the painting disappears into total darkness. The artist here restates his identity as a painter, and he does this against a background that shows two gigantic circles embedded in a wall. The circles have been interpreted as a reference to time itself and as an allusion to a famous artist of antiquity, Appelles, who reportedly was able to draw perfect circles freehand. The circle also can be taken as an allusion to eternity. As a mandala, it suggests the backdrop of timeless archetypal forms against which the mature painter works in time and space. In this painting, Rembrandt por trays his frail

Rembrandt, Self-Portrait, c. 1661-62. Courtesy The Iveagh Bequest, Kenwood House, London.

empirical reality proudly in relationship to symbols that transcend time, bringing his human limitations and mundane identity as a workman into connection with the divine. His imago is moving toward a union of opposites - time and eternity. As he looks out upon the world through the eyes of an artist, he is showing himself and the object world in a relation to eternity. This indicates that he is inhabiting a conscious attitude that links the time-bound human body-ego to timeless archetypal images of pure spirit. The light on Rembrandt's head signals what Jung calls deification.

As his position in the world deteriorated socially and economically-Rembrandt in 1660 was forced to move from his house to a more modest dwelling in a neighborhood of artisans and artists-it seems that the sense of gravity and serenity in his paintings increases. It has been noted by students of his work that, toward the end of his life, his painting becomes visionary. In these last years, he continued to paint for the odd commission and to struggle just as stubbornly as ever with his former creditors, who would not leave him in peace and who stubbornly insisted on payment to the last guilder. For the roof over his head and his daily sustenance, he became dependent upon his common-law wife, Hendrickje, and his son, Titus. Four years before his death, he painted a portrait of himself as a sort of old fool. In the self-portrait, he peers out of darkness with an expression of eerie laughter. It is a hard image to read. He may be showing himself as a drunken old fool; more likely, he is laughing with the gods. Again, his forehead is brightly illuminated, while much of the picture lies in darkness. The smile is almost a painful grimace, and the stooped shoulders indicate the weight of the burdens he must be carrying. Perhaps this is a holy fool. There is a theory that in this painting he is referring to the Greek artist Zeuxis's death. A story is told that Zeuxis died laughing when an ugly old rich woman paid him a large sum of money and then asked him to paint her as Aphrodite. This reference would imbue the self-portrait with the mirth of the artist who knows sublime beauty and the immense abyss that separates it from human narcissistic grandiosity and desire. The task of the artist, Rembrandt would say, is to paint the truth, not to create flattering images for wealthy customers. Rembrandt was in a brutally honest phase of his life, and human folly surely must have seemed to merit only scornful laughter-the laughter of Zeuxis, another archetypal painter.

Rembrandt, Self-Portrait, Laughing. Courtesy Cologne, Wallraf-Richartz Museum.

As his life entered its final few years, Rembrandt's conditions did not improve. His reputation as a renowned painter provided him little in the way of concrete reward. Yet, in his final self-portraits, he depicts himself as an artist who has joined the company of the immortals, exceeding even such illustrious contemporaries and predecessors as Titan and the Italian masters of the sixteenth and seventeenth centuries with whom Rembrandt had been competitive throughout his career. On the other hand, these self-portraits are statements of great personal modesty. The artist is brutally honest about his less than ideal physical appearance, yet he shows his figure as illuminated by divine inner light. In the final group of self-portraits, painted in his last years, including one that dates from 1669, the year of his death, Rembrandt repeatedly accentuates the crown of light upon and around his head. In a late masterpiece, he depicts himself as Saint Paul, for Protestant Christians the ultimate image of sanctity and nearness to God. (While Rembrandt is not known to have been an active member of any denomination, it is on the record that he was drawn to Mennonites, who at the time occupied prominent positions in Amsterdam. The inner life of contemplation and piety cultivated by this self-effacing Protestant sect must have appealed to Rembrandt.) Next to Jesus himself, Saint Paul ranked as close as a human could come to integrating fully the presence of God in human form. For Rembrandt to paint himself as Saint Paul was as near as he could approach to the idea of deification without falling into absolute sacrilege by claiming identity with Christ or with God Himself. In his Self-Portrait as the Apostle Paul, Rembrandt further extends his imago vertically.

One can conclude that Rembrandt pictorially displays in his self-portraits a transformation process that extends through his entire adult life. Beginning with pictorial experimentation, extravagance of gesture, and the drama of exotic costume-the elaborate and playful artifice of the puer phase-the images shift into portraits of greater substantiality in his personae as Dutch artist, as lover and husband, and finally as the fully realized adult man of power and authority. He attains his imago certainly by the time he is fifty years of age. He has become the fully realized personality and artist we know as Rembrandt. Meanwhile, however, from midlife onward, a series of crises in his personal life undermine his worldly position. After the crash of bankruptcy and loss of possessions and home, he enters a final phase of transformation- a further deepening and enriching of his imago. This phase carries him

Rembrandt, Self-Portrait as the Apostle Paul. Courtesy Rijksmuseum, Amsterdam.

beyond the meaning of all of his earlier self-portraits to images of self-acceptance, integrity, spiritual illumination, and a profound inner realization of the transcendent function-the personal relation between one's time-bound ego reality and the transcendent realm of the archetypes. His last group of self portraits, painted during the fifteen years before he died, increasingly show images not only of the artist as fully realized and in masterful command of his materials, but also of the man Rembrandt as a fully realized spiritual being. As one commentator points out, in these late paintings it is "as if the painter were merging into his painting."[2] Using the specific images and the notions available in seventeenth century Amsterdam, Rembrandt depicted the process of psychological transformation as the emergence of an archetypal imago that combined the vocation of the artist and the spiritual illumination of the saint.

The imagos that people realize in their individual development are based on archetypal forms which, while themselves relatively timeless and unchanging from age to age, nevertheless are shaped and conditioned by history and culture as they find actual expression. As we jump forward from the seventeenth to the twentieth century, we discover in Pablo Picasso an artistic self-imago different in some obvious respects from that of Rembrandt, but one nevertheless grounded in the archetypal figure of the Creator, as creative artist.

An artist arguably as talented as Rembrandt was, Picasso in some ways was the obverse of Rembrandt in terms of psychological and spiritual development. These two men were separated by a couple of centuries, and enormous changes occurred in European culture during that time. One factor that complicates this comparison, of course, is that so much more is known about Picasso's life than is available on Rembrandt's. The profusion of detail can have the paradoxical effect of obscuring rather than illuminating major transformational themes. One can miss the forest by concentrating on the fascinating trees. Picasso's love life and his relationships with wives and mistresses, for example, have received a disproportionate amount of attention. This is important information, in that he did become himself in part through these intimate relationships, but it also can be misleading if his poor interpersonal skills become the main focal point. Character becomes

---

[2] P. Bonafoux, *Rembrandt: Master of the Portrait*, p. 109.

so highlighted that one cannot any longer see the self-imago. If we look at self-imago formation as the emergence of the self in adulthood, we find that Picasso, like Rembrandt, achieved a full metamorphosis, but the features of the self-imago he became are different from those that Rembrandt embodied. This is true even though both self-imagos partake of the archetypal form of the Creator, as creative artist. This difference is cultural and not archetypal. It is the difference between traditional European religious culture and modernity.

Modernity is characterized by secularism, fragmentation and an absence of a unifying spiritual center. Picasso's art, which breaks whole images into pieces, abstracts them and then reassembles them in a novel form, is the mark of modernity. This is what it means to be modern, and it is the reason that Picasso is often considered to be the artist of the century. He gives the experience of fragmentation, dissociation, and loss of soul its most bold expression. The traditional person demonstrates a more or less straight individuation trajectory. It encompasses a prolonged metamorphosis at midlife and arrives at a distinctly spiritual self-imago in old age. Rembrandt is an example. The modern person's life, on the other hand, typically reveals many attempts at consolidation, a pattern of continual self-deconstruction through analysis followed by attempted reintegration, and often a final ironic statement about anxiety and emptiness. The intervals between intense cultural effort (i.e., work) are filled with physical gratification and/or addictions, while ultimate value is placed upon commercial success or individual creativity for its own sake or for celebrity. This is the collective tone of modernity, and it characterizes Picasso's life.

The question is: can one speak at all of transformation and emergence of the self-imago in the context of chaotic and narcissistic modernity? The answer: Only if we look deeper. There we may find the archetypal outlines of self-imago formation. For this, too, Picasso is a prime case study. If Rembrandt moves from darkness to light and realizes deification in the imago of the archetypal painter-as-apostle (as Saint Paul), what can we see in Picasso's process of transformation?

Picasso, throughout his adult life, was a person in perpetual creative movement. John Richardson, his great biographer, writes:

> Picasso liked to mark important anniversaries by doing a painting which would signify a change in his work as well as in his life. Around the time of his twenty-fifth birthday (October 19, 1906), he executed a group of self-portrait paintings and drawings, which . . . unveil a totally new Picasso: a sunburned Dionysos in an undershirt, his hair en brosse, all set to challenge and subvert the tradition of European art up to and including Cezanne, whose self-portrait had partly inspired this image. How cool, how laconic the artist looks, before he embarks on his messianic mission.[3]

According to no less standard an authority than the Encyclopedia Britannica, "While other masters such as Matisse or Braque tended to stay within the bounds of a style they had developed in their youth, Picasso continued to be an innovator into the last decade of his life."[4] His output was prodigious. At his death, he still retained in his personal collection some fifty thousand of his own works from all the periods and in all the styles and media of his lengthy career as an artist.

Picasso is considered to be one of the most transformative figures in all of art history. With a few artist cohorts, he changed the direction of Western art decisively, and "virtually no twentieth-century artist could escape his influence."[5] While Rembrandt perhaps painted better than anyone before or after him, Picasso changed the course of painting itself, like some mighty Hercules redirecting the flow of a major river from an ancient bed into an

---

[3] J. Richardson, *A Life of Picasso*, vol. 2, p. 9.

[4] "Pablo Picasso: Assessment;" in *Encyclopedia Britannica*.

[5] *Ibid.*

entirely new one. This is the very definition of transformation: to shift the flow of energy radically from one channel, one form or metaphor, into another. The total quantum of psychic energy poured by humankind into artistic expression - whether painting, drawing, sculpture, or ceramics - may not have changed as a result of Picasso's labors, but the forms that contain and express this energy were altered utterly. Picasso was a transformer on a vast collective level. Of course, it must be recognized, too, that he was expressing the Zeitgeist. He was able to rechannel Western art in this way because the changes going on in the collective life of the West were reflected in this art. Perhaps it would be more accurate to say, then, that Picasso's gift was to be deeply attuned to the times and to develop and elaborate a style of art that perfectly reflected them. Art changed because culture was changing, and Picasso was one of the chief innovators expressing this change.

If we consider Picasso's artistic production from the viewpoint of his own personal psychological evolution over the course of his long creative life (he was born in 1881 and died in 1972, a span of ninety one years), we can find a wealth of evidence to support the notion of transformation and imago formation. There are many youthful moltings in the first half of life that begin and end his famous "periods": the Blue Period, the Pink Period, the Cubist Period, etc. Each period is a significant manifestation of the young Picasso, and each plays its part in preparing for the following stages, until an adult imago finally is achieved. After midlife these moltings cease. There are no more distinctive, extended stylistic periods. In the second half of life, Picasso uses many styles. He changes styles of painting constantly, breaking old molds, inventing new ones, and ranging over the entire spectrum from classical and representational to abstract. But he does not remain committed to any one of them beyond an individual work. His self-imago as an artist now transcends style and technique. Style no longer dictates how he will paint or sculpt or etch; rather, his artistic ego moves freely from one style to another as mood or occasion demands. Picasso, now the complete artist, moves freely and with creative abandon, like a butterfly, among all the media and styles available to him.

One can compare the psychological development evident in Picasso's self-portraits to that seen in Rembrandt's, but the usefulness of doing so is limited. Picasso, too, was a masterful painter of his own image, but his explicit self-representations are rather limited in number and do not extend beyond his youth (except for those done at the very end of his life, to be discussed later). Much like Rembrandt in his early self-portraits, though to my mind less flamboyant and cosmopolitan, Picasso in these paintings plays with images of himself, experimenting with his appearance by dressing up in different costumes, by grimacing, by role-playing and modeling himself to himself. He is trying on identities, wearing them for a while, and then discarding them. To quote John Richardson, he shows himself as "a romantic vagabond, a glamorous jeune premier, a decadent poet, a top-hatted dandy and much else besides."[6] None of these roles fits the young bohemian artist exactly, certainly not permanently, but all show facets and possibilities for a persona. Picasso especially is fascinated with his eyes, a feature that in later works would become a signature item.

After the age of twenty-six, Picasso's own self-representational image dissolves, reappearing in a multitude of enigmatic references, disguises, and ambiguous self-disclosures. In a sense, all his work now becomes subtly autobiographical, and every portrait can be interpreted partially as a self-portrait. This strategy opened to Picasso a whole new world of possibilities for self-disclosure, subterfuge, ambiguity, and symbolic self-representation. "Picasso often 'inhabited' his creations without any reference to his physiognomy, vesting himself in a bestiary of natural and fanciful creatures, in objects like pipes or doorknobs, and even in patterns (such as varicolored diamonds of the Harlequin's costume) or other

---

[6] J. Richardson, quoted in K. Varnedoe's "Picasso's Self-Portraits;" in *Picasso and Portraiture: Representation and Transformation*, p. 113.

abstract signs,"[7] to use Kirk Varnedoe's exquisite wording. This strategy may indicate a keen intuitive grasp on Picasso's part of psychological projection and of the subtle intermingling of subjectivity with representations of the object world. It certainly also communicates a Hermetic identity and a playful cast of mind.

Picasso (much like Rembrandt) quite early in life attained a strong measure of self-confidence and was able to assume a vast array of images without fear of losing touch with his identity. While his personal image is not often represented explicitly, it is implied throughout the oeuvre. There are also, of course, elements of camouflage, denial, self-deception, and defensive distancing in this mercurial elusiveness. Again, this elusiveness of explicit identification is programmatic for the modern person. It is a style that characterizes politicians as well as artists, women as well as men, old as well as young people. It is neither good nor bad; it is simply modern. Depth psychological theory sees the person as made up of multiple centers of consciousness, none of which occupies the central position all the time. Thus, at the core of this theory, the human personality is seen as elusive.

Since I cannot possibly offer a complete account of the development of Picasso's full adult self-imago, I will generalize: the main problem was how to combine the opposites he discovered within himself into a unified image that would embrace his full reality. An early play of polarities shows itself in a pair of self-portraits from 1901. One of his most significant early statements, "Yo, Picasso" "[I, Picasso"], painted when he was twenty, shows the artist as a handsome Spanish painter with a bright orange red tie dramatically flaring out above his colorful palette. Strong facial features and prominent piercing eyes indicate the confidence and bravado of the young artist. He could as well be a famous matador, so proud and self-assured is his expression, the set of his jaw, his outward gaze. In the Blue Period, which arrives the same year, we

---

[7] *Ibid.*

find a contrasting self-portrait that depicts a sallow face, hollow cheeks, eyes sunk back in their sockets, and only the red lips indicating any life at all. The painting's background is an unrelenting blue. The body is covered with an oversized black coat buttoned to the top. It is the image of a vagabond or a suffering contemplative- at any rate a depressive, with a sweet half-smile playing across his features who is gazing directly at the viewer. To move so quickly from a self-portrait depicting a confident matador-painter to one showing a sickly hollow-cheeked depressive indicates a certain amount of identity confusion- or diffusion-in the young Picasso, before he achieved his more distinctive and adamant imago as an adult man. It is only later, when he has worked through his Blue Period and is able to shed some of the illusions he may have had about himself, that he is able to discover and draw upon a surer and more all encompassing self-imago.

In 1906, when he paints Self-Portrait with Palette, he shows his face, significantly, as a mask. Picasso has discovered the primal qualities of the African mask. He described this important discovery to Malraux:

> The masks weren't just like any other pieces of sculpture. Not at all. They were magic things. But why weren't the Egyptian pieces or the Chaldean? We hadn't realized it. Those were primitives, not magic things. The Negro pieces were intercesseurs, mediators; ever since then I've known the word in French. They were against everything- against unknown, threatening spirits. . . . I understood; I too am against everything. I too believe that everything is unknown, that everything is an enemy! Every thing! I understood what the Negroes used their sculpture for. . . . The fetishes were . . . weapons. To help people avoid coming under the influence of spirits again, to help them be come independent. Spirits, the unconscious (people still weren't talking about that very much), emotion- they're all the same thing. I understood why I was a

painter. All alone in that awful museum, with masks, dolls
made of the redskins, dusty manikins. "Les Demoiselles
d'Avignon" must have come to me that very day, but not
at all because of the forms; because it was my first
exorcism painting - yes absolutely![8]

Richardson reads the Self-Portrait with Palette as triumphant
self affirmation that bears "witness to Picasso's Dionysiac exaltation
at this time."[9] As noted earlier,[10] this portrait announces Picasso's
challenge to the whole tradition of European art to date. It is also,
however, an image that mediates transcendence. It is magic. Picasso
has discovered the power of the archetypal unconscious, and he has
included this feature importantly in his identity. This is an early
appearance of an archetypal imago (the surfacing of an "imaginal
disk," if you will), a sort of foretaste of things to come.

In the same year, Picasso made a bold move by painting the
face of Gertrude Stein as a mask. When people criticized him for the
obvious fact that Gertrude did not look like that, Picasso replied that
someday she would! He was painting an imago before it had fully
emerged from the larval stage. This is the face of Gertrude Stein that
posterity remembers. It is an archetypal image, her imago. Picasso's
strategy in portrait painting can be read as an attempt to capture
the noumenal essence beneath the physical surfaces of the
phenomenal presentation and thereby to reveal the unconscious
structures which only a probing, intuitive eye can discern and which
only the future will manifest more fully.

In 1907 another self-portrait followed, which developed the
masklike face and further "Africanized"[11] it. In this period, Picasso
assumed strong leadership in the artistic avant-garde in Paris. He
painted one of the most important and revolutionary works in

---

[8] Picasso quoted in Richardson, Life of Picasso, vol. 2, p. 24.

[9] Ibid., vol. 1, p. 71.

[10] Ibid., vol. 2, p. 9.

[11] K. Varnedoe, "Picasso's Self-Portraits" p. 138.

Picasso, Self-Portrait with Palette. Courtesy the Philadelphia Museum of Art.

modern art history, "Les Demoiselles d 'Avignon" (1907), which also includes a famous mask face placed upon the figure of one of the prostitutes. At this time, he was emerging from a major molting (the Blue Period) with a powerful self-expression of archetypal dimensions. Again, like Rembrandt, Picasso put his developing self-imago in terms of mythic images, which have the capacity to combine physical presence with a strong statement of archetypal transcendence. Besides dazzling Paris, the artist was revealing himself in this image and unearthing the elements of his future imago.[12]

In order to find a vocabulary of images that could represent his forming imago in the fullest possible way, Picasso was forced-by his needs, by his temperament, by cultural circumstances, and by his place in contemporary history - to break free of his Roman Catholic Christian heritage. He had to reach back to the origins of Western culture and even beyond, to the earliest origins of humankind in Africa. The myths of the Greeks and the masks of Africa came to define the imagery that Picasso would deploy to paint his imago as it emerged in the second half of his life. Roman Catholic Christianity, which absolutely ruled his native Spanish culture and also dominated the religious world of his adopted France, was too limited to contain his psyche. It was also, of course, much too identified with a moribund tradition and with right-wing politics to be of any use to the artistic sensibility and psychology of a Picasso. Unlike Rembrandt, Picasso was not spiritually or psychologically contained in a collective religious tradition, and this is what gives his life and work such iconic significance in the twentieth century. They mirror the condition of modern people generally. Picasso would have to find other, non-Christian images and stories to express his contact with the collective unconscious. These he found

---

[12] J. Richardson, *Life of Picasso*, vol. 2, p. 9, on this portrait, writes: "Inspiration for this portrait (now in the Prague National Gallery) did not come from any of Picasso's previous exemplars- El Greco, Cezanne or Gauguin-but from Van Gogh and a totally new source: the cinema. The artist was a past master of self-dramatization, and the look of menace on Picasso's face derives, at least in part, from the stylized close-ups in the silent movies of which the artist was such a fan: close-ups where the eyes, graphically accentuated, as here, in black, double for the silent mouth and articulate the hero's sangfroid, the villain's glee, the artist's mad resolve. This work is the quintessence of the Andalusian mirada fuerte, the strong gaze, that Picasso turned on people he wanted to conquer, seduce, possess, and, not least, shock!"

in Greek myths and African masks. These images allowed him to produce work that was *bien couillarde*, "ballsy." After discovering African masks and Greek mythology, Picasso would have no problem giving his work "the potency, physicality and heft that the word [*couillarde*] implies."[13] Vitality and potency- libido-would flow from Picasso's brush as he embraced these images and worked them into his painting.

In the paintings of the many women who passed into and through his life, Picasso created an astonishing wealth of images that are a fusion of the other's reality and the painter's psyche. Who can say where one begins and the other leaves off-which pieces belong to Picasso and which to the women? These are neither portraits nor self-portraits. Picasso was painting at the Rebis level, where the two personalities mingle and unite in a single image, an alchemical union. They are "Picasso's women;" not in a sense that implies ownership but rather as representations of perceptive and deep psycho logical experience. For example, in the image of his wife, Olga Khokhlova, he painted his fear of the devouring woman; in the portraits of Marie-Therese Walter, his regressive longing to return to the womb; in portraits of the model in the artist's studio, his engorged Minotaur passion. In short, these paintings depict the whole range of his anima moods and his emotional reactions to woman. In them he also created timeless images by stating their noumenal essences in color, geometric shape, and abstract symbol. By placing both eyes on one side of a flat surface, for instance, he shows the whole person, conscious and unconscious. By accentuating the breasts, the vagina, the womb, he demonstrates his obsession with sexuality and the essence of the feminine, as this was shared and revealed in the relationships.

Of course, Picasso's perspective is very one-sided and stated entirely from the male point of view. Picasso was palpably masculine. I do not wish to gloss over the widely publicized

---

[13] *Ibid.*, p. 103.

problems Picasso had with women, and they with him, for he was indeed a Spanish male whose machismo was deeply ingrained. Yet the several marriages, the many liaisons, and the short and longer love affairs did give Picasso access to the depths of his own soul as he explored his own nature and many dimensions of relational energy.

The chief icon Picasso arrived at to depict his mature imago was the Minotaur. (A lesser figure was the Faun, another the Monkey.) The use of these part-human, part-animal images as self-representations in many paintings, drawings, etchings, and works in other media constitutes the most extensive artistic expression of his adult imago, the culmination of his inner transformation and his deepest point of contact with the archaic basis of the human psyche. What biblical imagery was for Rembrandt, Greek mythological imagery was for Picasso. Especially in the images of beings half-

Picasso, Minotaur image. Courtesy Galerie Berggruem, Paris.

human and half-animal, and particularly in the figure of the Minotaur, Picasso found figures ample and complex enough to express his full psychological wholeness. I read these as images of the archetypal self. The animal image grounded Picasso in the archetypal. It is a kind of apocatastasis, a restoration to the original archaic man.

We should not too quickly assume that Picasso, in the image of the Minotaur, is presenting himself simply as bestial. The Minotaur was a child of Poseidon, Lord of the Sea, and Pasiphae, Queen in the Palace at Knossos. To discover the image of the Minotaur as a self-imago is also to become one with the divine (or at least the semidivine) and to gain access to the creative power and energies of the archetypal realm of the collective unconscious. Picasso's transformation is not a traditional spiritual one like Rembrandt's, in the sense of enlightenment, higher consciousness, and triumphant transcendence over the vicissitudes of the physical and material world. There is no evidence of achieved serenity in Picasso's self-portraits or in the biographies written about him. But there is abundant evidence of powerful and abiding connections to the archetypal unconscious, not the least of which is Picasso's enduring creativity and vitality deep into old age.

Picasso's Minotaur pictures can, I believe, be read as the emergence of his adult self-imago. His most concentrated expression of the Minotaur image came about in 1933-34, when he was in his early fifties, in the etchings that are contained in the Vollard Suite. At this time, he was ending his marriage with Olga Khoklilova and had just recently fallen in love with the voluptuous young Marie-Therese Walter, with whom he soon would have a child. The Minotaur image remained a special personal reference for the remainder of his life. It combines the spiritual nature of the artist and the bestial nature of the physical man-ideal. It is for Picasso an image of a union of opposites. This internal self definition guided him throughout his remaining years and allowed him the freedom to have and to express his psychic wholeness.

One final image. Picasso painted three explicit self-portraits in the year he died, one of which has been called by many an icon for the twentieth century. Like "Guernica," this painting is a powerful symbolic statement about the human condition in a time of extreme anguish. The image shows a large ragged face set directly atop a pair of naked shoulders. It depicts, by his own account, Picasso's fear of death. Like his mask paintings, it is apotropaic, an attempt to exorcise the fear of the unknown, to diminish the power of "the enemy," in this case identified as death. In the image, the eyes are dominant-wide open, filled with terror, the pupil of the right eye dilated and shot through with blood. The sharp lines around the eyes also speak of chronic fear, and the mouth is clenched shut as though to choke back a scream. It is a face inhuman, or nearly so, resembling that of an ape, per haps, or a monkey (another of Picasso's favorite self-representations).

Yet it also is human, the visage of a man staring starkly ahead into the menacing maw of death. Picasso joked with a friend that this painting was his way of exorcising his fear of death,[14] and yet one wonders how effective the exorcism was. To me, this mask speaks of meeting death head on, without the consolation of religion or the comfort of family and friendsnakedly, individually, consciously. In this final image, Picasso shows himself as essentially human, stripped of illusions and the dignity they would bestow. Rembrandt also reached this place of brutal honesty with himself

---

[14] Death is the ultimate threat to the ego and its integrity. Again, Picasso resorted to a mask that would exorcise his fear. It is evident that he warded off more severe forms of psychotic disturbance by using art as therapy. In 1932 Jung commented: "As to the future Picasso, I would rather not try my hand at prophecy, for this inner adventure is a hazardous affair and can lead at any moment to a standstill or to a catastrophic bursting asunder of the conjoined opposites. Harlequin is a tragically ambiguous figure . . . Harlequin gives me the creeps" (Jung, "Picasso," par. 214). While Picasso's psychological life between 1932 and his death in 1972 was turbulent and subject to extreme tensions, it does not seem to have resulted in that "catastrophic bursting asunder of the conjoined opposites" that Jung feared might happen. Probably Picasso owed this to the success of his art therapy.

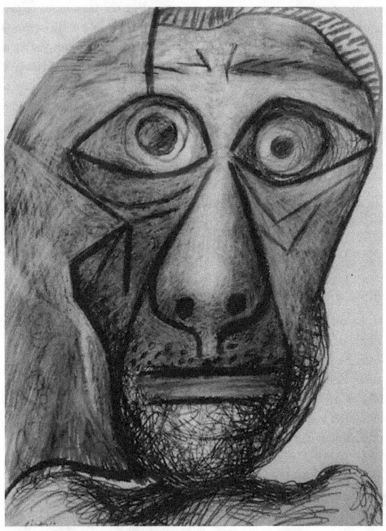

Picasso, Self-Portrait, 1972. Courtesy Fuji Television Gallery.

and his onlookers- an old man, bloated, wrinkled, and gray-but his containment in religious iconography held him back from the stark prospect of annihilation and destruction depicted in Picasso's last self-portraits. This has become a symbol for twentieth-century people because so many have had to face their personal mortality without faith in God or a personal afterlife, immediately and without hope marching to war and going into gas chambers and ovens. This has been a century of unrelenting deconstruction and analysis, and Picasso gives us an image that portrays the end station on this cultural path. It is the imago of a man undressed and devoid of illusion, facing the end of life in a state of panic. It is a picture of sheer animal terror. But it is also a mask, and perhaps it has some power to exorcise the demon of death. In Picasso, the imago's link with the animal side of his nature led logically and inexorably to the animal's instinctive reluctance to die.

It is possible that a study of imagos would help to explain biographies by illuminating an important psychological line of development in adulthood. It must, however, be considered as analysis at a relatively abstract macro level of detail. It helps to make sense of the details if one can discern the general pattern into which they fit. The self-imago speaks of the inner terrain of a person's life and indicates the general boundaries of the pattern that libido expenditures assume in the second half of life. It is a psychic formation that usually appears during middle adulthood and functions to orient, define, and direct psychic energy. The self-imago is a living, evolving psychic structure with roots in the archetypal unconscious and ultimately in the self. It both frees people to be what they most deeply are, and it defines who and what they are and what their lives are about. We should be careful not to consider the imago too narrowly, as fixed and defined.

In chapter 2, I alluded to Jung's adult self-imago formation as he described it happening in his active imagination experience with the transformative image of Aion. Jung's life has not been read as iconic of modernism in the way Picasso's has. Despite the Swiss regularity and predictability in his everyday existence, however, Jung was subjected to the same spiritual and psychological forces of modernity that influenced Picasso, insofar as these were generated in Europe by a general cultural abandonment of religious belief, by loss of faith in the idea of progress, and by the urgent need to find adequate images to express selfhood outside the frame of traditional religious culture. Jung was a thoroughly modern man, but we must note that, while he lived his adult life in the same century as Picasso, his cultural context was Swiss Protestant. His lifelong containment within bourgeois Swiss family life and in the firmly established profession of medicine gives his biography a tone much different from Picasso's with its Spanish background, Parisian color, and unfettered bohemianism. Both men felt the necessity to burst the bonds of tradition - indeed, to challenge and transform it. In Picasso's case, it was the artistic tradition that was challenged; in Jung's case, it was scientific and religious traditions. Jung did not depict his various moltings and major transformations in self-portraits on canvas as Rembrandt and Picasso did. Rather, they can be traced, for the most part, in written accounts of his inner experiences - dreams, active imagination, fantasy images - and, most importantly for this chapter in an architectural statement that I shall consider as a portrait of his self-imago, the stone tower at Bollingen.

Of the three lives considered in this chapter, Jung's was the most self-consciously aimed at and articulated as psychological transformation. Rembrandt left nothing in writing to indicate his state of self-awareness, and Picasso shunned psychological interpretation and verbal self-disclosure. Of the three figures, Jung alone offered an explicit account of his psychological process and a personal statement of its meaning. His own life became a kind of psychological laboratory for him, and he carefully observed and recorded what transpired there.

As a transforming and transformative personality, Jung shows some of the same traits in his relation to psychology that Rembrandt and Picasso demonstrate in their relation to art. All three figures took up their chosen professions in an established context that contained famous exemplars, models of career building, methods for proceeding with the work of their vocational choice. And all three transformed these given models and patterns into a unique expression of their own. One could describe them as rebels who, once they thoroughly had mastered their craft, used their enormous individual talent to defy the collective rules and go it alone. But this would describe adequately only the first half of their lives, the caterpillar stage. The adult self-imago, which follows a vigorously expansive youth, defines the personality's essence and indicates a personality's wholeness. In the cases we are studying here, the adult self-imago emerges only after the way has been cleared for a novel and relatively unrestrained individual development. As neither Rembrandt nor Picasso could paint happily on commission and follow the career path usual for artists of their time, so Jung broke the standard mold of psychiatrist and psychoanalyst, resigned his academic position, and sought his own way of being a modern psychologist. Rembrandt eventually assumed the self-imago of archetypal artist combined with the spiritual enlightenment of a Saint Paul. Picasso found in the Minotaur image the combination of opposites that allowed him full expression of his adult being, and eventually he assumed the mask of a death-haunted modern Everyman. What was Jung's destiny, his final self-imago?

It is noteworthy that all three of these figures reached back to ancient classical images to define themselves. Classical images carry the charge of the archetypal psyche. Chapter 2 discusses Jung's report of turning into the mythic figure Aion during an active imagination in 1913. This had been preceded immediately by an image of crucifixion, in which Jung was identified with Christ, and it led to the healing of his anima Salome's blindness. This is Jung's most dramatic account on record of deification, of actual union with archetypal images and energies. Occurring in Jung's thirty-ninth year, this extraordinary occasion was a crisical moment during the onset of his midlife transformation. The ensuing metamorphosis would change his identity and set him off in directions that could not have been foretold in his larval stage as a young psychiatrist and Freudian psychoanalyst. Of course, the imaginal disks were there from the beginning and can be discerned throughout his biography, but the fully formed self-imago did not emerge as a symbol until 1928, when Jung was fifty-three. This self-imago would allow Jung to transcend his times and his cultural conditioning and assume his place as one of the great healers of soul and spiritual teachers of the age.

One can detect a distinct change in the tone of Jung's publications after 1928. His early writings begin in 1900 with the publication of his doctoral dissertation on so-called mediumistic phenomena. They go on to include a book on dementia praecox (schizophrenia), the studies in word association, many papers on psychiatric topics, contributions to Freudian thought, and, in 1912, the culminating work of the early period, *Wandlungen und Symbole der Libido*. These are purely rational, academic, and scientific works. *Wandlungen* verges on the revisionary and is a bit disorganized and extravagant in its claims and hypotheses; nevertheless, it is a work of remarkable intellectual power, a tour de force. Then there follows an era of relative silence during the years of midlife crisis and World War I while Jung is intensively engaged in his Red Book project that was never published in his lifetime, and then in 1921 there was the publication of *Psychological Types*, a summary of his psychological thinking to date and a major contribution to the study of character and psychodynamics. In 1928, a sharp rhetorical shift becomes apparent with the publication of his "Commentary on 'The Secret of the Golden Flower.'" In this brief work, published in conjunction with Richard Wilhelm's translation of a Chinese alchemy text, Jung for the first time takes on the rhetorical mantle of the spiritual teacher, and his writing never will be quite the same again. At fifty-three, he has found his mature voice, which in the following years will become recognized universally as the voice of a psychological and spiritual master. At times he will play it down before a specific audience, but this voice is what will draw students from all over the world to study with him, the sage of Küsnacht. As a result of his midlife transformation, he has become "Jung."

We can study the period of transformation in Jung's life with some precision because he offers a lot of detail about it in his autobiography. As described there, the period of pupation fell into two major phases. The first phase (1912-16) consisted of opening up to the unconscious psyche with all of its frightful, teeming variety and symbolic richness, and Jung was flooded with psychic material and nearly overwhelmed. The second phase (1916-28) was calmer and was characterized by a centering process, which appeared first as a series of mandala images and then culminated in 1928 in a dream (the "Liverpool dream"[15]), which conveyed to him an image of the self. For Jung, this landmark dream's message was that he had gone as far as he would go at the time in plumbing the depths of the psyche. He had found the irreducible center. And thus he arrived at his defining myth, conceptualized later as the self. Articulating this myth and living out its implications would occupy him for the remainder of his life. The image and the concept of the self centrally defined the adult Jung and constituted his adult self-imago. From this imago and the perspective on psychological reality it offered, Jung created his later contributions to depth psychology.

The notion of the self became the dominant theme in Jung's writings after 1928. It is importantly featured in his alchemical studies, which begin 1928 and conclude nearly 30 years later with the publication of *Mysterium Coniunctionis*. It is most explicitly and systematically expounded in *Aion*, published in 1951, where Jung picks up the image of this mythic figure that he had personally experienced so vividly in 1913. In this work he employed it to establish a vantage point outside of time, as it were, from which to look at Western cultural history and the Christian era. Jung used this association with the symbolic ruler behind astrological time to reflect upon the inner history and meaning of Christianity in the Age of Pisces and to speculate about the Platonic Year to come, the Age of Aquarius. At the heart of this work's agenda, however, is Jung's

---

[15] C.G. Jung, *Memories, Dreams, Reflections*, pp. 197-98.

account of the structure and dynamics of the self as an archetypal factor that, like Aion, exists outside the ego's world of time-space categories. This factor shapes the psychological structures and unfolding developments of individuals as well as the Zeitgeist of whole epochs. *Aion* conceives of the personal and the collective historical dimensions of human life as united in a meaningful set of rhythms and deployments in time.

What Jung attempted in his writings on Christianity and Western culture was to dream the collective myth onward, to take it beyond its present state through a transformation process into a new era of its internal development.[16] Rembrandt accepted his age as given; Picasso lived the myth of the modern man; Jung tried to go one step farther. Perhaps the heroic side of Jung expressed itself in this undertaking, for through books, letters, and lectures he actively engaged the biblical tradition and offered the West a new religious symbol in the Quaternity to carry it forward in its potential internal development toward completion and wholeness. This effort to transform the central religious image of Christianity - its image of God as a Trinity - is passionately inscribed in his book *Answer to Job*, arguably Jung's most controversial published work and one that cost him several important relationships with Christian clergy (not least, that of the highly regarded Benedictine priest, Victor White). This text has been seen by some thinkers as the basis of a new doctrinal development in Western religion[17] and by others as a statement of Jung's unwarranted grandiosity.[18] In any event, it was an attempt on his part to generate a transformative dynamic within Christian theology and culture. A central thrust of it is the rising star of the feminine within an ancient patriarchal tradition.

---

[16] For further discussion of this, see my book, *Jung's Treatment of Christianity*.

[17] See E. Edinger, *The New God Image*.

[18] See V. White, "Jung on Job" and E. Weisstub, "Questions to Jung on 'Answer to Job.'"

Jung's tower at Bollingen. Photograph by Ruth Ammann.

Besides expounding the concept of the self in his writings and psychological teaching, Jung also represented it in concrete material form in an architectural undertaking, the stone tower at Bollingen. In 1922 he bought a piece of property at the upper end of Lake Zurich which, he notes, "formerly belonged to the monastery of St. Gall."[19] It would become his own personal hermitage, "a confession of faith in stone."[20] Over the course of the following twelve years, in four phases, each separated by four years (1923, 1927, 1931, 1935), a structure was built of locally hewn granite. Jung considered it a representation of the self. For our purposes, we can consider it a self-portrait of Jung's self-imago.

The first part of the tower initially was conceived as a simple African hut and was intended to concretize "an idea of wholeness, a familial wholeness in which all sorts of small domestic animals

---

[19] C.G. Jung, *Memories, Dreams, Reflections*, p. 223.
[20] Ibid.

likewise participate."[21] This part of the tower would cling to the earth and embrace the body and the instincts. Jung here was grounding his self-imago in physical existence, not unlike Picasso's elemental relation to body and instinct represented in the Minotaur. For Jung, the self included flesh and blood, the physical body.

In 1927, he erected a tower-like annex that became the central feature of the building, now a "tower." The spirit had begun to rise from the maternal ground, and the masculine next appeared. This annex was extended in 1931 to include a private room, a space of interiority and retreat, upon whose walls he painted the image of Philemon, the winged bald sage who, he says, taught him about the objective psyche.[22] This came to be "a place of spiritual con-centration"[23] where he could enter the realm of timeless symbols and the eternal spirit. Thus, body and spirit -maternal hearth and kitchen, tower and upper room - were united in the emergent structure.

Finally, in 1935, the building was filled out with a courtyard and loggia by the lake that connected it to the surroundings. The tower now remained in this form until 1955, when, after the death of his wife, Jung added a storey to the small central section. This, he says, represented his ego-personality, the "extension of consciousness achieved in old age."[24] It was an extension upward. This same "extension" is what we find in Rembrandt's late self-portraits and also, though in a distinctly "modern" form, in Picasso's last self-portraits. In its final form, the Bollingen tower represents the expression of Jung's self-imago as it was constituted after midlife and realized in the second half of life. It is a statement in stone of psychological wholeness. In a sense, Jung's self-imago embraces both the spirituality of Rembrandt's late statement in his self-

---

[21] *Ibid.*, 224.

[22] *Ibid.*, 183.

[23] *Ibid.*, 224.

[24] *Ibid.*, 225.

portrait as the Apostle Paul and the physicality of Picasso's final image.

There is a strong stylistic flavor of European medievalism and Christian traditionalism in the Bollingen tower, yet it also bespeaks modernity and post-modernity. It contains a mixture of styles - primitive, pagan, and classical, as well as medieval. This combination of "quotations" could be read as an anticipation of the vocabulary of postmodernism. But Jung would probably eschew all such labels and classifications. In his own terms, he was was intuitively groping his way toward a statement of psychological wholeness. He was seeking a combination of elements that would hold his own inner opposites together in a creative tension and would embody an image of wholeness in which even his remote ancestors would feel at home (hence no plumbing or electricity). Like his inner world of dreams and symbolic images, the tower embraces the ages and touches on many polarities: mother/father, material/spiritual, ancient/modern, traditional/individual, male/female. It is a testament in stone to his psychic self-imago.

In preparation for death, Jung found an attitude, created from dreams and visions, that would carry him confidently with the grace of a flower falling to earth and reconnecting with its original underground rhizome.[25] What he achieved in life was the realization of an archetypal self-imago that contains both spiritual wisdom and earthy grounding. He lived a full human life and became a sage, a teacher for his age and for ages to come. Like Rembrandt and Picasso, Jung himself was transformed by the ageless images of the collective unconscious. In turn, he sought to place his grain of sand on the scales of history and so move the eternal spirit one more tick in the direction of full incarnation.

---

[25] C.G. Jung, *Memories, Dreams, Reflections*, p. 4.

Men Under Construction[1]

A Short Preface

My junior high school in Grand Forks, North Dakota, was blessed with an inspirational science teacher with a great sense of humor. We loved her. I don't remember her name, sadly, but recall that she was a tall and sturdily built woman in her 30s who had not married and seemed totally dedicated to her vocation as a teacher. We learned about modern physics and astronomy from her, and she opened our eyes to the wonders of the scientific discoveries of the twentieth century. One day she came into class and told us a story from her weekend. She had been driving down a long and boring highway in North Dakota and decided to take a coffee break. Pulling over into a rest stop she saw a car marked as military with a sign on the back that read: "U.S. Marines. We Build Men." She went into the café, looked around, and saw the Marines from the car. Walking up to them boldly, she called out: "Build me a man!" We all laughed when she told us this story, and for some reason I've never forgotten it.

It raises the question: Do boys naturally grow into mature men, or do such men have to be built? Are men products of nature or of

---

[1] Originally presented as lectures at the C.G. Jung Institute of Chicago in 1988 and later published in a book by this name in 2020.

culture? In other words, how much of individuation is an *opus contra naturam*, an artifact of culture and individual will? And what role do the archetypes of the collective unconscious play in masculine development? The answer to this will depend in part on whether one takes archetypes to be a part of human nature or a cultural influence. I lean toward the former but recognize the powerful effects of culture on all human beings, especially in the first half of life.

The stages of male development observed cross-culturally and through historical time seem quite similar. They proceed from infancy and boyhood through adolescence and young adulthood to mature adulthood and old age consistently, although in somewhat different renditions due to cultural and geographical factors. The same stages are evident and marked. This argues for inherent nature governing the development from boy to man. However, this patterning of development is always strongly assisted by social and cultural influences and pressures. So, it may be that the Marines do indeed build men (culture), but it must go along the lines of inherent patterns and tendencies (nature) that make this model of a man possible.

Of course, if you argue that archetypal patterns are mainly cultural artifacts and not inherent in human nature, then most features of development are due to culture while nature plays little role. But there is still the physical body, and this is without doubt a contribution of nature and the evolution of the species.

In my view, individuation in both men and women is a complex interweaving of physical, psychological, and cultural factors. How a person develops, matures, in other words individuates, depends on a multifactorial panoply of forces. Each factor contributes to the dynamic process, and each makes an essential contribution to the final result. In the pages that comprise this volume, I try to give due respect to all of them, but my primary emphasis is on the psychological. I recognize that the individual psyche is by no means independent of the body; it is a part of the culture it inhabits. But too often the psychological is overlooked in favor of physical and cultural factors, and I would like to contribute to a rebalancing of the picture. It is in this spirit that I offer these reflections.

Introduction

The general view among non-specialists in developmental psychology is that a person moves through several eras of development – childhood, adolescence, adulthood - and enters a stage of psychological development at a certain age, takes up the tasks appropriate to that stage, solves them (or not), and then moves on to the next stage. This is perhaps true in a very broad sense in the first half of life and follows, more or less, the observed stages of biological development from infancy to adulthood. But it is misleading as an accurate description for how people grow into themselves over the course of an entire lifetime. Psychological development is messier than that. We don't pass through and leave discrete stages as such, but we do develop—only it's not by opening and closing doors in well-ordered sequential stages. Psychological development, which I will hereafter refer to also as individuation, goes forward sequentially but in a pattern of cycles. The image of the spiral is closer to the reality we experience and witness than the image of a straightforward passage through chronological eras that move unilaterally in one direction through time. A "stage" is a way of speaking about a period in life when certain issues seem more pressing and prominent than others. A name like "childhood" or "adolescence" becomes attached it. The problem is that we find ourselves engaging the same issues again and again throughout life, and if we are indeed developing, then with each pass we make a little gain in consciousness, or freedom, or integration. But we can be sure that we will pass that way again, over the same ground as before. If we are doing our work, then each passing is a little more conscious, a little deeper, a little truer to the self we are.

Erik Erikson proposed a theory of eight stages of psychosocial development that are evident in the course of a lifetime. Every student of psychology learns these stages by heart. Most famously, Erikson wrote about the stage of identity development that occurs during adolescence. This is typically a turbulent period in people's lives, and sometimes it involves a crisis filled with angst and uncertainty about what kind of person one is ands wants to become. But it is certainly the case that the question of identity plays a role in every transitional period, sometimes with more intensity, sometimes with less. We go through a process of identity formation as small children, and we are engaged in the process of identity formation and reformation in midlife and in old age. Each time the question of identity comes up in our lives, we make a little more progress on it. We might see ourselves more clearly, or simply differently, with new aspects emerging out of the mist, new formations appearing, or with old aspects coming more prominently to the fore. Identity is a work in progress throughout our lives. We never leave the issue of identity behind once and for all. We circumambulate this question as identity changes and expands its scope. It is the same with intimacy, the next stage in Erikson's program. We have to deal with it in childhood and throughout life, not only after adolescence in early adulthood as Erikson positions it. So it is with all the stages on Erikson's list.

When I speak in the following pages of the development of men "out of the mother" and "out of the father" into a relatively free space of choice and relatedness, I am not saying that these developments follow a strictly linear sequence from "a" to "b" to "c" without residues. I am going to insist, rather, that one never completely frees oneself from the mother or from the father, and that there are only relative freedoms from them, and one has to keep working at these issues throughout life. Still, there are important change in one's sense of self and purpose, and development does occur.

Jung's advice on the subject of insoluble developmental problems was that we cannot overcome them directly, we can only outgrow them. I would recommend this strategy: learn to love the insoluble problems of freeing yourself from mother and father, because these problems are worth the time and effort and are worthy of your most careful consideration. You will pass over them innumerable times in the course of your life, each time with more consciousness, seeing more deeply into the implications and dynamics, each time loosening a deeper strand of the limitations these complexes have created. The goal of the development I am going to propose, the *telos* of a man's inner development, is to achieve as much freedom from them as possible, true freedom, in order to release the full panoply of potentials in the self. And the traps and seductions and illusions of freedom along the way toward that freedom are almost infinite.

I look on this work as a statement of vision of what men can become, rather than a research-based social scientific report. Further research is, of course, invited and welcome.

The Five Stages of a Man's Life — A Brief Overview

The diagram below sketches a model of psychological development in a man over the normal lifespan, assuming an achieved age of 80+ years. As it shows, his psychological movement passes through five major periods, or "stages," in the course of the individuation process.[2] This model provides the general framework for discussing the developmental issues and challenges I will be considering in the following pages.

Diagram #1 shows discrete circles that designate stages, but it should additionally be arranged in the form of a spiral as in Diagram #2.

The circles nest inside one another, rising gradually and progressively emerging from one to the other. The transitional areas between the stages are shown in Diagram #1 at the intersection of the contiguous circles. The circles and links in the model are

---

[2] I will use the term, "individuation," throughout these pages to speak of full-lifespan psychological development. It is a term used by Jung to indicate the process of personality development from birth to death.

Stages Of A Man's Life

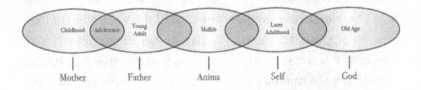

Son → Husband / Father → Hero → Missionary → Sage

Diagram #1.

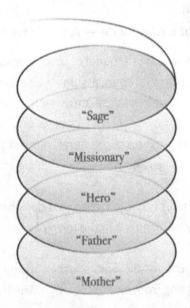

Archetypal Dominants Of
The Life Cycle

Diagram #2.

stretched out or condensed in time according to cultural and other factors such as life expectancy.

The initial phase of a man's development, which covers infancy and childhood, is dominated by the mother. I refer to this stage as "in the mother," since the child's conscious horizon is more or less enveloped in the atmosphere of the maternal. It is a period of containment and nurturance. The transition from this stage to the next takes place in adolescence, which begins around the age of 12 and lasts until a solid residence has been taken up in the next stage. This is a first step in the lifelong process of separation.

The figure of the father dominates the second stage, and I will speak of it as "in the father." The psychic horizon here is framed by the patriarchal attitude, either personal or cultural. Separation from the second stage and transition to the third stage begins around the age of 35 and lasts until approximately the age of 50. As the maternal dominates the first stage and the patriarchal the second, the soul, or anima, features as the dominant figure in the third stage.

The fourth stage, which lasts roughly from the age of 50 to the mid-70s, concerns the development of the ego-self axis and is characterized by the emergence and increasing consciousness of the self as an important psychic factor. This stage moves gradually, and usually without a major break in consciousness into the fifth and final stage, in which spirituality and the "God problem" enter as the main themes of further individuation. I call this "late stage individuation."

Each of the dominant figures in these five stages—Mother, Father, Anima, Self, and God—presents specific typical problems and challenges that have to do with the sense of a man's identity. In stage One, he is "mother's boy." As he frees himself from this stage, he moves on to become "father's son." There may be a formal rite of passage that marks this change in identity. During the second stage, he often becomes a father himself, even while his identity remains that of son of the father. In the midlife stage, there is a further demand for separation from parental figures as his sense of identity shifts to that of the hero, whose task is to rescue his soul, the anima, from domination and extinction by the patriarchal world. His identity as hero is diminished in importance as he moves into later adulthood, which I will designate "missionary" because he now finds a mission in the world, which directs his vision outward beyond himself to embrace collective and cultural issues. This is the era of significant engagement with the world. As he moves into old age, this missionary identity gives way to religious questions of ultimate meaning. His sense of identity shifts to "sage" as he becomes a wisdom figure for others.

As I said earlier, each stage pushes psychic material forward into the others. We carry our past with us even as individuation moves further and deeper into full selfhood.

The First Circle: Mother
The Age of the Boy

This first stage in a man's development, which I will speak of throughout these pages as the "mother stage," forms a platform for all future psychological developments to come and is extensive and complex, consisting of several phases and sub-phases, many of which may be repeated in various forms in later life. It covers the period of childhood, from birth to teens, in which the mother and "mother-child problems" occupy center stage. Here the male child is "a mother's boy" and, ideally, feels loved and admired by her totally.

I will not go into the details of the several phases of early childhood development (much about this topic exists in the psychological literature) except to mention some issues affecting masculine development specifically. By "mother," it is important to understand, that I mean more than a single caretaking person. The whole surrounding environment of a child is "the mother," in the sense that it is a containing and nurturing context. The personal mother merely symbolizes this total environment, for better or worse.

In the early years, the first significant person in a man's life is (usually) his own biological mother. She is the first significant "other" with whom a physical as well as psychological relationship is established. This relationship is often referred to as "attachment," following the name given it in the pioneering work of John Bowlby, and it begins already prenatally.

The infant's first extra-uterine experiences of the world are normally centered on the actual mother and are colored importantly by her reception of the newborn. The quality of this reception lays down over time a critical foundational element in a person's basic attitude toward the world and has lifelong consequences. Erik Erikson names the crucial emotional issue of this phase of psychological development "trust vs. mistrust." If the reception is welcoming, stable, and nurturing, and if the infant is sufficiently healthy and responsive, an attitude of trust develops in the young persona. The infant can relate to the world (here represented by the mother) with feelings of trust. A cordial, welcoming reception will encourage a positive outgoing attitude toward the world, while ambivalence shown in a cool or negative reception may produce or strengthen an already existing tendency toward avoidance of relations with the outside world. In summary, the attitude of the mother toward the infant is generally seen as critically important for the future quality of object relations. The relationship to the world established at this stage of life will play a considerable role throughout a man's life.

While still contained within the "mother world," which typically continues until early adolescence, a boy will show strenuous efforts to develop a separate sense of self and autonomy. A boy's efforts to separate himself from his parental caretakers (the "mothers") begin early on and normally gather considerable energy around the age of two ("the terrible two's"). Then, when the three- or four-year-old boy discovers significant physical differences between himself and his mother, he intensifies the separation process from her on a psychological level with the noted gender difference coming prominently into play. A mother, who of course is well aware of this difference and the coming need of her son to separate from her, may facilitate this process or she may try to hinder it. Ambivalence on her part concerning separation can set the stage for emotional conflicts in the son. Is it OK to leave his mother or not? How far can he stray and still remain attached? On the other hand, an anxious mother, anticipating separation too soon, may begin to take distance too early and leave the boy with a feeling of insecurity and abandonment.

There are some typical problems that arise from the nature of the relationship between a mother and son. I will describe a few that I have observed in my practice. This list is by no means exhaustive, to say the least.

1. The man with an absent mother. I recall the case of a man, "Ben," who was thirty years old when he came into my practice. His mother had been heavily medicated and hospitalized with severe mental illness during his early childhood. At the time I saw him, he was sexually underdeveloped and had several addictions, mostly around eating and alcohol but also involving excessive fantasizing and daydreaming. Having been a fairly good student in school, he was now studying for the priesthood. This course of study was not going very well due to his inability to stay focused. One of the most striking things I noticed about him was what I felt as his "vacancy." In sessions, he would sit down and almost immediately go into a fugue-like state, staring ahead vacantly and unresponsively, as if in a sort of self-induced hypnotic state. When I asked him about it, he said he was "processing." Sometimes, he said, it was "prayer," because he felt that he was communicating with spiritual beings like saints or angels. In one session, upon going into this state he reported to me that he was having a vision of "Our Lady," the Mother figure honored by multitudes in his church, and he was connected to her by an umbilicus through which "food" was passing into him.

Ben was a man whose mother had been incapable of receiving a child into her care. The image of the archetypal Great Mother came to him as a substitute for the missing personal mother, and She offered food and nurturance to him. The psyche compensates for the absence of a real mother by offering a symbolic one, and the neglected child finds refuge there and remains embedded in the archetypal world until a way can be found to exit from it and enter into relationship to individuals and communities. In contrast to a man who has too strong an attachment to his real mother and stays at home well into his adulthood, this man's difficulty was that he could not form an attachment to his mother because she was not there, and so he became attached to an imaginal surrogate. He remained "in the mother" by projecting this archetypal image on to religious objects and institutions.

2. The man with an ambivalent mother. A man aged 33 came into therapy because he felt completely stuck in his life on every level. While he was constitutionally very creative and artistic, bordering on brilliant, he had been unable to engage with the world in an effective way. He remained cocooned. He could not bring himself to present or sell his paintings. His father had not invited him into his business because of the boy's close tie to his mother and his unsuitability for the rough and tumble life out there in the competitive world of commerce. In his adolescence, the boy had dropped out of school, left home, and started to make his way in life completely on his own. He exhibited behavior similar to Ben's in sessions, including fugue-like states and discomfort and distrust when engaged in dialogue. Deep narcissistic injuries and traumas from childhood were evident in his reactions to others, including myself. His relationship to women was severely stressed: he demanded that a woman be completely virginal, a Madonna, but once in a relationship he constantly berated her and tried to prove that she was a whore and therefore unworthy of him, which drove her away, of course, and left him living alone again.

His dreams showed that he was "stuck in the mother." In one, he was trapped in a grocery store (a mother image) owned by the Mafia (symbolic of the mother's animus). Finally, his father came to the rescue, providing him with the suggestion to pay the Mafia off in order to escape. Thus, his father offered a way out of the mother trap. The dream father was more active than his actual father had been. To me, this suggested a possibility that his transference to me might provide a way out of his stuck condition. The question was how to pay off his mother's controlling animus and get free of her. In the end, he did not succeed, sadly. I felt badly and regretted that I had been unable to help him in his search for liberation.

In this case, we discovered a mother who allowed her boy infant to form an attachment to her but at the same time harbored a deep hostility to men, typically because she herself had been wounded by them and by the patriarchal bias of society. Most importantly, she had a deeply troubled and conflicted relationship with the boy's father, and this led her to draw her son into a tortured marital drama by making him an ally against the father. Since the child was male, however, she saw him both as ally and enemy. This ambiguity was frightening to the son, since sometimes the mother was too close, threatening incest, and at other times she was distant and murderously rageful. Her unpredictability destabilized him and created turbulence in his relationships, especially with women. The father—designated as enemy—could not help, so the son was trapped in the home with a frighteningly unstable mother. The father was probably envious of the child because he seemed to have gained access to the mother's intimacy while he was locked out, and consequently a negative and hostile relationship developed between father and son. The father rejected him and the mother threatened him. He was stuck between them.

3. The man with the faulty-mirror mother. A 50-year-old professional man who was successful in his profession and married with a family of three children had an enduring problem of being unable to feel himself as a man. When looking at himself naked in the mirror, he could not "see" his penis and had no sense of it. He grew up in a family dominated by a strong-willed mother, and his father was weak by comparison and passive. In his adult years, he dealt with his inability to feel his masculinity by looking intently at other men whom he admired and trying to find in himself the qualities that attracted him. He was trying to find himself in the

mirror of these projections. He searched for his masculinity by looking outside of himself. It was a more or less hopeless quest since the missing qualities inevitably remained "out there" in the other and could not be located within. This often brought on spasms of despair.

A mother will typically mirror her child, looking at him with loving eyes and enjoying him for his being, not for abilities or achievements (which will be the father's role) but simply for what he is, in and of himself. One aspect of his nature that is to be also enjoyed by the mother is his maleness, and her positive mirroring of this will enable a strong development of his masculinity. If the mirror is faulty, however, the mother may enjoy him as an infant, cute and cuddly, but she cannot positively mirror and enjoy his maleness as he grows older. She may ignore or suppress acknowledgement of his sex and his male qualities as they appear in childhood. She thus rejects his masculinity, possibly because of her own difficulties with sexuality in her relationships with men. She may dress the boy as a girl and cast him in the role of a daughter she would have preferred. The father is, again, passive, distant, or missing. The boy will have difficulty identifying with his own masculine parts, even if he has no difficulty identifying with other parts of his personhood such as his intellect.

4. The man with a guilt-and-shame-inducing mother. This type of mother does not neutralize, distort, or deny the masculinity of her son, but rather creates an atmosphere of guilt and shame about typical masculine traits that her son might display. When typical boy behaviors such as aggressiveness, independence, and explorative-ness appear, she reacts negatively, shaming the boy. As a man, if he is primarily attached to her rather than to his father (that is, a "mother's boy"), he may seem to some women to be a paragon of gentleness and goodness—but too good to be true. Women like him, but they do not fall in love with him, lacking as he is in basic masculine qualities. He is still "in the mother," and were he to depart from the mother's injunctions, he would feel terrible guilt. Such a

man tends to stay close to the female-dominated home and is often service-oriented in his behavior and career. He cannot be his full masculine self, because he is afraid of his mother punishing disapproval and of shaming looks. This constraint operates subtly, pervading daily behavior as a maternal super-ego.

5. The man with the perfect mother. This mother permits the son to attach to her and gives her son enough nurturance and mirroring to keep him from discovering her negative side. Usually she accomplishes this by encouraging him to project the negative feminine outwardly onto someone else, which produces a split for the son between the good woman (herself) and the bad woman (all others). This son becomes the classically mother-bound son. He sees his mother as totally positive—virginal, pure, good—and other women as much lesser than his mother—problematic, sexual, witch-like, and so on. Thus he idealizes his mother and denigrates other women, often remaining a bachelor and caring for his widowed mother, or cherishing an ideal memory of her. The father is usually rather inconsequential, weak or absent, or thoroughly denigrated by the perfect mother. The son only sees "her sweetness" and gets trapped in it. He feels he must stay with her and protect her, and he feels guilty about any possible relationship with another woman. Typically, she encourages this sense of responsibility. If he is to marry, she encourages marriage to a weak, unchallenging woman. A classic example of the perfect mother is portrayed in the opera, *Carmen*. Don Jose's mother is allforgiving, meek, and non-sexual, in sharp distinction to Carmen who is her complete, and extremely attractive, opposite.

In contrast to all these problematic mothers is the so-called "good enough" mother. She is not the perfect mother because she gives her son her real self, gradually, at a rate that he can handle. She is devoted to nurturing in the beginning, but in time she weans him, allows some distance, permits him to see her anger, her imperfections, her negative side, in short, to see her more and more as she really is. Secondly, she maintains the strength of the early bonding in an appropriate way, which will stand him in good stead throughout his later development. In this, she fosters his ability to achieve intimacy and trust in relationships especially with women. A man's capacity to be open and intimate generally depends substantially on the development of his trust in women, which is first established in his relationship to the good enough mother. Third, she confers on her son a sense of self-confidence, which he can take with him when he leaves her. The mother is the son's first experience of the world and its reliability or lack thereof. If a man is able later to count on his inner good enough mother, his ego will be well-grounded and his sense of self-worth will enable him to proceed through life with resiliency, confidence, and the ability to relate successfully to the world.

In time, the good enough mother will show her son her negative side, which helps him to separate from her. If the mother remains too one-sidedly positive, there may be an irresistible temptation to stay at home with her. The good enough mother shows her negative side in her weaning of him or "abandoning" him to the father or babysitters, and eventually he understands that he is meant to go into life on his own.

The gift of the good enough mother is that a man can be enough at home in his body and in the world to feel and understand his impulses and instincts. In addition, the good enough mother bestows the confidence that he can meet his needs and gratify his desires with success. Therefore, he will know when he is hungry and can seek something to eat; he will know when he wants and needs intimacy and can seek out a suitable partner; he can feel his anger or sadness and can act on them if necessary; he can be active, even aggressive, when a situation calls for it; he can destroy in order to create. When confronted with the negative features of life, he is able to protect himself through his wits and his own knowledge of the world. This type of mother has enabled him to leave the parental household because he has the basis for self-sustenance.

In an optimal development, a man's sense of self is constellated adequately in the Mother Circle so that he is able to move out of the parental home and into the wider world. He can now enter into the Father Circle, the realm of career, development of skills, and the challenges of society. Here, he can express his ambition. In the next stage, he will need to learn to relate to the expectations and requirements of the prevailing culture, which will bring the father into a position of central importance.

The Second Circle: Father
The Age of the Son

If a mother provides her son with the basis for a solid inner sense of self, a father helps him to discover and relate effectively to the outer world of society. As with the term "mother," I am not speaking here exclusively of the actual father but rather of the "fathers," in general, who appear in a man's life in a variety of figures, such as teachers, ministers, politicians, and other leaders, not all of them necessarily biologically male but definitely of a masculine-patriarchal cast in attitude. The feminine side of the self for a man typically constitutes the quality of his inner life, which covers such matters as his experiences of intimacy and soul, that is, his private and inward subjective space. The masculine side typically takes up the dominant space in his ego and persona. In the persona he shows himself to others as a man: he dresses like a man and he acts like a man in a manner acknowledged and approved by his specific culture. The father, a loving and instructing representative of the masculine principle, functions as a bridge to the outer world and helps him to adapt to society positively and to adjust himself to collective expectations. His father figures guide him in learning how to be a man in the real world of work and taxes.

Mother and father contribute, therefore, fundamental structural strands in a man's psychological genetic makeup. They are essential building blocks of a man's personality structure. Moreover, the autonomous and unconscious mother and father complexes are major psychic energy centers that return to affect consciousness over and over again in a continual and lifelong enactment of his psychological life, behaviorally and attitudinally. Like the *leitmotifs* of a Wagner opera, their influences resurface and thread through all the phases and stages of life. Mother and father exist both as real individuals and as complexes and archetypes, each level contributing emotional and psychological influences on the early years of a man's life and forever after.

At the beginning of life, the mother world constitutes the entire object world to which the infant relates. Inner world and outer world are one, and there is no serious division between subject and object. Jung calls this type of relationship, where subject and object are entangled to the point of identity, "participation mystique" ("mystical participation"). It is the earliest form of object relations. While the father is equally primary in the structural formation of the personality, temporally he arrives on the scene later. His image appears as from out of a mist as a second primary figure in the world of the infant child. The father relationship reaches deep into infancy and is lifelong, just as is the mother relationship, but as a significant figure with meaning, he is introduced slightly later in life. With the arrival of the father, the psyche begins the process of differentiation among objects and between inner and outer. Mother is intimate, familiar, close; father is impersonal, strange, and distant. This is the early picture of psychic experience.

The world, at first whole, gradually becomes differentiated and divided as discrete objects begins to emerge in consciousness, and this evokes a variety of reactions. According to Melanie Klein, a first differentiation is made in infancy between "good" and "bad." She locates this discrimination in the infant's relationship to the mother's two breasts. There is an alternation between "good breast" and "bad breast," one breast being felt as nurturing, warm, and comforting, while the other takes on the quality of being persecutory, poisonous, and attacking. This is the origin of the distinction between good and bad, the earliest work of the differentiating function of consciousness, according to Klein. Jung would not necessarily disagree as he sees ego consciousness gradually emerging from the unconscious in the course of infancy. Klein proposes a rather violent and emotional beginning to psychological life. Later researchers like Daniel Stern have taken a more sanguine view of these first beginnings of conscious awareness of material objects. This phase, however, takes place within the original ouroboric (tightly enclosed) relationship between self and other. It represents the beginnings of a differentiation in the inner world.

A different kind of differentiation is made when the "third," that is, father, is introduced into the mother-infant setting. This is not a differentiation within the mother world but between the mother world and the father world, inner versus outer. The differentiating function of consciousness now begins to create another axis: that between woman and man, feminine and mas-culine, inner and outer. In the unified world of original wholeness, these features exist only as latent possibilities. The original primordial state of oneness becomes divided between good and bad, and then when the figure of the father is introduced into the infant's world, between inner and outer, between mother and father. This yields a fourfold structure for consciousness, which the child will use for basic orientation: good vs. bad, inner vs. outer. The latter distinction becomes the distinction between fantasy (inner) and reality (outer). This later yields two types of thinking: imagination and directed thinking.

It should be said that these same differentiations occur for both girls and boys, but their development diverges because boys tend to go on to identify with the father and girls with the mother. Through her identification with the mother, a little girl sustains a sense of continuity in her identity and tends to remain more inward, imaginative, and close to her mother, while a little boy experiences a rupture in his world as he parts with his mother and as he tends to move outward into the world to be near his father and toward directed thinking. These are gross generalizations but I believe they cover a large majority of cases.

In optimal male development, or what we could refer to as the highly desirable but elusive "normal" development, a mother introduces her son to his father and creates an atmosphere of inclusion that bring the father into what was the dyadic world of mother and infant. This avoids a split and results in a triadic social structure that can be stable and enduring. Ideally, she presents the father as a positive figure and not as a threat to the intimacy between her and her son. In doing so, she helps her son to idealize his father as a figure of pride and high esteem whose importance casts an aura of value on the family as a whole. This initial idealization is absolutely essential for further development because the son is then able to draw upon his native masculine tendencies by identifying with his father and striving to imitate him, feeling that being like him is a good thing and that mother will be supportive and not feel abandoned, wounded, or critical. Out of this idealization the boy's ambition is born. The son's ability to idealize his father and to strive to be like that ideal, provides a motive for further development of his personality.

Later on, usually in early- to mid-adolescence, the son "outgrows" his personal father, discovering some deficiencies and becoming disillusioned with him. At this point, idealization passes on to other male figures such as teachers, coaches, political leaders, and so on, who seem greater than the father and who represent the son's next step out into the world. Again, ambition is constellated in these idealizations as the boy strives to become like his ideals. The relocation of the son's idealizations helps to release the son from his actual father and his parental nest. He can fly away and test his own wings. The father's role at this point, optimally, is to allow himself to be supplanted as his son's ideal and to understand that it is appropriate for his son to move on. Nietzsche observed that it is the mark of a good teacher that his students outgrow him and that he enjoys their development. It is, likewise, the mark of the good enough father that he can enjoy watching his son outstrip him in some ways.

Having been outgrown at this stage, the father will come back in later life, often at midlife, in the memory, imagination, and dreams of his son. He may have died by this time but in the psyche his continued presence is assured. He returns not as the historical father who has been idealized and outgrown, but as a self figure. The archetypal self becomes personalized in this way, moving from the hidden depths of the unconscious to the concrete memory image. Whereas the self may appear in dreams in abstract form such as stars, circles, squares, numbers, and so on, it now may appear in personalized form in the figure of the father.

The Role of the Father: Initiation

The essential role of the father is to initiate his son into manhood, or at least to assist crucially in the initiation. The father accomplishes the earliest phase of this initiation simply by appearing in the world of the mother and by offering himself as an alternative point of orientation, enabling differentiation between the masculine and the feminine, the outer and the inner. He next offers himself as an object of idealization. Not all fathers find it possible to allow themselves to be idealized, and this refusal creates a deficit in the son's development. Idealization places some pressure on the father to live up to a projection. This pressure, which grows stronger as his son gets older, demands that a man live up to an ideal, which can limit his freedom. In this sense, children can be said to create their parents, although some fathers strongly resist this development. A father may reject such idealizations if there is too great a discrepancy between his own (possibly poor) self-image or his lack of maturity, and the ideal image reflected back by his son. He may feel trapped or caged in.

By idealizing his father, the son separates himself further from his mother (and sisters). He may at this point feel that he is better than they are and assert superiority on the basis of the masculine prowess he shares with the father, becoming grandiose about his fantasies (as dragon slayer or superman, like his dad) and feeling full of himself as a male. The idealization of the father operates at several levels—physical (he is bigger, stronger), cognitive (he is smarter, more capable of doing things), and social (he has a wider circle of friends and colleagues). The idealized father is seen as having great knowledge of the world—he lives "out there," he knows about places outside the home, and he can fix things that mother can't. The son will take note of his father's professional or social position and compare that invidiously with the mother's domestic roles. The son thus builds a positive father complex and identifies with his father's masculine presentation of himself as a man in the world, which then become strengthened as other more feminine parts become recessive and fall away into the unconscious.

Eventually, the father will have to allow himself to become de-idealized. This often occurs suddenly and surprisingly. A word will be said, something will be seen, or the father will disappoint in a certain critical way that the son does not quite understand, and the son will consequently feel disappointment and becomes disillusioned. The father is not as great as he had imagined.

The first step in initiation is, then, identification with an ideal; the second is loss through betrayal of that ideal. In the identification stage, the son learns to claim his phallic power and feel his masculine strength, later connecting this to his creativity and fertility. In the second step of initiation, betrayal, the son is released from bondage to the father. The betrayal is essential to prevent the son from being forever bound in the father. James Hillman in his important paper, "On Betrayal," retells an old Jewish story. A father takes his son to the basement of their house where he tells him to climb up on one basement stair and jump into his father's arms. The son complies, and the father catches him. The father then tells him to repeat the action, this time climbing up two steps. The son climbs, jumps, and is caught. Again, says the father, another step higher; and again the son climbs, jumps, and is caught. This is repeated until the son has climbed quite far up the steps. He jumps once more; but this time the father does not catch him. The son falls and is hurt; he is enraged and astonished. The lesson, says the father, is that this is what life is like; moreover, he, the father, will not always be there to catch his son. Thus, the son is released from dependency on the father by an act or instance of betrayal. That betrayal, of course, must come at the right time; and the son must have the wherewithal to grow from the experience and move on into independence. If it comes too early, or too consistently, a negative father complex will develop and with it an aversion to all paternal authority. But the good enough father is able, at the right moment, to show his negative, untrustworthy side to his son and to allow his son to suffer the consequences. All initiations have an element of risk and possible catastrophe. Without that, it is not a true or effective initiation. The outcome of initiation must be a man's sense of his inner resilience, strength, and reliability to deal with life's trials without collapsing.

The Initiated and the Uninitiated

If I contrast the initiated with the uninitiated man, it should be recognized that no man is totally one or the other. These concepts represent the extreme ends of a spectrum based on the relationship with the father. Nonetheless, in observing men, one can often see a clear difference between those more fully initiated and those who are not.

The initiated man has incorporated the masculine in himself as an *inner* structure. It is a part of his self-definition and feeling of self. He has gone through an initiation process or trial, in which he was challenged and found himself able to identify the masculine in himself—feeling his phallus and its strength as a part of himself, and feeling his strength and prowess as a man. Moreover, he has not become bound in dependency to a particular father figure but can use father figures or strong masculine images as points of reference. He is able to use his literal and his symbolic phallus in his life and can therefore stand his ground against other powerful male figures who challenge him. Able to stand on his own two feet, he can make independent judgments, face authority, and carry authority himself. He is what people call "self-confident." Thus, he can be a father— or a manager or a boss or a leader. He is neither dependent on his mother, from whom his father helped to free him, nor on his father, from whom he is freed through initiation.

The Uninitiated Man

The uninitiated man, in contrast, tends to stand beside or outside the circle of masculine authority, as if not quite pulled out of the mother world into the world of the father. He has difficulty feeling his own phallic power or masculine strength. He has a problem with ambition, exhibiting either too much or too little. Tending to look outside of himself for male power figures to identify with, he seeks to bolster his masculine strength vicariously. Examples can be found in the followers of strong leaders who put themselves in the service of such powerful male figures in order to absorb phallic authority by proximity. Similarly, some seek that authority through identification with a powerful corporation or institution. The uninitiated man cannot idealize his own works and prowess, even if they may be quite exceptional in the eyes of the world.

There are two general types of uninitiated men. One type seeks protection as a follower, ever asking for advice and looking for support from strong men in a constant search for a father figure to hide behind. By contrast, the other type is rebellious against male authority figures, asserting seeming independence that actually is counter-dependence in that it needs the other in order to stand upright. This type is unable to idealize a mentor; he approaches potential father figures negatively, often with anger, or he falls immediately into competition with them. This man ends up a loner. At first glance, he may look initiated, but on closer scrutiny one gets the sense of weakness and lack of inner structure. Often, he is subtly mother-bound, such that if the woman on whom he depends is withdrawn he collapses into addiction or attempts suicide.

In fact, most men are located somewhere along a spectrum of initiation. Initiations take place throughout life, beginning with the classical one in adolescence. Later initiations may come about with the assistance of a mentor in college or graduate school, or of employers and institutions in professional life, or in relationships when they end in betrayal and a break. This lifelong process of initiation takes place in the world of the father. The father is the first initiator. If he lays the groundwork well, his son can experience later idealizations and betrayals in a way that will allow him to grow.

Fathers and Sons

As there are types of mother (see previous lecture), so there are types of father. This sets up specific problems regarding a man's transition out of the mother world into the world of the father.

The Absent Father. A man's adult psyche may show a lacuna where the father image should be. The "father effect" is simply not there. This is a man without an internalized image of a father although he may have some memories of one. But the effect of a father in his psychological development is absent. His actual father may have been physically absent, for instance, off to war or living apart as the result of a divorce, or he may have been a non-functioning father for all intents and purposes although in the household. As a result the son is "rudderless" in adulthood. If he had a good enough mother, we could say he has a strong, tight boat, but he does not know where to go with it; he lacks a sense of direction. The absence of ambition to succeed in this world is derivative of this problem. The father was absent as a figure for the son to idealize so the son will not have experienced ambition to be great and heroic like his father, and later on he misses also the feeling of mastery and accomplishment that result when such ambitions are fulfilled. The sense that accomplishments in the real world are better than fantasy achievements does not arrive in this man's life as an effective means for getting him to make the transition out of the mother world.

In the absence of a good enough father, as with the case of the absence of a good enough mother, the psyche compensates by creating an archetypal image of the missing figure. The resulting "divine" father may be so far removed from everyday life that no modification of the lofty ideal is possible, and the son can thus never hope to achieve any of the ideals symbolized in the image. Arthur Colman refers to such an image as the "Sky Father," a purely symbolic father. The real father, who would have functioned as the carrier for idealization and later for gradual modification of the ideal, is absent.

A "rudderless" man, then, is stuck with the problem that if a task is good enough for him to attempt, it will be too great for him to accomplish—or else the contrary: if the task is something he can accomplish, it is beneath him and not worth the effort. Such a man is not necessarily totally dysfunctional, but he does not live up to his inherent potential.

A son of the "rudderless" father has a similar problem, because his father, though able to have a family, cannot pass on the sense of ambition and direction that he himself lacks. The son of such a father may look promising but may also be rudderless, although less so. As a scholar, for instance, he may stop at a master's degree, though the doctorate would be fully appropriate and within his ability. He has identified with the "rudderless" father, and that identification is unbroken because the rudderless father will not have completed the initiation process for his son. Like his father, he has the underlying problem of grandiosity, low self-esteem, and inability to master the small steps that lead to great achievement.

The Abandoning Father. Though this man has some similarities to the man with no father, there are subtle differences. This father may not physically abandon the child but tends to leave him with the mother. He has difficulty in allowing his son to idealize and identify with him, and so he fails to initiate him into the men's world. This father is often a *puer aeternus* ("eternal boy") himself in that he lives more in a world of possibilities and fantasy than in actualities, more in potential than in actualizing potentials. He is often too busy with his own projects to attend to his son. He is distant and cold and does not expect anything of his son. Part of initiation is the expectation of performance by the son; the father makes demands and shows conditional love (as opposed to the mother's classical unconditional love). His conditions on a son's acceptability, if appropriate to the son's stage of development and ability, provide opportunities for achievement and the experience of mastery by the son. The abandoning father is too uncaring and too casual. He does not care whether the boy gets an A or a C in school; he is uninvolved. He cannot, therefore, be an initiation master, who must care what happens to the boy. He is negligent, possibly an alcoholic. The son of an alcoholic father experiences his father as an abandoning father (and a threatening one if the mother and children are endangered by his drinking), because he is involved in his own addiction and mother-bound problems.

The Oedipal Father. Freud described the father-son relationship in terms of the classic Oedipus complex. In this view, the son comes to occupy a privileged place with the mother, creating jealousy in the father. The father becomes a threat to the son because he wishes to assert his priority with the mother and tries to separate the son from the mother. This creates what Freud called castration anxiety in the son. This fear becomes the basis of what Freud called the super-ego, so the father is internalized as a threatening image, indeed as an enemy of the son's success in life.

It is true that if a newly married husband and wife have had a close bond with each other, the introduction of a child can create a great change. The father no longer has exclusive and unlimited physical access to his wife because a baby gets priority. A mother's powerful attachment to her children may, at least for a time, outweigh her feelings of closeness to her husband. Feeling that, the father may pull away and distance himself, or he may become very competitive with the children. He can become intolerant, anxious, possessive, refusing to share the mother's love. And he refuses to initiate his son into manhood. The son faced with an Oedipal father has a father who is an enemy rather than an initiation-master.

The Oedipal father tends to be extremely repressive. He puts his sons into situations where they cannot grow. In family businesses, one sees children held under the father's thumb. He will not relinquish his power position and limits his children to positions of subservience. This type is graphically depicted in early Greek myth. The Sky God, Uranus, reacts with fear to a prediction that his son, Cronus, will grow up to overthrow him, so at the son's birth to the Earth Mother, Gaia, he attempts to forestall this by shoving the son back into the earth, symbolically back into the womb, and keeping him there. The father cannot endure the thought of being surpassed by his son and fears reprisal by the son. In the myth, this does indeed come to pass when Cronus eventually breaks out of bondage and succeeds in castrating his father. This pattern later repeats itself when Cronus is castrated by his repressed son, Zeus.

A son with an Oedipal father will develop a negative father complex and later project it on to men in authority over him. He will very likely be rebellious against them and try to overthrow them.

This kind of father is, in Jungian terms, a *senex* father, distant, cold and repressive.

The Too-Good Father. This is a father who is one-sidedly positive and does not allow his shadow side to show. He does not betray his son in any way but always accommodates and protects him. This has the effect of keeping the son at home and dependent on him. The message is: "I have this great, wonderful house and you will never do as well outside." The effective communication is: "You can't make it on your own, you aren't good enough, so you had better stay here with me. You need my protection, and I'm glad to provide it." The father offers comfort and security, but it is undermining because it prevents the son from testing himself in the real world and establishing his own sense of worth. This set-up is often seen in privileged classes. For sons who are heirs to fathers of great position or fortune, it is very difficult to achieve a true initiation and be released from "the father's house." If the father's house is too rich and accommodating and if the father is too good, if betrayal never happens, the son becomes father-bound.

The Third Circle: Anima
The Age of the Hero

We move next to the third circle in a man's evolving psychological development. It is the stage of the hero and presents another major challenge with which he must come to terms: the anima.

What is the anima? If the mother and father complexes constitute two basic structural strands in a man's personality, the anima can be thought of as a dynamic, transformative force. The anima constellates a man's creative energy and initiates the hero's journey in his development. The anima is generally imaged as feminine and conceptualized as the contrasexual feature of a man's masculine gender identity. She is his inner other, his soul mate.

It is important to note the essential difference between the anima and the mother complex. Both are feminine in nature, but the anima plays a very different role from the mother in a man's life. Whereas the mother stabilizes and contains his personality, the anima is dynamic and motivates him to find his own unique direction in life. The anima is the archetype of life itself, the life force. The Latin word *anima* means soul. She animates the psychic body as a force of vitality. She demands liveliness and change and ever further development, and she provides the energy and drive for the transformation that a man must go through in order to pivot his identity from the father world to becoming his own man, free and independent. And, as all men know who have experienced her, she is not rational.

The anima demands that a man make an unqualified commitment to himself and to his own life. This is a challenge to responsibility. Men understandably have difficulty in taking this step because it means leaving the security of the world of father and mother. Out of fear, they become conservative and hold themselves back, keeping "a foot on the brake." They may have a problem with making the sacrifices demanded by the anima. They have reservations and doubts, fearing for a lack of inner resources to accomplish the task she sets before them. It seems impossible, not physically but psychologically and spiritually. It is brushed off as a silly dream, an illusion. They become frozen in established habits of mind. They renounce the heroic and settle for the conventional.

In myth, fairy tale and imaginative literature, the anima's challenge is classically depicted as the task of winning the hand of the beautiful young woman or freeing her from captivity. Marrying her symbolizes a man's achievement of making a lasting connection to the soul and committing himself to her "till death do us part."

While the process of confronting, winning, and integrating the anima belongs classically to midlife, a man will meet up with the anima throughout life in different forms, usually in discovering a remarkable woman with suitable features and attributes and projecting his anima onto her. This can begin early in life. A little boy can fall in love with a playmate or an older woman who is not his mother, such as a nurse, a teacher, or a cousin. In adolescence, the anima may appear when a boy falls in love with a movie star or a beautiful unattainable woman. In all cases, he will experience the archetypal passions of romantic longing, jealousy, and helpless infatuation. Eventually, he may meet the anima in a more accessible form and persuade her to marry him. One of the purposes of the anima is to draw a man out of his familiar parental context and into an unfamiliar interpersonal and cultural world. She stimulates "exogamous libido"—non-incestuous Eros—so that he leaves mother and father behind and ventures out into the wider world. The classical, full-blown "anima call" occurs at midlife, after a man has established himself in the father world and has made all the necessary investments in his life as a member of collective society.

There are many literary examples of the irrational power of the anima in a man's life. One of my favorites is Shakespeare's Cleopatra. At her beckoning, Mark Antony abandons his role as a dutiful member of the ruling triumvirate in Rome and lives with the exotic Cleopatra in her home in Egypt. Eventually he loses his life for her sake, and she for his. It is a cautionary tale about the dangers of anima possession. One of Jung's favorite literary anima figures was the larger than life feminine character in H. Rider Haggard's 19th century novel, *She*. Also set in Egypt, this story takes place in the dark interior of the country where a man discovers an immortal feminine figure known as "She Who Must Be Obeyed." Her power is overwhelming and utterly irresistible. Moreover, she is ancient and privy to the secrets of death and rebirth: she can go up in flames like a phoenix and transform herself into a youthful maiden. When she calls, a man finds her irresistible. For Jung, this figure illustrated the power of the anima in setting the course of a man's life. He himself alludes to such an experience in his famous Red Book.

When a man meets the anima in life, he feels an overwhelming desire to get close to her. She represents a promise of trans-formation and fulfillment. In her presence, a man discovers himself as if for the first time. He is a new man. The anima promises trans-formation, physical and spiritual. If he can only unite his life with hers, he feels, she will make him a new man and even immortalize him. However, he will also feel danger in her vicinity—she can destroy him.

The anima is an ambiguous figure—attractively wild and destructive and at the same time rejuvenating and creative. When she makes her appearance at midlife, she ignites a meltdown of fixed structures and identifications. She claims a man as her own and draws him into the fire of her transformative energy. As a muse she inspires poetry and big dreams. A goddess, she elicits absolute devotion. The troubadour movement of the Middle Ages was an anima manifestation on a collective level, and she is the Beloved of the Romantic Tradition. She is represented in mythologies throughout the world—as Aphrodite, Freya, and Parvati, to name only a few.

The devastation that ensues when she is rejected or lost is dramatic. In Richard Wagner's "Ring," the first work, "Das Rheingold," tells of Wotan's promise to give Freia, the Love Goddess, to the grotesque Giants, Fafnir and Fasolt, in payment for the construction of his grandiose palace, Valhalla. Among the gods, the loss of Freya creates a crisis because it means they will gradually age, lose their beauty and die. A single day without her sees the apples in her orchard wither and rot and the gods becoming old, ill and decrepit. The rest of the drama follows from the gods' urgent quest to retrieve her and to bring back her powers of rejuvenation. She is the anima of the gods, and as such she is the source of life, of *joie de vivre* and *élan vital*.

It is in relation to the anima that a man experiences his profoundest sense of play and creativity, as well as his most complete freedom and sense of release from mundane cares. If an anima-endowed woman accepts a man into relationship with her, it is as if he is allowed reentry into paradise. She is the source of joy, of life itself and all its pleasures.

Anima versus Persona

It can be safely assumed that the anima will be the enemy of the persona. Persona defines a man's social identity as it is formed in conformity with others' expectations and rooted in his acceptance of roles and positions as offered by the father world. Persona takes shape through a gradual process of imitation, education, adaptation, and identification. It is based on mirroring what is seen in the immediate social environment or alternatively reacting against the surrounding milieu. It is not a superficial aspect of the personality.

It originates in early childhood. In order to relate first to his mother and father, a son becomes a certain kind of little person and begins to develop a social identity, positive or negative, within the family context. Among peers, he eventually finds a niche as a particular kind of boy—the smart one, the handsome one, the athletic one, the popular one, the bad one, and so on. These are all personas, and they constitute the interface between a man and the social world surrounding him. They signal the world as to what roles this man may be expected to fill.

While parents are the earliest and most important contributors to this social identity, peers are later very important as well. Erik Erikson's definition of "psychosocial identity" offers an apt account of the persona: it is an agreement between oneself and important others regarding who and what kind of person one is. In adolescence, as Erikson famously wrote, the persona becomes an acute issue as the adolescent focuses intensely on what his peers think of him. The persona question is: "How do I relate to the group, and how do others in the group see me?" Loss of face amounts to disgrace and can lead to severe emotional consequences.

At its best, the persona gives a man the security of knowing that he has a place in the world. It provides a basis for his social standing in the community. From this position, he can exert power and influence. In addition, it provides a tool with which he can try to master his inner life. Through identification with his persona, anything in his inner life that does not seem to fit his picture of himself can be pushed aside. He is thus able to channel his energies into his work and build up a material position in the world.

The anima's entrance on the scene creates tremendous tension and instability as she challenges a man's commitment to the persona and opens a breach in his defenses against troublesome yearnings for deeper emotional satisfaction. She can motivate a man to leave mother and father, wife and family, and all official duties in order to abandon himself to the sheer joy of life in a moment of exuberance and passionate excess. In the world of opera—think of La Traviata—

the anima typically rules. A typical operatic conflict involves a man torn between his duty to father, king, mother, or wife and his love for an unconventional woman. Such a conflict in life arises from the difference between the intentions of anima and the conventional demands of persona.

When the persona is firmly in place and the ego has strongly accepted and identified with it, the anima classically comes in to compensate—to blast away, so say it more dramatically, the identification with the persona. The purpose of this is to initiate a man's individuation. The classic story of individuation begins at midlife when the persona clashes with a will demanding that the man become more than his persona—unique, special, and different from the collective average. This source of this demand is the anima, thus she always appears as unconventional.

The appearance of the anima typically induces the "meltdown" of a man's persona structures and identifications. She calls for fluidity and flexibility, which contradict a man's entrenched notions and habits. Those fixities become the targets of her aggression, and the more deeply embedded they are the more she will attack them. She is then at her most dangerous, but the potential is also present for her greatest creative contribution to the possibilities for transformation and individuation. A collateral danger is that a man becomes anima possessed and loses all common sense and rationality. This is a kind of madness. On the other hand, the individuation potential lies in undergoing a transformation that forever frees a man from his previous dependencies and from identification with his persona. By bringing him out of this bondage to the past, she will lead him ultimately to the self. As the father was a bridge out of the mother into the outer world where the son established his persona, the anima is the bridge inward to the self. This is the meaning of her implacable opposition to the persona.

The uninitiated man will relate to the anima primarily with fear. She is too much for him because he has not integrated enough of the father's gift of masculinity. He is not able to claim an anima figure in real life even if he will dream of one in his fantasies. Initiation into the masculine prepares a man for his encounter with the anima.

On the other end of the spectrum, the man who has been well initiated into the masculine world of the father and is exceptionally successful in his persona adaptation runs the risk of "selling his soul" for the sake of gaining power and social position. The anima lure is so demanding of major change in direction and attitude that he will not even remotely consider the possibility of transformation. He remains stuck in the father world and cannot individuate further.

The anima, it must be emphasized, is not a derivative from the mother complex or archetype. She is *sui generis*, a psychic being unto herself and having her own independent foundation in the self. Actually, the anima is opposed to the mother. Part of the anima's function is, in fact, to free a man decisively from the mother and all she represents. Nor is the anima derived from the father, although a father's anima has a powerful effect on his son. The father's anima has a role to play in the relationship with the son—she can bind the son to his father. But again, the role of a man's anima is to separate him from his father as she does from his mother. She is an individuating power and demands that he become his own man, free and clear.

One can mark a distinction between three different kinds of bondage in men: the mother-bound, the father-bound, and the anima-bound. A mother-bound man, as described earlier, is typically weak, non-assertive, soft, and restricted in his phallic activities both with women and at work. A father-bound man is typically identified with the patriarchy and its structures in the social world: He is conservative, rigid, dogmatic, and tied to the persona. He is the man who sits at the right hand of the father and stays there, slowly going grey and becoming withered. The anima-bound man is typically a romantic and a dreamer. He is moody, unrealistic, overly emotional and sensitive; he is a permanent adolescent. It can happen that a mature and fully initiated man becomes temporarily anima-possessed through falling in love with a young woman who carries his anima projection. When this happens, he loses his judgment and values; he daydreams and finds it difficult to pay full attention to the details of daily life. He becomes inflated, dreaming big and unrealistic dreams about a perfect future together with his anima woman. He may be inspired to write poetry or sing youthful songs; he uncharacteristically spends money freely and without thought. Powerful emotions of sexual passion and murderous jealousy assault him, and extremes of ecstatic joy and despair alternate in rapid succession. He is temporarily anima-possessed.

A mother-bound man cannot feel these excesses. He does not fall powerfully in love with an anima woman because the mother effectively blocks the anima. The mother sits in the doorway, guarding the threshold. The man is locked in the mother's house, and the anima cannot enter. A father-bound man will, on the other hand, fall into anima-possession, since the purpose is to free him from the father complex and its insistence on conventionality. If he is strongly tied to the father, seated at his right hand and identified with an adapted and well socialized persona, he will manage to resist the possession. He will remain true to the father's world of collective rules and social norms.

A man's individuation task at midlife is to use the anima experience differently from the way he did in adolescence. In adolescence and early adulthood, the function of the anima is to "trick a man" and take him away from the mother and into a relationship with a woman, into marriage and family life. At midlife, the anima's function is to loosen identification with the persona. A man then can open an inner space where depth psychological experience has a place to operate. At this stage of life, the anima experience becomes the opportunity for further development of a man's personality. As long as a man is identified with the persona and with his social roles in the world, personality is nothing more than an inconvenient nuisance. It just gets in the way. It has no functional value and is regarded as "mere emotionality." Personality has no place in the world of business deals, legal transactions, or peace treaties. The anima is seen as an enemy in the father world of the bottom line.

How can a man reconcile the two? They form a pair of opposites that must be held in tension. Dealing with the anima experience at midlife calls for establishing and holding this tension between desire and reality. This is a classic conflict and a man has to wait it out and tolerate the pain. Eventually an option will open up that offers a decision that would be neither exclusively a persona nor an anima decision but a "third" possibility that alchemically combines the two or transcends them.

The anima typically introduces inflation in a man's sense of himself and makes him feel bigger than life. She creates an illusion that he is "God's gift," and he feels wonderful in her presence, powerful and healthy. In a sense, this is not altogether bad. It gives the courage and energy to undertake heroic tasks for her sake. The paradoxical nature of this condition demonstrates the problem with deciphering the messages of the anima: which are true and which are nonsense? A man does feel himself to be God's gift, yet he knows he is one of billions of such gifts; he can be a hero for her, but his capacities may be exaggerated beyond his possibilities. The experience of being unique and special and capable of heroics does put him in touch with something true and can be useful if picked up and used in the right way. Thus, in one way, the anima brings inflationary illusion, but in another she reveals truth as well.

The anima in her own nature is not realistic according to the standards understood by the persona and the man's ego awareness. She would turn the world into a chaotic place where each man would be a law unto himself. This is the philosophy of anarchists and dictators. A man who is possessed by the anima feels he can do as he pleases. Reality contradicts this approach to the world, however. Sooner or later he will run afoul of the rules of society and face the consequences. A man cannot tell a judge he was under the influence of something other than law or that he "forgot himself" and be let off the hook of impersonal justice.

Odysseus dealt very successfully with the anima in his encounter with Circe. In a manifestation of the negative trans-formative power of the anima, Circe turns men into swine. Such men, who have completely believed the anima mirage and given in to the enticement of pleasure fulfillment, can be said to have lost human consciousness; their ego has been demolished. With Hermes' advice, Odysseus is able to make a relationship with her, getting her to commit herself to his safety and the welfare of his men before he goes to bed with her. He and his crew are then able to remain on her island renewing themselves before continuing on their journey, thus gleaning the rejuvenating benefit of the anima experience without falling prey to her negative, destructive capabilities.

The anima is the unconscious, which needs to be brought into a human relationship. Jung often said that the unconscious does not know what the ego and the ego world are about and must be taught. One of the roles of the active imagination is to accomplish that instruction—to tell the unconscious what the needs and demands of real life are, because she does not know and must be convinced. One needs Odysseus' strategy of beginning with tough bargaining (he holds Circe at sword point, threatening her and extracting promises before bedding her) and then knowing when to give in. When done successfully, a man can contain the effects of the anima, neither falling into them or acting them out, nor repressing and ignoring them. He then develops the inner capacity to be inspired and creative. The anima becomes his own animation, and gradually personality comes into being. Learning to love his moods, his musings, and his creative, unconventional thoughts, he begins to learn the joy of giving in to irrational notions. It is very releasing to allow oneself to be irrational. A man can be a poet with life, becoming unpredictable and inconsistent. It is exhilarating and playful—the anima becomes a playmate as the man learns to play in his inner world.

Playing and intimacy are closely related. If one cannot play, one cannot become intimate. A man's attractiveness to a woman depends very much on his ability to be intimate. Through the anima, a man can learn to become intensely intimate. On his integration of the anima, a man can enhance his inner capacity to enter a playful mood and become childish without fear.

The anima, when she is developed in a part of a man's life as a companion or inner felt-presence, tempers his anger and disappointment in life. By the time a man is middle-aged, he has usually built up a great store of anger and disappointment about his life. Perhaps his children have not turned out as he would like; or his wife is no longer what she was. Maybe he himself is not what he was physically or mentally, or his career has not been what he had hoped. He may have become embittered and generally ill tempered. The presence of the anima counteracts all that, giving a kind of mellow feeling and soothing the anger. She allows for play and offers a sense of being able to start over.

She permits intimacy in momentary relationships, on a weekend or at a luncheon, without requiring the presence of a woman to enable becoming relational. Men characteristically have great difficulty becoming intimate and relational without having a woman to accomplish it for them. The formality of an all-male group, for example, can be radically changed with the advent of an anima woman. A man who has integrated the anima is able to achieve intimacy and relationality without reliance on a woman. He can make his own relationships, which can be *eros* relationships; he can become intimate with men and women and children and beasts because he has that inner capacity.

The anima also enables a man to be imaginative. As the spinner of images and fantasies, she helps him to let himself entertain illusions without necessarily believing in them. The ego and the anima forge a bond in a permanent relationship. A man then becomes a personality and consequently leaves the patriarchy, which is his identification with the father. As long as the anima/princess is attached to the king, a man cannot get out of the patriarchy and win his soul away from his persona attachments. On winning her away from her embeddedness in the patriarchy, the hero has his own soul. A man, then, has his personality, including his affectivity, his emotional life, and his interiority.

Failure to Win the Anima

At this point, it is useful to restate the observation that the embodied anima is an unconventional female. If the man is too much still in the mother, the anima, because she is physically female, will resonate too closely to the mother and threaten further regression into the mother. It is for this reason that a man still stuck in the mother cannot truly fall in love with an anima woman. Not only does the mother sit at the doorway and block the anima, but because the anima is physically female, she is too close to the mother. A man thus must resist the female or risk further regression into the mother. He will not, then, see a woman as attractive, because that would bring him too close to incest.

If a man is too much in the father, the unconventionality of the anima woman is what threatens him, not the fact that she is female. It is a more conscious threat, then. In the movie *Fatal Attraction*, we see a man drawn into a wild, destructive anima with disastrous consequences, which is how a man yet embedded in the father will perceive the dangers of the unconventional female. A man too much in the father can successfully fall in love, marry, and lead a conventional family life, but he cannot afford to experience the anima fully because she threatens his bond to the father. Behind this, clinging to embeddedness in the father and the patriarchy, is actually the threat of regression into the mother; for if the father bond is loosened, the bridge out of the mother disappears; and the son is drawn back into the mother. The consequences for such a man, lacking the inner resources from having integrated the father in order to leave the mother, may be massive regression or psychotic break. His commitment to the world of the father is based on a defense against the mother. The separation from the mother has not taken place enough for him to let go of the father. Because the anima's unconventionality seeks to free him from the father, she is a profound threat; and he will resist her.

To the mother-bound man, then, the anima is a threat because she is female. To him, she appears as a witch, an evil monster. To the father-bound man, the anima is a threat because she is unconventional. To him, she appears as a seductress and a deceiving siren.

Among mother-bound men, we can identify four positions along a spectrum from more to less mother-bound. First, we note the man without an anima. This is a man deeply embedded in the mother and not at all attracted to women, to the point that he simply does not see them. Typically, his father has been absent or unable to help his son out of the mother. Actually, he is the man described above in the chapter on the mother as the man without a mother. He is embedded in an archetypal mother. His real mother was not there enough for him to be drawn out into the object world. His anima is in the unconscious. She is "unconstellated," belonging to the *massa confusa* of undifferentiated material in the unconscious.

Somewhat less embedded in the mother is the man with the prematurely integrated anima. He tends to be effeminate. There is an identity mix because male and female were not strongly separated at the earlier stage of leaving the mother and identifying with the father. Masculine and feminine elements are mixed, so that the ego takes on a coloration that is slightly more feminine than normal. While it might seem that he has integrated the anima in his connection to the feminine, there is actually a lack of differentiation between the masculine and the feminine. He may be rather aesthetic, exhibiting certain feminine and maternal characteristics. He sees the mother in females. The female body remains identified with the mother's body: a woman's breasts are her breasts, and the vagina is horrifying and threatening rather than sweet and alluring.

Third, we come to the man with a lesbian anima. He is in love with women who prefer other women. He can be attracted to women and make love to them, but he does so as if he himself were a woman. His lover must also be a woman; *eros* is a woman-to-woman experience. Again, this is a result of remaining "in the mother."

Fourth is the man with the fleeting anima, the Don Juan. He seems to be a man's man, powerfully attracted to women, sexually active, and generally promiscuous. While he may exhibit behavior that suggests a love of women, there is actually no underlying love of a specific woman at all. There is sexuality without *eros*; there is no affection for them. The anima is still not constellated optimally. He is a heartless lover, who is actually still mother-bound and has not identified with the father. Differentiation between masculine and feminine has not yet taken place definitively.

Among men still in the father, I will describe two positions. The man with the perfectionistic anima is so tied by love of the father that the passion of the anima does not have a feminine form. He is fiercely committed to the father and the father's world. In the fierceness and the dedication to ideals and notions of perfection and spiritual purity, one senses the anima. The love involved, however, is not feminine but rather like the love as the Holy Spirit that passes between the Father and Son in the Trinity. Certain classical forms of Christianity have a powerful exponent of that type of commitment to the Father, such that the anima stays in the father world and within the father-son bond. This type of man may marry a woman in order to be close to a powerful man; the woman's father is the one he is really in love with.

A variation of the man with a perfectionistic anima is one who is himself perfectionistic, dedicated to high ideals and purity of a spiritual, ascetic, or aesthetic nature. Certain kinds of writers or artists fall into this category, exhibiting great refinement and perfection. One misses the anima messiness in their spiritual, precise, Olympian work. Another example is the enthusiastic priest who only loves God the Father, has dedicated heart and soul to the highest ideals of religion and philosophy, and who has seemingly transcended sexuality or transmuted it into religious enthusiasm.

At the other end of the spectrum of men stuck in the father is the man with a conventional anima. By definition, however, the anima is unconventional. In this case she has not appeared fully or authentically, having been unable to reveal her full presence because the man is trapped in the father. This man is married conventionally, his wife is conventional, his children are con-ventional, and his career is conventional. Everything is middle-of-the-road; he is dedicated to maintaining the status quo and enhancing the persona and patriarchal values. The anima's unconventional presence in this man is occluded by the presence of the father; he is actually married to the father. This man is not interested in separating the anima from the father, since he is committed to staying married to the father.

When a man is sufficiently separated from the world of the mother through initiation into the world of the father, and when the male identity is secure and consolidated enough as an inner structure so that he can leave the father, he can then allow the anima to approach him nakedly and powerfully. He will not need to be defensive towards her. He will be able to pursue the task of winning her from the father; and once she is won, he will be able to marry her. The marriage of the hero to the anima means that a relatively stable and permanent relationship comes about between a man whose masculine identity is firm and the feminine. He is able to be in the world of the fathers, the persona world, and to be effective in it, but not be totally *of* it. He is able to be un-conventional, to be playful, to let himself float about in fantasy and liminality. He can become intensely intimate without fear of losing himself because he has the necessary inner structures. He can be creative and think unconventional thoughts; he can experiment and risk his feelings.

Once this relationship with the anima is established, they can have children. The child born of this relationship between the anima and the ego is a new self. Anima development means developing the personality through intimate contact with and knowledge of his emotional life. This is the era of integrating emotional life, of becoming a personality. The man with a developed relationship to the anima has a personality and is a personality. As a result of that, he is able to go on to encounter and experience the Self as a new being.

A Brief Aside

One of Jung's first discoveries occurred when he was a resident early in the 1900s and doing research with the Word Association Experiment (WAE). Using this instrument, he found that similarities in the organization of complexes could be identified in families. The responses of a mother and a daughter, for example, would indicate very similar complexes. This finding could be said to be the beginning of family systems theory. Although Jung never followed up on it in any major way, other researchers have found evidence for continuities of complexes through generations. They are called cultural complexes or in some cases generational complexes. A trauma to a family at one point in history, for example the suicide or homicide of a father, can perseverate through generations. The collective memory of the event and the impact on the wife and children can be passed on to two, three, four or more subsequent generations. This phenomenon has been extensively studied in countries within the former Soviet Union.

One of Jung's early studies concerned the role of the father in the destiny of the individual.[1] Jung discussed the influence of the father complex on children, both daughters and sons. His discussion

---

[1] C.G. Jung, "The Significance of the Father in the Destiny of the Individual," in *CW* 4.

was based on the finding that family systems rest upon complex structures and that these complexes are passed on from parents to children. This transmission of unconscious complex arrangements down through the generations is well described in the colloquial expression, "the apple doesn't fall far from the tree."

The way a father relates to his own anima and his level of anima development will thus have an impact on his son and the way the anima will constellate in the son. This is not biologically genetic but is passed on through psychic influence and transmission, through subtle behavioral gestures and modeling. In identifying with the father, the son introjects not only the persona of the father but aspects of his unconscious as well. The father's internal dynamics— the relation between his ego and his anima, and the way he has dealt with "the anima problem" in his own life—will have an impact on the son's approach to the same inner figure.

Optimally, the father will have dealt with the anima effectively, integrated it, and become a personality, so that his relationship to the anima had become one of free exchange between consciousness and unconsciousness. If the father's *eros* is free and not bound in the father or mother structures, the son will experience this. The son may witness this in seeing the father not being bound to the wife (he is not "henpecked"), which would indicate a mother-bound anima. Or, the son might witness father-boundedness in seeing his father as conventional or perfectionistic. Optimally, a son would see in his father a free and integrated anima development, and he could witness in his father a freedom to love and work, unbound by either matriarchy or patriarchy. If a son sees a free father, his chances of being able to free his anima later in and for life will be that much greater.

A number of problems, as we have suggested, can appear. If, for example, the father's anima is attached to the patriarchy, the father will be conventional and perfectionistic. The son might then have a tendency to rebel against that or else to follow in his father's footsteps by imitating him. It can also happen that the father's anima compensates for a cold mother. She may have been an emotionally cold woman married to her opposite—as often happens—that is, to a warm and extraverted type of husband. The father becomes very close to the son at an early age, while the mother remains more or less distant in the background. A maternal father compensates possibly with too much intimacy and *eros* toward the son, which will create later problems. The son will become too emotionally bound to the father and search for father figures who play a similar role rather than functioning as mentors to guide him further into the world, thus retarding development of his independence.

Problems will also arise if the father's anima is locked up in the mother. The father might be the Don Giovanni type, for example, in which case his anima image is free from his mother, but not its affect. In other words, he can pursue women and have sexual relations with them, but the feeling of being in love is blocked. Underneath his promiscuous behavior, he is mother bound; his *eros* is still truly attached to the mother. If the son sees his father is of this type, philandering while his wife becomes hurt and embittered, the son usually is unable to identify with his father. He takes the side of his mother against the father in what becomes a family struggle. Because he sees his father's anima projections rampant in the world, his own sexuality becomes inhibited. He tends to become a "good boy," defender of his mother and mother-rights, and overly faithful to mother figures and women's prerogatives over a man's freedom of *eros* and movement. His own sexuality tends to be blocked. He is likely to take care of mother or mother figures against father, even marrying a woman in order to take care of her. With the father being himself so mother-bound, development of his son's independence and freedom is, again, retarded.

In the circle of the anima, typically, a man experiences this psychic figure through projection, often onto an unconventional woman with whom he falls in love. As his anima, she represents his future psychological development into the so-called classic phases of individuation. He has the problem, however, of how to relate to this figure who is carrying the soul for him in projection. The question is whether to go off with her, marry her, and have children with her, or to treat the experience symbolically as an inner challenge, as the onset of a search that will take him to the inner depths of the psyche rather than to an outer relationship, which may end up only repeat prior relationships. How may he solve this anima problem in such a way as to create the optimal individuation step? This question arises in addition to and complicating further the obvious ethical and moral questions attendant to the situation.

When a purely inner solution is sought, the man takes the experience as a constellation or projection of the anima and uses classical Jungian methods for working with it (such as active imagination, dream analysis, and so on), avoiding any action on the interpersonal level with the "outer person," so to speak. This strategy usually results in sterility; there is no "child" of the relationship. It becomes virtually autoerotic. Outer manifestations of this outcome are often states of depression, lack of animation, rage, a kind of unfulfilled, woundedness or sense of deprivation.

If a purely outer solution to the anima problem is sought, a man may get a divorce, marry again and possibly begin a second family. If his actions are the result of a purely outward solution, based on impulse and instinct lacking any reflection on what he is doing, they will be repeated again and again. The relationships will develop along very similar lines; the reasons a relationship does not work out with one woman will be the same reasons one will not work out with the next. If children are born, they are problem children.

What kind of solution, then, should be pursued? What is the answer?

Occasionally, one or the other of these two solutions turns out to be the best in a specific situation. The child born of the union between the ego and the unconscious is a *spiritus rectus*—a guiding spirit. This child represents the self and will be able to guide the ego in its further quest for meaning and purpose. The resolution of the confrontation between the anima and the ego must include somehow, at some level, a marriage—a sense of a permanent bond between ego and anima—be it predominantly inner or predominantly outer, or both.

An example of this symbolic child is Hermes. The product of the love union between Zeus (married to Hera, representing the law of marriage) and the nymph Maia. As the offspring of the patriarchal dominant, Zeus, and the unconventional other woman, Maia, Hermes will become a crucial figure in Greek mythology and later in alchemy. Born in a cave, Hermes does extraordinary deeds on the first day of his life. He creatively invents the lyre out of a turtle's shell and then, hungry, goes to Apollo's herds to steal some cattle (he is god of thieves). Mightily angry, Apollo takes Hermes before Zeus the judge. Zeus reconciles the brothers, and there is an exchange of gifts—the lyre for the cattle. Apollo becomes, then, the god of music as Hermes becomes the god of shepherds. Through this relationship between Hermes and Apollo, the Greeks found a balance between a spirit of rationality represented by Apollo and the liminality of Hermes, the god of irrationality, thieves, night, sudden inspirations, shamans. Where Apollo operates on rationality, Hermes operates on chance and synchronicity.

By reconciling these two children of Zeus, the Greeks sought a balance between these two attitudes toward life, both of which are necessary to a man's wholeness. Without Apollo's rationality, a man has little stability; but without Hermes' spirit, a man lacks inventiveness and inspiration. Had Hermes not been accepted into the pantheon, the irrational outsiders might have engendered a revolutionary overthrow of the "regulars." Thus the inclusion of Hermes in the pantheon is an attempt by the Greek spirit to reach an inclusive, pluralistic, and democratic solution to spiritual variation in the population. In Christian tradition, the same accommodation is achieved in the variations among the saints.

Eventually Hermes becomes the guide, a messenger god carrying Zeus's messages to mortals. Psychologically speaking, he represents intuition. If one is well connected with Hermes, one knows what the Self wants and can consult the Self on the complex decisions of life. Hermes personifies, then, the *spiritus rector*—the consultative guiding spirit between the ego and the Self. The messages from the Self can take the form of dreams (Hermes is the god of dreams), synchronicities (chance events), or doors opening—which are often how life's problems are solved. Hermes sets the process in motion.

The Fourth Circle: Self
The Age of the Mature Man

In the fourth circle, we move from the age of the hero to the age of the mature man, and here the Self presents the central challenge. At this point, we are considering a man who has reached the fourth circle of personality development, which is quite advanced. Most men in everyday walks of life have not come this far. Commonly, they are caught still in some way in the circles of the mother or the father or remain fixed in the hero identity. If they register the psyche at all, it is in an unconscious and projected form, perhaps in the movies or on television where the psychic world is acted out before their eyes. They have relatively little self-awareness or consciousness of an inner world and its features. They do not pay attention to their dreams and spend no time in trying to understand their meaning for their own lives. They are living in two dimensions, not in the third as offered by contact with the unconscious.

We are now speaking about the second half of life and the movement toward the fifth circle, which is concerned with life's ultimate transcendent meaning. Men who have entered into these late stages of individuation have had a good deal of life experience and have achieved considerable self-awareness and consciousness. Often, they are highly successful professionally and socially. They have also arrived at a sense of inner reality and an awareness of the complexes—the attractive pull of the mother, the father, the anima, and so on—and they have separated and come to terms with them. Such a man is in command of himself but also aware that he is not in charge of his destiny. The ego has entered into a subservient relationship to the greater personality, the Self.

Out of the confrontation and interaction with the anima that takes place in the third circle, a *spiritus rector* is born in the fourth. The presence of this psychic function has several typical features. A man who is connected with an inner guide no longer takes his most important cues from the collective or the consensus of the group (persona considerations), either with regard to his individual life choices or his public positions. He is Self-directed, oriented from within by a personal vision for himself and by ever emerging greater self-knowledge. He has his own myth. His vision for life is not necessarily based on a dramatic "road to Damascus" experience. It could be less explicit and function as an intuitive sense of self that orients him. The guidance function may be partially unconscious to him. It operates like an internal gyroscope.

The *spiritus rector* is an uncanny guide. This is because it does not appear to be rational by usual standards. Its directives and messages imply a large unconscious plan or vision for life, a pre-set course of a life process that is not culturally determined and therefore not predictable. By making choices on the basis of strong intuitions and a felt sense of Self, an unconscious life plan emerges and is revealed over time. Socrates referred to this as the voice of his *daimon,* which he would consult when he had to make crucial decisions in his life, as when the Athenian court gave him the choice of drinking the cup of poisonous hemlock or going into exile. The *daimon* would only respond in the negative, otherwise it would remain silent. When Socrates asked if he should accept the hemlock, the *daimon* was silent. So, he drank it without question or hesitation. Choices made on this basis are not rational in the usual sense, and Socrates had a difficult time defending his decision because it appeared to be suicide. His choice, however, followed his life plan: had he left Athens and gone into exile, he would not have been true to the fundamental essence of who Socrates was. He would not have been Socrates.

The *spiritus rector* gives one the felt sense of "this is me" or "this is not me." Writers will often say that it took years to find their "voice." Though they may have developed technical skill in school, they acknowledge that it is a different matter to discover their own signature style. That style, their "voice," involves a distinctive way of putting things, a rhythm and pattern of verbal expression that sounds true to them. The styles of Hemingway and Faulkner, for instance, are very different. This was not consciously worked out by their respective egos. Hemingway did not start out as an author by consciously deciding to write short sentences; he found that he was simply being Hemingway by writing that way—the taciturn macho male, the heroic fighter, and so on. A writer's style will be consistent with other things about his character, and it will represent his essence. This unique signature is the gift of the *spiritus rector*.

The manifestation of the *spiritus rector* is not restricted to intellectuals and accomplished artists. Everyone is capable of being an artist-in-life. As a man makes key choices in the second half of life, these begin to sketch in his essential features as a mature man. They are no longer mimics of his father's or his mother's styles. At midlife he begins to transcend those early influences.

Problems arise if a man lives his life without the integrity conferred by the *spiritus rector*. It is possible to deny or override its direction. A man can live instead by a conventional code of behavior, orienting himself according to the demands of the persona instead of the inner voice of the Self. One quickly notices in such men of a lack of courage to be authentic. In fact, these men are plentiful in all cultures. Such men may have lived socially successful and culturally circumspect lives, but they are not individuated men and they leave no unique impression when you meet them. They are company men, cut-outs of stereotypical patterns. The unique images that remain of such men as Carl Jung and Sigmund Freud, for example, are based on their essence. They each evolved a unique style by following the uncanny guidance of a *spiritus rector*. This factor pervades all levels of activity right down to the most concrete decisions of daily life. They are originals, not imitators.

This guidance is not rational, but that does not mean it is crazy or absurd. It means that the decisive choices in life cannot be simply derived from antecedents. If one knew everything possible about a man's genetic make-up and cultural and psycho-social history, one still could not predict what the *spiritus rector* would guide him to do next. If one knows enough about a person's background, his general character may be somewhat predictable from early on, but the details of his individuation process cannot be forecast. The mysterious essence of a man's personality is unknowable until it is made manifest in life. This sense of who one is, deeply, becomes more conscious to a man in the second half of life, after he has left his mother's lap and his father's home, has met the anima and discovered his personality, and has gone on to develop a sense of his own voice through tuning in to the *spiritus rector*.

As the essence of the Self becomes more consciously available to a man, its position moves from the unconscious toward the conscious side of the psyche. It's like the rising of the sun—distant but obviously manifest. The birth of the Self in consciousness is the result of the relationship established to the anima earlier, which has opened the door to the unconscious so that the *spiritus rector* can become a conscious function. The anima now becomes a psychological function as mediator and is no longer anthropomorphized or imaged as a feminine figure, but rather operates as a communication link with the Self. The anima, as such, has given way to the *spiritus rector*. She has opened the way to the Self and created a realm of inner space. This results in a new childlike ability to play spontaneously and be creative in an adult fashion. Think of Goethe in his later years.

Sometimes a vocational call for the remainder of a man's life will come about as the result of a strong encounter with the unconscious, that is, in a vision, a big dream or an impressive active imagination. I describe this kind of experience in the book, *In MidLife*. When Odysseus descends to the underworld to meet with Tiresias and ask for advice about how to return home to his beloved Ithaca, the blind seer tells him how to get home but says he cannot remain there permanently until he has completed another task. He instructs him to take an oar and travel so far inland that he finds people who do not know what oars are, and there he is to plant the oar in the earth. In short, Odysseus is asked to become a missionary of Poseidon, the god of the sea, whom Odysseus had offended by killing his son, the Cyclops Polyphemus, and who had therefore persecuted Odysseus by driving him hither and yon across the high seas without a chance of making his way home. He must take up this mission in order to expiate the wrathful god.

In other words, after one has gone through midlife a man does not find a permanent resting place or comfortable home. Instead, there is an imperative to do something more and not primarily for oneself. The imperative is one of service and has the aura of serving a purpose something beyond simple individual self-actualization. It means service to a deity, that is, becoming an agent of the Self.

After his midlife crisis, Jung said that he knew that he no longer belonged to himself alone but that he now belonged to the generality. He felt the need to share his experience and to speak about it in order to lead the consciousness of others further. He spent the rest of his life writing his books on psychology based on his midlife experience as recounted in *The Red Book*, named by him *Liber Novus*, his "New Testament." It became his mission in life to explicate the reality of the psyche. St. Paul's conversion and its consequences for his life can be seen similarly. In the moment when he was blinded by a bright light on the road to Damascus, he experienced a dramatic call from the Self that sustained him and gave his life meaning for the rest of his days. He poured his energy into his mission and became the Paul that we know from his later letters. He found his personal myth by understanding and incarnating the meaning of this numinous experience.

An important ethical question poses itself at this point in our reflections: How is a man to tell the difference between what I would call "a true mission" and a misguided mission that would be an enactment of pride, wounded self-esteem, early trauma, and resentment? The latter is also irrationally driven by unconscious complexes and may assume the trappings of a divine imperative. As was the case with Hitler, an "inner voice" can counsel evil. One can fall into the hands of evil and be as controlled by it as by good, and have the felt sense of being guided by a *spiritus rector*. It is question of who or what one serves. Hitler will stand out forever as a man who was possessed by the spirit of evil. Sometimes the only thing that helps a man distinguish between the light and the dark is offered by a tradition of morals and ethics.

The vision brought by the *spiritus rector* in the form of a more conscious sense of the life plan helps a man organize his energy for the future. It provides a general orientation, though not usually specifics. It offers a symbol, and symbols suggest possible channels for the flow of psychic energy. A man without a guiding vision or personal myth does not know where to put his energy and so is dependent on others or on culture to give him direction. The emerging consciousness of the larger Self, given through the agency of the *spiritus rector,* is essential for channeling energy in an individual way in the second half of life because it suggests where meaningful activity is possible. Because the *spiritus rector* is a living presence in the psyche, it constitutes a continuous source of direction and inspiration. A man can go back to it in inner dialogue and be renewed in its vision. The symbol is supported by the anima, the life force, so it is invested with vitality.

A man's ground plan will become evident to him if he listens to the *spiritus rector* and pursues its direction honestly. Honesty is authenticity. One could say this is living authentically, as the existentialists put it, or religiously as Jung would express it.

The great Danish philosopher, Søren Kierkegaard, arranged the stages of personal development in three phases: the aesthetic, the ethical, and the religious. The first stage is based on the pleasure principle and seen in typical form in Mozart's opera, *Don Giovanni*. A man in this stage is locked in the mother circle of psychological development. He is a *puer aeternus*. The second stage introduces a sense of ethical values. Here, a man guides his life by the law and a corresponding sense of right and wrong, and he develops the ability to make difficult moral decisions in a lawyer-like manner. He is in the father circle and committed to the rule of law and living an ethical life. This stage is succeeded, or transcended, by the religious stage by means of what Kierkegaard calls a "leap of faith." This man is a hero, a "knight of faith." He manifests at a time in life when laws are inadequate or irrelevant to his challenges. The voice of the *spiritus rector* dominates in this stage, and it calls for obedience. The voice of the Self is not derived from the law but is rooted in the archetypal depths of the psyche. A man's sense of meaning is now contingent not upon pleasure or the satisfaction of instinctual desires, nor upon obedience to the law, but upon primary consideration of fulfilling the will the Self. A vision grips a man and leads him beyond the limits of the law. Kierkegaard's biblical example is Abraham, who hears God's voice commanding him to sacrifice his son, Isaac, which countermands the law of fatherhood. He has left the circle of the father archetype and has entered the circle of the Self. It is a radical step into obedience to the Lawgiver and not to the law.

While there are many mundane instances of the guidance the *spiritus rector* provides in daily life, this step into the religious follows the *spiritus rector* into another realm of being, the spiritual. The moment when the ethical imperative is transcended by the spiritual imperative is ambiguous from the point of view of the law. It cannot be evaluated, justified, or defended by rules or law; it is its own imperative.

Earlier stages are not necessarily left behind in these later circles. They can be relativized in some important ways, but a man does not leave his shadow behind, that is his human flaws and weaknesses, his unsolved problems with mother, father, and anima. Earlier circles may now not be so bright but they are not ever completely deleted. There is always a residue of unresolved material in every life, even in that of a great person.

The Fifth Circle: God
The Age of the Sage

Moving into the discussion of the fifth circle, I will explore a stage of development that few men reach consciously, although everyone who lives into old age enters into it in one way or another, because it poses the question of the meaning of a man's life. We can see this stage expressed graphically in the biographies of famous men, such as the Russian novelist Leo Tolstoy and the philosopher Ludwig Wittgenstein. Both men in their own way took up the question of life's meaning and the question of God. Whether a man looks to established religious traditions or ventures into this search individually, the purpose is the same: to come into contact with the Ultimate, with the Ground of Being to use the phrase of Paul Tillich, and to search for the answer to the question of life's meaning.

As we shall see, this late phase of the individuation process involves deep engagement and struggle with the transcendent Self. This is not a simple matter of learning to meditate and to clear the mind of distracting thoughts. In truth, it means confronting the deepest paradoxes within oneself and within the cosmos, which are two aspects of a single reality. In this engagement one finds light and dark, the sources of life and death, and the energies of creation and destruction. One can think of it as a dialogue with the God within and beyond the limits of the psyche. In speaking of dialogue, I follow the Jewish thinker Martin Buber's writing on this subject and also Jung's account of his engagement with the biblical God image in his late work, *Answer to Job*. It is a serious engagement, an *Auseinandersetzung*.

It is because one connects to the *spiritus rector* in the fourth circle that one comes upon the problems of opposites in God and the Self. If one fails to achieve this connection in the fourth circle, one simply accepts conventional views and these more fundamental problems never arise. The experience of the *spiritus rector*, however, leads one to an encounter with the mixture within the Self of good and evil, masculine and feminine, and other polarities and paradoxes.

The advance of a man's age into the 7th and 8th decades and beyond typically brings an increasingly urgent need to gain a more complete perspective on the meaning and patterns in one's life, to develop a picture of the whole. Dark, brooding questions about what it all means and what it all amounts to are typical of people of advanced years at a certain stage in their reflections. They may be diagnosed with depression, but it is not that simple. This mood is not without meaning, and it is not fundamentally biological in origin. It is existential. As they review their lives, these men often dwell on certain key decisions and turning points in their personal history, for good or ill, in attempts to come to terms with the choices they have made in life. Often this is presented as a moral issue: Did I do the right thing? Or it may be more of an emotional question like: Did I follow my passion enough or did I avoid its call? This reflection in old age is an attempt to find answers to the question of meaning in the specific life that has been lived and to come to a just and balanced appreciation of it. The soul is placed on a scale and its weight measured against a feather, as the ancient Egyptians thought of judgment in the afterlife. This can be a long and drawn out reflection. The alchemists called it *meditatio*, the long meditation involving inner dialogues with good and bad angels, and it begins with *nigredo*, the realm of the raven in alchemical imagery.

Beyond simply reflecting on their personal lives, men in old age turn philosophical and consider the meaning of human life itself. Why do human beings exist at all? Is our presence on this planet, our beautiful and awesome Earth, a good thing or a bad thing? What is the meaning of human consciousness in the vast universe of stars and galaxies? Of course, these questions are unanswerable, but they are important to ask as one approaches the conclusion of a long life. The perspective a man reaches as a result of this long meditation will be an important piece of the heritage he leaves to the generations following. Will he leave behind a sad and embittered image, or will it be a hopeful and encouraging one? Or a balanced one, combining both positive and negative features? For certain, it can't be faked.

The attempt to expand one's consciousness to include all aspects of reality in its multiplicity is the work of searching for wholeness. Wholeness is a master term. It refers to reality inner and outer, and its symbol is the mandala. Striving for wholeness implies stretching consciousness to include a maximum perspective on reality and to see it with a minimum of distortion, neither rationalizing evil away nor trying to turn it into good, nor cynically turning good into bad. The attempt to stretch consciousness to the point of containing reality as it presents itself in all its aspects is a man's attempt to achieve wholeness. That is the fifth circle.

The struggle with God in old age becomes an internal dialogue. That internal dialogue may be expressed in a variety of ways, possibly as teachings or as writings or verbal statements of wisdom about life. Unfortunately, when old people try to teach the young in inappropriate ways, the young are disinclined to listen. But when they embody wisdom as tribal elders, perhaps they need not say anything further. Rather, they may embody in their being and their actions an achievement of the inner balance among the opposites. In doing so, they can influence those who come in contact with them because they will constellate Self projections even in their silence and will thus function as models. By their simple presence, they carry the projections of the wise old man and the Self. For themselves, it is important to have struggled through to some congruence with the Self.

An older person who has done this work will be able to exemplify a radical freedom to be essentially what he is. Older people often observe that after a certain age they no longer have to worry about what others think. It is important, however, to distinguish between being *what* one is and *who* one is. The question of who one is, is an identity problem that is personalistic and egocentric. *What* one is, is a Self definition. Being what one is, rather than only who one is, presents a much closer approximation to the Self. Such people are not trapped in social role definitions.

This image of the wise old man, or sage, is one that includes potential for further growth, creativity, and wisdom, in contrast to the image of old age as a time of increasing deficits in ability. If taken in the right spirit, such physical deficits can even function as stimulants to another kind of development and as part of the struggle with the Self. The contributions to culture that old people make are unique and special. A culture is blessed if it possesses figures that can carry the projection of the wise old man because they can orient people toward meaning and purpose.

I often think of Jung's biography as an illustration of the struggles that transpire in the fifth circle for a man in his later years. Toward the end of his life, Jung became more and more engaged with two fundamental issues: the problem of evil and the problem of uniting the opposites. He took these up specifically in his late works *Answer to Job* and *Mysterium Coniunctionis*. In the first, he speaks in a very personal voice and with great passion and drama. In the second, his style returns to the usual analytical and interpretive mode. Describing how *Answer to Job* came to be, Jung says he was "gripped by his *daimon*." While recovering from a bout of illness, he wrote feverishly and finally announced to Aniela Jaffé, his secretary, in a letter from his Tower in Bollingen: "I have landed the great fish." The composition of this text was both a personal struggle for Jung with the problem of evil and a message to his contemporaries about the need for further evolution in Western religious history and culture.

In *Answer to Job*, Jung discussed the idea of the evolution of the God image. This evolution comes about as a result of a confrontation between the ego and the Self, or in traditional terms between man and God. It is characteristic that in the last part of life psychology becomes equated with theology. One can no longer keep the strict division between the personal and the theological. As ego and Self merge, ego and transcendent world also become one. Earlier in life, this would result in inflation. Late in life this becomes wisdom.

From our perspective, we see Jung as an old man in the fifth circle in the process of confronting another dimension of life beyond the personal level of ego-consciousness. His aspiration is to advance a collective unconscious-conscious dynamic that reaches far beyond his own individual life and his times. If the individual has evolved far enough, he may gain leverage to move religious tradition and the collective view of God to another level of wholeness.

Jung was also attempting to resolve questions of good and evil in his own life, and he had to deal with the despair of old age. The wells of creativity can dry up in old age, although tremendous amounts of new creativity can also still appear, as they certainly did in Jung's late years. The old person will be dealing with the shadow—his own, his tribe's, his culture's—and can easily become lost in the darkness and fall into despair. Jung also experienced this in his late years. But if he remains engaged in the project of individuation, he will go on to forge what Jung referred to as a *Weltanschauung*, a fundamental attitude toward life flowing from a worldview that includes good and evil and that expresses the whole Self. He becomes a wise old man, the embodiment of an archetype within a cultural context. He performs the role of elder, as is so dramatically seen among non-technological, natural peoples—as one who represents the wisdom of the generations, the tribal gods, and the highest religious values.

Concerning the Transformation
of God Images[1]

> "Religion is following the hints from God."[2]
>
> C. G. Jung

Introduction

Evidence that God images can, and do, change over time has been widely available since the advent of modern historical consciousness. The detailed scholarly reconstruction of the past that took hold in the eighteenth and nineteenth centuries has occupied thinkers in the West ever since. Whether they saw the change as bad and a sign of decay or deterioration from a former state of purity (Adolph Harnack, for instance, who commented critically on the Hellenization of Christian theology that took place in the early centuries of the Common Era), or as evolutionary and a sign of development and maturation (John Henry Cardinal Newman), or as a confirmation that God images are illusory and mostly bent to the service of non-

---

[1] First presented as lectures given at the 2001 Annual Summer Conference at St. Hilda's College, Oxford University and later published by The Guild of Pastoral Psychology, Guild Lecture No. 278. It has been slightly revised for this volume.

[2] C.G. Jung, as quoted by A. Lewis.

religious motives of one kind or another (Feuerbach, Marx, Nietzsche, Freud), the historical reality of change in God images generally, and in the God image of Western religion specifically, and the resulting consequent changes in culture and in religious sensibility and outlook, have been widely noted and intensively discussed. In recent times this issue has come under especially intense discussion, due to the urgent interest in including feminine images of the Divine in Christian theological reflections and even in its most fundamental doctrines.

The question of what such changes might mean, both theoretically (i.e., theologically, philosophically, and scientifically) and practically (i.e., psychologically, sociologically, and religiously) is critical, and largely unresolved among contemporary thinkers. It is a question that left open and unanswered can cause confusion and anxiety. If as permanent-seeming a cultural object as a God image is subject to change and mutation, what is stable? Is there no fixed and intact spiritual foundation that people can rely on? No "Rock of Ages"? Is absolutely everything in flux? And if so, where might we be headed? Can we detect patterns, a direction perhaps? These are some of the questions raised from the realization that God images change over time. Uncertainties abound. Moderns were made anxious by this state of affairs; post-moderns have sometimes attempted to celebrate it.

Jung picked up on the theme of the changing God image in his writings and developed it in several novel directions. I will review some of his ideas and use them to grapple with the question of what a changing God image might mean. The origins of Jung's profound interest in theology and the history of religions can be traced all the way back to the *Zofingia Lectures* of his student days in Basel. Religious themes and images also fill the pages of his first major psychoanalytical work, *Wandlungen und Symbole der Libido* (translated into English first as *The Psychology of the Unconscious* and later with revisions in the *Collected Works* as *Symbols of Transformation*). The transformation of the God image is a central theme in *The Red Book*, which Jung composed during his midlife period. These reflections were considerably expanded as he gained experience and depth of vision in his later years. In several of the works of his maturity such as *Aion* and *Answer to Job,* he focuses intensely on the question of the changing God image in Western religion, both historically and in modern times. Some of his most trenchant observations on this subject were expressed in his correspondence. Edward Edinger, in his book *The New God Image,* comments on several of the key letters in Jung's extensive correspondence with several theologians and clergypersons who also had a pressing interest in this issue. This book and other of Edinger's many writings provide a useful basis for extending a Jungian reflection along the lines I will propose here.

In what follows, I will ask four questions:

1. What is a God image?
2. Why does a God image change?
3. How does a God image change?
4. What does it mean, psychologically speaking, when a God image changes?

These four questions are linked and revolve around the central hermeneutical problem: A changing God image – what does it mean? The answers I offer to these questions derive principally from Jung's understanding of the human psyche and its relation to what religions call God or the Gods.

What is a God Image?

God images come in many forms. To consider them, one must include the material ones such as statues, icons, paintings and other graven images, and also the literary ones as described in Sacred Scriptures, ancient epics and visionary literature, and theological treatises. A brief survey of world religions would yield a list of scores of God images; an extensive review would reveal hundreds, even thousands. A God image appears whenever people attempt to portray or describe, or to give definition to, the *mysterium tremendum,* an experience of the numinosum, which we commonly refer to as a God. The cluster of attributes ascribed to a specific Deity defines the God image under consideration. Even a Deity like the biblical Yahweh who forbade graven images and demanded to remain invisible and transcendent received specification in such names as Father, Creator, Sustainer, Bridegroom and Husband, and Shepherd.

Many of the God images found among the world's numerous religions have similar features but differ in detail and nuance, depending on the social and cultural context in which they are embedded. For instance, there are Father Gods and Mother Goddesses, Savior Gods, Sky Gods and Goddesses, Earth and Underworld Gods and Goddesses. Categorization of them is possible and instructive.

In addition to the God images of the religious traditions, there are those found in the dreams and visions of individuals, historical and contemporary. These recipients of a revelation might keep it private or perhaps share it with a few chosen friends. These private experiences may have features similar to those that are enshrined by cultures, and most of them can be similarly typed and categorized.

What is the essence of these multitudinous God images? Can we define "God image"? Here is an attempt: *A God image is a numinous symbol that claims for itself absolute and cosmic standing.* In Jungian terms, it is a symbol of the Self rather than a sign for the ego. This means that as a symbol it points beyond itself as a concrete image and can open ego-consciousness to the eternal and the infinite and thereby connect the ego to the Self.

For some God images a claim is made by human beings that they are superior to other God images, and even that they should be the only God image. This argument for superiority was made famously by Akhenaton for the sun God, Aton, while the later the monotheistic religions took this theology even a step further, insisting that there is only a single Ultimate Deity. Other religions are pantheistic and contain and revere many God images simultaneously and inclusively (Hinduism, for example). Just because a God image is one of many in a pantheon does not make it less transcendent. Each God image may be considered a facet of the Ultimate without giving undue privilege to any one of them. Some God images are highly abstract and theological, having been refined by many intent minds that have created a consensual and dogmatic image, as is the case with the Trinity of Christianity. Other God images are visual and concrete, and have remained so in the religious traditions that hold them as sacred. In the latter, the image is a symbol that communicates or makes visible the transcendent. Whether abstract of concrete, a God image is a numinous symbol that captures and conveys an intuition or feeling of awe-inspiring, absolute, cosmic, eternal Being. As symbols, these images mediate a dimension of Being that lies beyond the confines of humanly perceived boundaries of time and space in the sensory realm. In Paul Tillich's words, they represent "the ground of Being." One can think psychologically of all God images as representing certain features or aspects of the ultimate and undefinable reality of the Self.

The following are two examples of a God image, the first from the Bible, the second from a contemporary woman's orally reported dream.

From the Book of The Revelation of John:

After this I looked, and lo, in heaven a door stood open! . . . At once I was in the Spirit, and lo, a throne stood in heaven, with one seated on the throne! And he who sat there appeared like jasper and carnelian, and round the throne was a rainbow that looked like an emerald. Round the throne were twenty-four thrones, and seated on the thrones were twenty-four elders, clad in white garments, with golden crowns upon their heads. From the throne issue flashes of lightning, and voices and peals of thunder, and before the throne burn seven torches of fire, which are the seven spirits of God; and in before the throne there is as it were a sea of glass, like crystal.

And round the throne, on each side of the throne, are four living creatures, full of eyes in front and behind: the first living creature like a lion, the second living creature like an ox, the third living creature with the face of a man, and the fourth living creature like a flying eagle. And the four living creatures, each of them with six wings, are full of eyes round and within, and day and night they never cease to sing,

"Holy, holy, holy, is the Lord God Almighty,
who was and is and is to come!"

....

And between the throne and the four living creatures and among the elders, I saw a Lamb standing, as though it had been slain, with seven horns and with seven eyes, which are the seven spirits of God sent out into all the earth; and he went and took the scroll from the right hand of him who was seated on the throne. And when he had taken the scroll, the four living creatures and the twenty-four elders fell before the Lamb, each holding a harp, and with golden bowls full of incense, which are the prayers of the saints...

...And I heard every creature in heaven and on earth and under the earth and in the sea, and all therein, saying, "To him who sits upon the throne and to the Lamb be blessing and honor and glory and might for ever and ever!" And the four living creatures said, "Amen!" and the elders fell down and worshipped.[3]

In this example, which is a classic image from the New Testament, the foundational document of Christianity, one clearly

---

[3] Revelation 4-5.

recognizes the essential features of a God image: a) numinosity (awesome power, wonder, fear on the part of the human observer), b) absolute (i.e., ultimate ontological) standing, and c) cosmic proportion. The Book of Revelation states that this image was presented to the author in a vision. This vision includes many familiar quotations from the earlier biblical tradition, but this does not disqualify it from being an authentic vision, that is, a spontaneous manifestation of the archetypal unconscious. The recipient of the vision was obviously familiar with the Hebrew Bible, and his unconscious brings these references into play. In the vision, they are combined and presented in a novel fashion and contain new information. It is, therefore, a new revelation of Deity.

This vision's symbolic nature is evident, moreover, not only because it contains familiar biblical images such as the four living creatures (a reference to Ezekiel's vision), but also because it gazes into the very heart of the *mysterium tremendum,* to which all genuine religious symbols point. A God image attempts to capture all that it can of the noumenal (i.e., essentially hidden and invisible) God, of God as God is in and of Him/Her/Itself, that is of Ultimate Reality. In this vision, recorded according to tradition by the Apostle John on the island of Patmos, we find a symbol of ultimate spiritual reality as presented to a human being's consciousness some two thousand years ago. The pieces of this vision taken all together represent aspects and facets of the Self as it was experienced in that place and in that time by an individual human consciousness. At its center are the One on the throne surrounded by the four living creatures (the Evangelists) and the Lamb of God (Christ) with seven horns and seven eyes. This recorded vision became one of the foundational documents for the theological doctrine of God as Trinity – Father, Son and Holy Spirit. In the process of reflection and debate that took place over several centuries, the vision was transformed into abstract theological teaching (dogma) to yield the Christian doctrine of God as Triune, Three in One. This God image that has been central to the Christian religion for some 16 centuries.

Leaping over two millennia, so replete with complexity and historical developments, I turn now to a second example of a God image. This one appeared in a dream told to me by a woman in her early sixties, a person not especially religious in a traditional or even a non-traditional sense, but highly sensitive and attuned to the archetypal images of the collective unconscious. She is what one would term today a spiritual rather than a religious person.

I find myself in a large throng of people who are milling around, moving slowly from one area to another, as though at a garden party. Gradually I become aware of a strange thing happening. Close to the ground and around our feet, a powerful charge of energy is moving rapidly through our midst. It dawns on me that this energy has a form, and that it is gliding among the people in a figure eight. I see that it is an enormous snake. The snake's beautiful face appears. It has the head of a woman. The body of the snake is covered with white orchids that are growing out of her. She confronts me. Her gigantic face comes near, her dark eyes fix me in a stare, and I become afraid. Beyond the fear, though, I feel tremendous awe and wonder at this marvelous and remarkable being.

"Who are you?" she demands of me. "What do you do?"
I give my name and tell her that I am a psychotherapist.
"Oh, so you are an architect of souls," she replies.
I am surprised at this designation and listen further.
"You are like Julius Caesar and . . . ." (She names some other historical characters whom I cannot recall after I awaken). She must see the look of astonishment on my face because she goes on to say: "Of course, you could not know that Julius Caesar was an architect of souls in a much earlier lifetime."
I now understand that this snake has been around since the beginning of rime. Her memory holds a record of all the souls who have ever lived, and of all of their various

incarnations and specific identities. Some souls have lived more than once, or even many times. I am surprised that she has placed me in a category with Julius Caesar and even more astonished that his underlying identity was an "architect of souls." Clearly, I do not understand something important here. I am dumbfounded and shaken to be meeting a consciousness that has been around since the universe began.

For a while we simply look at each other. I admire the beautiful white orchids that cover her massive body. I also realize that she is immensely powerful and could annihilate me in an instant. But I decide to take the risk and venture to say:

"You now have an opportunity to do great good, because you are at a point in your evolution where you are on the way to becoming fully conscious. You are more than halfway there."

Surprised at my own boldness. I wonder how she will take this comment.

Her face lights up and she smiles. This is a blessing. Great streams of energy are exuding out of her.

Like the God image reported by St. John in the Book of Revelation, the giant snake image in this dream is a numinous symbol of the Timeless and Eternal, and it portrays a being of vast power and cosmic dimension. Unlike the biblical God image, however, this modern one emerges from the earth and does not appear in the heavens, and it includes the notion of an evolving consciousness in the God(dess) figure. The cosmic snake does not show the quality of absolute omniscience and transcendence typical of monotheistic Deities, although she does have a memory of all that has happened to date in human and, perhaps, in cosmic history. The Serpent's consciousness is in process, however, and has now arrived more than halfway toward completion, according to the dreamer's assessment. The claim made for the God of the monotheisms has been, universally, that the God image named and worshipped is omniscient and omnipotent, anything but a work in progress. This modern God image, on the contrary, implies development of divine consciousness. History and the passage of time make a difference. Moreover, the relation between the human observer and the observed God image is also more dialogical. One can hardly imagine St. John conversing with the One seated on the throne, or with the Lamb, never mind commenting on their degree of completeness, or partiality, in any manner whatsoever. While it is certainly not correct to say that the dream ego and the serpent God image are on a par, or in any sense equals, the words of this dreamer to this God image would be unthinkable in classical religious experience, where the power and consciousness differential is so much greater.

One might hazard the hypothesis that ego-consciousness has gained considerable standing vis-a-vis the archetypal Self in the last two thousand years. This same increased standing of the ego in relation to the biblical God image is represented in Jung's contro-versial *Answer to Job*, where, in a number of famous passages, Jung takes Yahweh to task for his lack of consciousness.

To answer the question posed earlier, "What is a God image?", we can conclude that it is a symbol that captures an important aspect of the Self. Presented to the ego, a God image offers the benefit of an impersonal symbol, which mediates between the ego and the Self. The connecting link between the ego and the Self—the so-called ego-Self axis—is made of God images. This is as critically important to recognize for the psychology of religion as it is for the therapy of souls. People use God images to establish a relationship to the Self. Activities like prayer and contemplation in religious life have a profound psychological value. The ego anchored in the Self enjoyed ultimate security. This explains why people become so attached to their God images and why they are so loath to give them up. Without a connection to the Self, the ego experiences emptiness, meaninglessness, and dread—in short, the psychological pathos of modernity and postmodernity.

Why does a God image change?

Do God images really change over time, and if they do *why* do they change? The answers to these questions are bound to be complex.

One could argue that collective God images (i.e., those embedded in and carried by culturally entrenched historical religious traditions) do not change in their essentials at all, ever. A religion may die and disappear from the stage of history, being replaced by another or by a competing religion perhaps (as happened in Egypt and Greece). Or a new religion may be born out of an older one (as happened in the instances of Christianity and Buddhism). But once established as fundamental doctrines and objects of collective veneration, religions' God images do not change over time. Because they represent the eternal, they must of necessity show evidence of permanence themselves. Moreover, the element of fundamentalism in all religions guarantees a relative degree of permanence.

On the other hand, a careful historical enquiry will show that religious doctrines and dogmas do show signs of development over the centuries. John Henry Cardinal Newman and others like the church historian Adolf Harnack have persuasively argued this view in the case of Christianity. Jung is of the opinion, as I will show later, that change in God images is more characteristic of Western religions than of Eastern ones. In addition, some people would argue that such developments in the God image are not for the better but that they are in fact devolutionary corruptions of an original, pristine God image based on an authentic revelation. This was, to some degree, the opinion of the Protestant Reformers who were intent on returning to the New Testament and the accounts found there of religious experiences for guidance in their lives and theological writings. Others have held that they are evolutionary and progressive and thus add important features that were understated in the earlier doctrines. Cardinal Newman was of this opinion, and the Roman Catholic doctrine of the infallibility of the Pope to enunciate new dogma based on evolutionary developments in the thinking of the Church is in line with this notion of progress in defining the God image.

In modern times, this tendency toward change in God images has been greatly complicated—perhaps augmented would be the better word here—by philosophy and psychology. Kant and Schopenhauer turned philosophy decisively away from metaphysical system-building and certainty to the phenomenological, the directly experienceable, and the individual. William James's well-known study, *The Varieties of Religious Experience,* builds on this foundation. James collected and studied the religious experiences of ordinary individuals and analyzed them without judgment from a psychological perspective. Jung wholeheartedly embraced this return to the study of primary religious experience and its effect on the individual psyche. Many of his writings affirm this commitment and exemplify this approach.

This insistence on experience and the empirical has had the effect of opening the doors to new God images. If a person experiences a God image and it functions to offer meaning, who can deny its psychological validity? The experience is subjectively true for the individual.

When new revelations of the Divine appear, the old God images of collective religions become subject to revision and questioning. This does not mean, of course, that Popes, Cardinals, and others among organized religions' administrators and guardians readily accept modifications in traditional God images. Yet, pressure for change and modification of established traditional God images may well have an effect on traditional images nonetheless. The urgent pressure recently in some mainline Christian denominations to include feminine imagery in prayers to the Godhead and to embrace inclusive language in worship has made considerable inroads in theology and has certainly altered liturgical language. In the end, the leaders of religious traditions must go where the people go.

To address the question of why God images change, I would like to consider two familiar examples of change in a prevailing God image. The first took place over a period of at least three centuries, or perhaps as many as five if one counts the preceding century as preparation, and goes on to the full completion of doctrinal and creedal formulations. I am referring to the change in God image that took place in the birth of Christianity out of the parent religion, Judaism. Admitting that there were a multitude of complex sociological, historical, and psychological dynamics underlying this development, we find a change during the period from l00 B. C. E. to 400 C. E., from Yahwist monotheism to Father-Son-Holy Spirit Trinitarianism. For those who were Christians, the new God image was seen to be an extension, or a further revelation, of the old one, in that it included the previous one and folded it into a new formulation. This new formulation included the incarnated Son of God, Jesus Christ, and the Spirit of God that descended upon the apostles after Jesus' death and continues to inhabit the Christian Church. The new God image, it was claimed by the early Church Fathers, was a further revelation of God's internal structure, which had been only partially revealed in the image of Yahweh.

The vision of God recorded in the Book of Revelation discloses this new God image. While the Father occupies the throne, the Lamb (who is the Son of God, the crucified Christ who died for the sins of the world) stands beside the throne, and the Spirit is dispersed in various figures surrounding the throne and also inhabits the Lamb. It would take the leaders of the Church several centuries to solidify and codify the new God image into the Trinitarian doctrine expressed in the great Creeds. In the end, the Christian Church formulated a God image that captured the new revelation of God as Love, as a suffering Saviour and an immanent, indwelling Spirit. While maintaining the element of transcendence and the patriarchal emphasis, symbolized by God the Father.

The God image of Yahweh changed. We may conclude, in order to reflect a new awareness of the Ultimate and its relation to conscious, human life. This shift was not based on an individual person's decision to change the prevailing God image of Judaism. It was a collective decision based on the religious and communal experiences of many people, and it took centuries to accomplish. The new God image emerged slowly over many generations from the collective unconscious of the people, gripped by a new revelation of the Divine. Those who continued their faithful adherence to the original monotheistic vision of ancient Judaism would deny its validity, and what resulted historically was a situation of two quite distinct God images—a parent one and an offspring— co-existing side by side, among peoples who often found themselves in a tense and, sometimes, vicious and bloody rivalry.

The second example of a changing God image famously celebrated by Jung in *Answer to Job*, where he wrote about the newly (in 1952) announced dogma of the *Assumptio Mariae:* "I consider [it] to be the most important religious event since the Reformation."[4] As Jung further noted, this dogmatic addition to the Roman Catholic understanding and vision of the God image was prepared for in the collective life of the Church for many centuries, and the foregoing prophesies and visions, cited by Pope Pius XII in evidence for its inevitable recognition as dogma, are much like those cited for the appearance of Christ in the Hebrew Bible by the New Testament writers.

Again, the change in God image reflects an attempt to capture a more complete picture of Deity in all of its complexity. With the addition of the Virgin's physical being in the Heavenly sphere, the Christian God image received two important new additions: a feminine aspect and a physical one. As though something important has been left out, the new God images add to, or complete, a picture of Deity. As further aspects of the Self emerge into consciousness, the God image changes to include them.

---

[4] C.G. Jung, *Answer to Job*, in CW 11, par. 752.

In response to the question, why does a God image change? we may answer: because it must in order to capture a more complete expression of the emergent Self. This notion can be tested. If it is true, then it should follow that whenever a new God image appears it will represent a feature of the *mysterium tremendum* that the immediately preceding God image(s) available did not include.

There is another reason as well why God images change. Over time they tend to lose their numinosity. At first their symbolic power—that is, their ability to communicate awesome energy and their consequent capacity to bring the ego into contact with the *mysterium tremendum*—is enormous. People are overcome by them, struck with wonder and smitten by the desire to submit and worship. The God image is rich with libido, charged to attract and persuade. In this phase, the God image is to the ego as container is to contained. The individual's psyche becomes housed, as it were, in the much larger and more powerful God image. Over time, however, the God image loses some of its numinosity because it becomes integrated by ego consciousness. Its wildness becomes tamed. As it is rationalized and turned into theology and doctrine, its capacity to link the ego to the unconscious diminishes. It gradually becomes more of a sign than a symbol. When people are born into old religious traditions they may merely memorize the teachings and catechisms. They go through the motions of ritual as a matter of course and routine, and often these formal acts of worship and adherence become more a matter of conformity to custom, than experiences of the Divine. Priests and theologians become, in time, more practical, rational, and quietly skeptical. They lose the sense of the mystical presence of the Divine in their rites and symbols, and as a result their psyches are less contained in the God image.

The container-contained relationship actually reverses, and the God image becomes contained in the consciousness of the individual. It is now an item of learning and knowledge. While this implies a growth of ego consciousness, it also leaves people with an unsatisfied hunger for mystery, for numinosity, for the unconscious. This is the present condition of many modern people in Christendom and in other traditional religious cultures. Modernity is founded on a strong and differentiated ego consciousness, scientific, rational and in control of emotion. From this absence of living symbols comes the restless quest of "modern man in search of a soul," as Jung describes this condition. This is fertile ground for the springing up of new God images. For, in truth, the unconscious has not been exhausted of content and energy. As the cosmic serpent dream cited above states, the collective unconscious is just a little more than halfway to full consciousness. There is still much more potential left to develop.

We must recognize, however, that classic God images (i.e., those held up and worshipped within the great religious traditions of the world) have enormous staying power. Religious Jews still enthusiastically worship Yahweh; Christ is still heartily declared to be the ultimate Lord and final statement about God by many faithful Christians; ancient Hindu deities still contain the psyches of multitudes of devotees in India; the world of Islam is vast and highly charged with religious fervor in many areas. What this tells us is that, on a mass, collective level, human consciousness changes very slowly. Millennia come and go, and there is little evident movement. The Enlightenment, the scientific revolution, modernity—powerful cultural movements that they are—have been highly disruptive of traditional patterns of religious life and belief, especially in the West, but on global scale they have not yet proven decisive. What they have shown quite clearly, on the other hand, is that change in all spheres of human life, including the religious and the psychological, can accelerate rapidly in certain periods of history. We seem to be in one of those periods now on a global level, and the probabilities of new God images appearing, and taking hold, on a collective plain are quite high. In times of deep cultural and social transformation, there is a strong likelihood that new God mages will emerge in order to capture the new features of the Self, that are brought into play by the transformation process. The other parallel movement, of course, is a strong defensive movement of regression back into traditional categories, as witnessed by the explosive growth of fundamentalisms throughout the world in the last decades.

How do God images change?

A new God image appears. Joseph Smith meets an angel who shows him a new scripture, and from this visionary experience arises the Church of Jesus Christ of Latter Day Saints (the Mormons), who now number in the millions and are to be found on all inhabited continents. John, on the island of Patmos, is taken "in the spirit" and hears and sees a new revelation, which has entered the iconography and dogmas about God in Christianity. Moses asks God for a name and receives "I am that I am" and, later, the tablets of Law on Mount Sinai. And so on. God images appear to people, usually unexpectedly and by surprise, and they create an impression of numinosity and indelible symbolic truth. They command obedience and worshipful attention. And always these new God images are set against the backdrop of other, older God images that have lost their containing, convincing capacities. Joseph Smith's revelation appeared against the backdrop of Christianity, John's revelation against that of Judaism, and Moses' revelation against the background of Egyptian religion.

If we think in causal terms about why this happens, it can be explained, at least partially, by the law of compensation. Compensation, as Jung defines and uses the notion, refers to the action of the unconscious, ultimately of the Self, upon ego consciousness to produce individuation, that is, greater wholeness in consciousness. Dreams function to compensate the one-sidedness of ego-consciousness, and over time they offer the ego an opportunity to change in the direction of greater integration of the Self. All the many small dreams of a lifetime are actions directed by the Self, to incarnate itself in the concrete existence of an individual. The several (or sometimes many) big dreams offered to the ego by the Self have a similar prospective function—to increase the ego's awareness of the Self. But big dreams also reach far beyond the individual's own personal individuation process, and address the collective individuation process of a tribe, a nation, or even humankind as a whole. For not only are individuals capable of increasing their consciousness of the Self, but also groups and collectives of various sizes and qualities. Containing collectives such as families, religious traditions, nations, etc., have the ability to raise or to lower, to enhance or to diminish, the level of consciousness of those who adhere and are psychologically attached to them. So the big dreams of people can have a compensatory effect on a collective, and can move its constituency in the direction of greater consciousness of the Self.

The curious thing about compensation is how seemingly unpredictable it is. Dreams, for example, are notoriously hard to foretell, at least in an exact way, even if one has a long and detailed previous dream series to go on. Jung (1989) in *Seminar on Dream Analysis,* it seems, was able to predict dreams to a certain extent because of his long experience with the psyche and his extraordinary intuition. But prediction, to be scientific, must be governed by thinking and by rules of reason that can be applied anywhere, anytime. Compensation from the unconscious can at best be predicted only with statistical probability. This may be because as with the weather, there are simply so many factors at work that it is practically impossible to take them all into account. But it may also be the case that compensation is controlled by a factor that is beyond our knowing altogether, by a *Ding an Sich* (thing in itself i.e., essence), the Self archetype per se, which has its own reasons and timing. And this consideration leads us to the centrality of synchronicity in compensation and individuation generally, and in changing God images specifically.

Statistically it would be probable that when a God image is no longer numinous and containing, when it has been integrated sufficiently by ego-consciousness to lose its symbolic aliveness and alluring energy, its ability to connect the ego to the Self: and when the one-sidedness of an individual's or a collective's consciousness has reached a critical degree of extremity, then a compensating God image will appear to carry the individuation process forward. But it seems impossible to predict exactly when this will occur, or what aspect of the Self will appear, or, in a group, from what quarter it will come.

Beyond that, God images do not change only because someone has a dream or a vision. There must be miracles, i.e., synchronistic events that match inner mental images and outer physical facts and events. Without miracles Jesus would not have become the Son of God, Christ, the Second Person of the Trinity. Miracles are essential in the change process from one God image to another. Why is this the case? In part, it is because they act as tangible confirmations of an inner realization. People are skeptical of purely mental happenings, and the psyche seems too evanescent to pin much reliance on it. There has to be physical evidence. Dreams and images come and go and they may momentarily move people, but we are not permanently affected and changed by them. Movies affect us for instance, often deeply, but we do not change our lives because of them, unless, that is, they are accompanied by synchronicity. Synchronicity tells us that there is objective under-pinning for the image, and that it is anchored in a reality beyond the human psyche.

Synchronicity ties the mental and the physical together. It is the fundamental principle behind incarnation. Without syn-chronicity one may have good intentions and firm ego motivations, and these may carry one a certain distance, but with synchronicity, an inner event like a dream or vision becomes indelible, and its penetration into historical reality does not depend upon the ego. It gathers flesh around itself, and it grows without the need of constant intentional nurturing. It becomes alive in its own right in a three-dimensional fashion, and it is grafted onto the tree of life by the hidden hand of the Self.

In the extensive and highly instructive correspondence between Jung and Wolfgang Pauli,[5] one sees these two scientists struggling to clarify the notion of synchronicity at great length. Before publishing his only major paper on synchronicity in 1952, Jung discussed it in detail several times with Pauli, who offered his critical appraisal and suggestions. The deepest point of contact between analytical psychology and physics, they found, lies in a specific location: in the joint unpredictability of happenings at the unconscious level of the psyche, and at the subatomic level of matter. In both areas one can make predictions only on the basis of statistical probability. Causal laws do not seem to apply, and prediction of a more precise nature is impossible in both instances. Pauli brought Jung around to defining archetypes as statistical probabilities of psychic functioning: ". . . the archetype represents nothing else but the probability of psychic events,"[6] Jung writes to Pauli from Bollingen in 1952. Pauli, as it happens, was especially blessed (or cursed) by numerous synchronistic events in his life, so much so that in scientific circles there were jokes about the "Pauli effect": Things behaved strangely in his presence, like the time a vase filled with flowers cracked spontaneously and fell over when he arrived late for the inauguration of the Jung Institute in Zurich.

Pauli's term for synchronicity (in the correspondence with Jung) was "radioactivity." Pauli was intent on finding what he called a "neutral language" for psychology, which he felt would make it suitable for joining the discipline of physics as a sort of little sister branch of research. This translation of synchronicity into radio-activity is suggestive. Here is how Pauli expresses his idea: "A process of transmutation of an active center, ultimately leading to a stable state, is accompanied by self-duplicating ('multiplying') and

---

[5] C.A. Meier (ed.), *Atom and Archetype*.
[6] *Ibid.*, p. 69.

expanding phenomena, associated with further transmutations that are brought about through an invisible reality."[7] In this letter of December 12, 1950, Pauli goes on to put this idea into language more related to analytical psychology : "The 'active nucleus,' familiar to me as a dream symbol, has a close relationship to the *lapis* of the alchemists, and thus in your [i.e., Jung's] terminology is a symbol of the 'Self.' The transformation process as a psychic process is still the same today as that represented in the alchemical opus, and consists of the transitions of the 'Self' into a more conscious state. This process (at certain stages at least) is accompanied by the *'multiplicatio'* - i.e., by the multiple outward manifestation of an archetype (this being the 'invisible reality'), which again is the same as the 'breaking of barriers through contingency' or 'transgressivity' of the archetype that you talk about in your letter."[8]

This last part of the sentence refers to Jung's previous letter of November 30, 1950 (again written at Bollingen), in which he says: "A further possibility is that neither mass [i.e., material objects] nor the psychic process possess such a characteristic [i.e., to co-opt the other] but that a third factor is present to which it must be attributed, a factor that can be observed in the psyche and can be observed from there - namely, the (*psychoid*) archetype which, thanks to its habitual indistinctness and 'transgressivity,' assimilates into each other two incommensurable causal processes (in a so-called numinous moment), creates a joint field of tension (?), or makes them both 'radioactive'(?)."[9]

Jung and Pauli are grappling with the question of how synchronicity (hence also individuation) takes place. The source of it lies in the "invisible world" and is conceived of by Pauli as an "active nucleus", by Jung as a "*psychoid* archetype." When activated, this energy center creates effects that "multiply;" on the one hand,

---

[7] *Ibid.*, pp. 66-67.
[8] *Ibid.*, p. 67.
[9] *Ibid.*, pp. 62-63.

they touch the psyche (creating images such as the numinous God images we are concerned with here), and on the other they affect the material world (where physical objects behave similarly). Hence we find "miracles" in the vicinity of newly emergent God images. Objective events in the material world take on symbolic meaning as they participate in the appearance of the new (psychic) God image. In this way, the new God images become incarnated, that is, are given shape and form in the material world.

A familiar example of this concatenation of psychic and material factors is contained in the story of Jesus' birth. Here we find a thick cluster of objective events and psychic factors, including the constellation of stars, to indicate the special moment in time (astronomy and astrology); a Virgin Birth (which denies the normal chain of causality), the appearance of angels (spiritual beings seen in visionary states), dreams that come to Joseph convincing him of Mary's rectitude and giving the child's name (an inner psychic factor), the appearance of Wise Men from the East (a social and political factor), and the actual physical birth of a child (a biological factor). All of these are woven together textually to state that this was a special time, a synchronistic moment of *kairos,* in which the "active nucleus" of the cosmos was creating multiple effects ("radioactivity") in the vicinity of Bethlehem in Judea. The four Gospels recount the many later synchronistic events in the life of Jesus of Nazareth, and the Book of Acts continues the story into the period of the early church, when miracles accompanied the work of the Apostles. These were the years of the birth of a new God image, coinciding synchronistically (again) with the beginning of the Piscean Age.

Compensation, then, working in conjunction with syn-chronicity, can explain the means by which God images change, or new God images emerge, convincingly and historically, in collectives and in the lives of individuals. This is how it happens. Not by the will of the ego but through the action of the Self. Perhaps we can reflect now more deeply on what it means when this happens.

What does it mean when a God image changes?

In a much cited letter to Elined Kotschnig dated June 30, 1956, Jung observes that the "religious spirit of the West is characterized by a change in God's image in the course of ages," while "the East holds a thoroughly static view, i.e., a cyclic view."[10] He further remarks that the notion of evolution is Christian. What does this changing of a God image mean, then? Is it only a local cultural and religious affair?

A key question is: Does a change in God image also reflect a change in God? Or is it change only in the human perception of God? Is the ego changing here, or is the Self changing? Most Christian theologians, even if they would admit to some development in the theological account of God, would not support the idea that there is evolution in God. They would rather be inclined to remind us that what we are seeing is a progressive revelation of God's eternal reality. Nevertheless, from the human – and the psychological—viewpoint, there is no difference between progressive revelation and the evolution of a God image, or even evolution in God in and of Him/Her/Itself.

Jung's Kantian reserve did not prevent him from entertaining the truly non-Christian hypothesis, that the changes seen in the images of God over ages may reflect an evolution in the *Ding an Sich* underlying these images. Rather than representing a progressive unveiling of a stable underlying reality, of a God in and of itself who does not change, the changes at the phenomenal level (the images of God as experienced by the human psyche) may reveal important changes at the invisible noumenal level (the reality of God). Keep in mind that this is a hypothesis, not a truth claim or an article of faith. This cannot be affirmed as doctrine or belief, otherwise the same mistake of ontologizing merely human mental images, severely criticized by Kant, would be repeated, and a new psychometaphysical project would be mistakenly launched. The idea of a change

---

[10] C.G. Jung, *Letters*, vol. 2, p. 315.

in God must rather be held as hypothetical, with an attitude open to future confirmation or disconfirmation based on accumulating evidence. As evidence is gathered, further interpretations and revisions may be ventured. This is an on-going hermeneutical project rather than a metaphysical one. For the moment, though, one can hold the hypothesis that a changing God image means a change in God. This would not be a local cultural bias, any more than other scientific hypotheses are. It is rather a venture in thinking and interpreting data.

In the same letter to Kotschnig, Jung writes that based on the evidence of paleontology the creator has spent some billions of years at it and "has made, as it seems to us, no end of detours to produce consciousness."[11] From this Jung draws the conclusion that "His behavior is strikingly similar to a being with an at least very limited consciousness. He has apparently neither foresight of an ulterior goal nor any knowledge of a direct way to reach it."[12] The method looks hit-or-miss, experimental, randomly creative, and it has produced no end of suffering along the way. Of course, this view assumes that the creation of consciousness is a goal. This could be questioned.

Scientific thinking would indicate that if we start with the present and work backward into the history of the universe, there is scant evidence of moral purpose or goal-oriented trends in the unfolding patterns of creation. There is little to warrant a conclusion that consciousness is the be all and end all of creation, or the purpose of a creator. There is almost nothing to persuade the rational skeptical mind of the existence of an intentional Being (i.e., God) who is trying to make something particular out of this material universe. Science, attempting to maintain rational neutrality, eschews presuppositions like teleology or purpose in nature. What is known about evolution and change can be sufficiently explained,

---

[11] *Ibid.*, p. 312.
[12] *Ibid.*

it is generally thought, as the result of a combination of random genetic and physical changes in nature, and the natural selection of the more fit of them to given changing environments. There is no need to suppose a plan or planner behind the scenes. Science and theology (at least Christian theology based on traditional doctrines and the Bible) have parted ways, and increasingly so since the early nineteenth century. Yet even if, for the moment, we do suppose that human consciousness is one important result, so far, of known cosmic evolution, the way here does not appear to be very efficient or rational.

If we shift perspectives, however, from change and evolution in the vast cosmos to historical evolution of God images in the West, Jung detects a pattern of development in them toward greater consciousness and responsibility. What could this mean?

As he lays his thinking out in the letter to Kotschnig, there is a discernable movement from "the playful and rather purposeless existence of the polytheistic deities in the Mediterranean sphere" to the "Jewish conception of a purposeful and morally inclined God."[13] This new God image, however, still showed "fatal un-reliability," and this fact led to prophesies of an "Advocate" or "Mediator," which were fulfilled in the identity of Christ. The New Testament portrays another new God image in the form of a "Loving Father in whom there is no darkness."[14] This God is one who incarnated Himself in human form, and committed the extraordinary and unprecedented act of self-sacrifice in order to prove His ultimate goodness.

The act of incarnation, furthermore, released a genuinely new development in the God-human relationship. When God became human, humans also received the potential to be God-like. Suddenly a new equation arose between the two terms, God and human. While pagan Greek and pre-Greek Gods might have shown

---

[13] *Ibid.*
[14] *Ibid.*, p. 313.

proclivities toward intercourse with humans and producing offspring in the form of semi-divine heroes, there never was the notion of a God incarnating Him or Herself in human form, giving up divine prerogatives (such as immortality and absence of suffering), and undergoing a genuinely human life process including physical suffering and death. The terms God and human were always kept separate and distinct, and it was wisdom, according to the Greeks, not to confuse them. In classical Judaism, too, God is seen as utterly transcendent and removed in essence from human life and the material world.

With the idea of incarnation, Jung writes in the same letter, came the recognition that "we have become participants in the divine nature and presumably heirs of the tendency toward goodness and at the same time subject to the inevitable self-punishment."[15] In short, the birth of a greater degree of consciousness of the good vs. evil distinction entered the human dimension as a result of the change in God image that took place some two thousand years ago. Human potential changed, too, with the change in God image. Moral consciousness became potentially stronger, and the capacity for goodness increased in the human psyche. This has been the contribution of the Jewish-Christian transformation of the God image in the West. It has meant an increase in moral capability on the part of human beings through greater consciousness.

The psychological development of moral awareness has been severely berated and criticized by thinkers like Nietzsche, who called for a return to pre-Jewish and pre-Christian guilt-free consciousness. Left-wing Freudians like Herbert Marcuse have similarly sought to overthrow the strictures of the Western moralistic "super-ego." And Western history itself has shown no end of departures from the vision of Goodness held up by Biblical theology and teaching, not to mention the horrific regressions to barbaric transgression and brutality, seen in such massive collective movements as Nazism in

---

[15] *Ibid.*, p. 314.

recent times. Yet it must be admitted that at its classic center, the Judeo-Christian tradition holds up a high ethical and moral standard of conduct, with a distinct accent on the Goodness of God and the potential holiness of at least select human beings {the patriarchs in the Hebrew Bible, Job, the Christian saints, etc.).

While the evidence for *telos* (i.e., purpose) from nature is scanty or non-existent, the changes in the God images of the West do reveal a progressive movement in the direction of strengthening Goodness in the God image, and of involving humans in this process. So argues Jung. There has been moral development here even if behavior in the large, on the scale of society and culture, does not always manifest it.

But even if we allow that the change in God images reveals this trend, the question remains of the extent of development at the noumenal level, in the *Ding an Sich* behind the scenes, in God. We must posit that this factor (God) was present before these images ever came into being, and will, presumably, go on after humans cease to exist. It is highly unlikely that humans invented God, and much more likely that God invented us, existed before we did, and will continue to exist after we disappear. This is the age-old perception about God, and it is reasonable. God is the noumenal factor underlying the patterns evident in the physical world (the so called laws of nature and mathematics) and the psychic world (the archetypes of the collective unconscious). This factor has priority, temporal and logical, to human consciousness.

What is the link between changing God images and changes in the noumenal factor underlying them? Here one must be content with uncertainty. The factor of synchronicity would seem to point toward a connection. When archetypal images are constellated in the psyche, Jung observed, synchronistic events become more likely, statistically speaking. There seems to be a connection, but it is indefinite and obscure. One can only guess that some sort of correspondence or linkage exists. This is not so much a matter of faith as an invitation to collect more data and continue with interpretation.

Supposing that changes in the God image do reflect, even if only obscurely and imperfectly, movement (evolution?) in the underlying *Ding an Sich* (i.e., in God), what are some implications for what lies ahead? Jung provocatively asks, again in his letter to Kotschnig: "How much of God - if this is not too human an argument - has been transformed?"[16] Given the vast stretches of time involved—billions of years!—the last few thousand years are rather trivial from a numerical viewpoint. It is quite reasonable to suppose, therefore, "that we are going to contact spheres of a not yet transformed God when our consciousness begins to extend into the sphere of the unconscious."[17] In other words, we can expect new God images of the "not yet transformed God" to make their appearance. These may reveal new regions of exposure on God's part to human consciousness, but these parts are "not yet transformed."

It is precisely here that the human work of individuation becomes critically important in the large scheme of things. As Jung uses the term "individuation" it means, both the personal differentiation of a unique personality from an unconscious background of potentiality and from a state of identification with family members and cultural objects, and a specific incarnation of the transpersonal Self. Each human life is an incarnation of God in human consciousness. This incarnation may be relatively full, or extremely meager and partial. The difference lies in the degree of consciousness attained by the individual. When a person becomes aware, even partially, of the God factor within, of the Self, then a God image becomes available, and the aspect of God reflected in this image enters consciousness. Each God image made available in this fashion adds to the full incarnation of the noumenal God within

---

[16] *Ibid.*, p. 314.
[17] *Ibid.*

humankind's consciousness as a whole. This is Jung's point about continuing incarnation made so eloquently in Answer to Job. It matters to God that humans individuate, for in so doing they are contributing to the cosmic project of bringing God fully into consciousness. While this sounds highly metaphysical and theological, Jung does not mean it to be so. It is meant to be empirical, verifiable by experience, thoroughly biographical in the lives of psychologically aware people. The data that holds evidence of this process lies in the stories of individuating people.

Individuation also works through a double movement between deintegration and integration. The phase of disidentification from earlier identifications leads to the absence of guiding images within the psyche. There is a state of alienation, or at least of psychological distance, from traditional cultural forms. This is the precondition for later integration of new ones. The ability to live without a God image is necessary in order to experience a new one offered by the Self, later to integrate it. People who are individuating often are void of guiding images and live in a state of psychic uncertainty. They are open to experimentation and new experience. Tolerance of liminality and ambiguity is the prerequisite for creativity as well as for the birth of new God images.

The "spheres of the not yet transformed God" that humans come into contact with, Jung cautions, may be dark and dangerous to oneself and others. In fact, this is likely to be the case since they are "untransformed" aspects. Transformation of these parts involves the process of integration, which takes them from their home in the abyss of unconsciousness and tethers them to ego-consciousness. As this process is taking place, there are a host of possibilities for acting out the partiality of instinctual urges and egocentric shadow motivations. As anyone who has done this work can testify, consciousness is not fully operational during the process of integrating new pieces of the psyche, and regressions and lapses are common enough to give the process a bad reputation. "Things have to get worse before they can get better," is a truism that springs from the mouths of many therapists as they face the questioning and pained questions of patients' families. Psychological integration is a messy business.

On the collective level it is no different. As portions of God become newly available in the form of new God images, the historical process shows the same kind of turbulence that an individual's life shows during periods of transformation (adolescence, midlife, old age). There are long stretches of liminality, dis-identification with earlier guiding forms, ambiguity and uncertainty, and there are periods when new images emerge and compete for attention. Then there is a time of digestion, integration, and linking the new with the old. For a culture this process may take decades, even centuries. In world historical terms, it certainly takes several centuries to complete this de-integration/integration cycle on a broad cultural plain. Can we predict where this process of integration and transformation will go on the world historical level? What sort of God image will come into focus in the coming centuries? In the short term it is certainly impossible to make such predictions. In the long term, perhaps—so long as we remain cautious about trying to pin down or predict the emerging images too precisely or exactly. Jung's term "wholeness" is a good candidate for consideration. His suggestion for a Quaternity is also ample and open-ended enough to be useful.

But can we count on a continuation of the moral quality of the God image being extended as more parts of the noumenal God become transformed and made conscious? Jung focuses on this direction of development in the evolution of God images in the West. But we also know of his violent disagreement with the Christian understanding of evil as *privatio boni,* as the absence of goodness. Our notion of evil must become more substantial, more essential, than that, he argued passionately and perhaps even it logically (as in his arguments with the much more logically consistent and better philosophically trained theologian, Victor White). If the God image by which we live is too one-sided in favor of goodness, Jung worried, the unconscious will surely react with compensation of equal and opposite magnitude and produce phenomenal evil. And so it did indeed occur in the twentieth century, a time of extraordinary outbreaks of collective evil in highly civilized and formally Christian cultures. Somehow the new God image must find a way to include the missing and denied elements of Deity, to ease the tension of opposites so regnant in the traditional image. Too much conscious emphasis on goodness will surely produce violent negative reactions.

God images do change out of human need, and our need is great. What God images offer is an answer to the deepest questions and dilemmas about existence and its meaning. During a time of disidentification with traditional God images and consequent liminality, such as our present lime certainly is, the cultural and individual ground for birth of new God images is highly fertile. The unconscious is bound to respond. But God images also change by the action of synchronicity, and not only by the imperatives of need and compensation, and they are, therefore, unpredictable in their exact timing. When they appear, it is an indication that a new aspect of the underlying reality of noumenal Being is available for integration and transformation, and here the human part becomes critical. Humans must incarnate the newly revealed God image in their individual consciousness and patterns of behavior, otherwise the transformation of God will not come about. This is the human task, first individual and then cultural.

I will conclude by recalling the dream of the world snake described at the outset of these reflections. The dream captures the notion of evolution in God's consciousness. The snake's level of consciousness has reached a point just beyond the halfway mark to its ultimate potential. Now, the dreamer says, it has the possibility of doing great good. This is, of course, the human hope, that the moral quality of the God image will continue to increase, and that goodness will grow in strength and ubiquity. One half of God is still to be transformed, and one does not know what that will mean in the future. If the balance can be tilted in the direction of "grace and light" and away from "the terrible temptation of power,"[18] then the tendency shown by changes in the God image over the last three thousand years in the West will be strengthened.

What does it mean when the God image changes? It means a time for active engagement in individuation on the human side and a time for new revelations on the part of the Divine. It means mutual transformation.

---

[18] *Ibid.*, p. 316.

Symbols as Transformers of the Psyche[1]

Since its beginnings in Freud's late nineteenth century clinical workshop, psychoanalysis has been concerned with the dynamics and the contents of repression. The concern has been to reduce repression, to bring the light of consciousness into regions where it was previously excluded, and thereby to vivify ego-consciousness, to extend its options for choice, and to increase the range and scope of personal freedom. In Jungian parlance, this means replacing signs with symbols. I will explain.

What gets repressed and remains repressed is a key issue for psychotherapeutic theory and also, or especially, for practice. For Freud, the chief content of repression was sexuality in its most basic, original and instinctual forms as he understood them. Oedipal sexuality and its attached contents of fantasy and thought were the prime targets of the repression dynamic. With their repression went much memory as well. This accounts, in Freud's mind, for childhood amnesia. Moreover, the repression of Oedipal sexuality lay at the heart of culture, too, and for Freud this accounted for civilized man's and woman's psychic discontents and miseries.

Umberto Galimberti, an Italian Jungian psychoanalyst, suggests that there are other, and perhaps more important and far-reaching,

---

[1] First published in *Practicing Wholeness*.

repressions than the instinctual/sexual. Following Jung, he points to the spiritual end of the psychic spectrum:

> Actually, repression is carried out not so much on the level of instincts as, much more, on the level of meanings. Opinion is decided in such a one-sided and rigid fashion that the individual does not retain the possibility of expressing himself in a different way, one that could even perhaps be definitive. . .
>
> More than being a playground for impersonal instincts, the human being is defined by the openness to meaning, and freedom is demonstrated much more by the extent of this openness than it would be by the full deployment of the instincts. . .[2]

"Meanings" and "ideas" can be the targets of repression, not only instincts. It is a task for psychotherapy, therefore, to lift the repression on the possibilities for meaning that the patient may deploy from within the domain of consciousness.

Images, dreams, and fantasies are known to be classic subverters of the various collective orthodoxies that are built on and support the continued repression of individual meaning. It is not surprising, therefore, that collectives of all kinds seek to discount the value that might be placed upon these products of unconscious process. In the history of the religions that develop strong orthodoxy (i.e., "correct teaching and doctrine"), one sees clearly a direct attack upon such subversive suggestions from the unconscious. In the biblical tradition, the ancient prohibition on images ("Thou shalt not make unto thee any graven image, or any likeness of any thing that is in the heaven above, or that is in the earth beneath, or that is in the water under the earth" - Exodus 20:4) was extended by some religious denominations to include the representation in art of any images at all, including inner images, not to mention mythical

---

[2] U. Galimberti, "Die Analytische Psychologie in Zeitalter der Technik," p. 91. (My translation)

figures. Dreams, too, were suspect and subject to the test of "correctness. " This repression of images attempted to channel all religious notions and all fantasies and dreams pertaining to ultimate meaning into ironclad formulations (i.e., dogmas). Any dreams or images or attempts to elucidate meanings from a different angle were deemed "false" - given by "false prophets" or by "false dreams" or "false teachers. " All such were seen as leading away from the paths of truth and righteousness.

In later centuries, the rigor of this same attitude was expressed in the Inquisition. The conviction of the orthodox was that truth and the authority for guarding it resided with the Bishops and was vested in their teaching function. Their authority derived from contact with the original sources of the tradition, the Apostles, and before them from Christ himself. That meant that anyone who had a new or "original" vision, a dream or fantasy or intuition that imparted meaning and claimed truth, would be declared heretical. Eventually this rule came to define heresy. A canon was established, authority and doctrine were consolidated, and heresies were declared out of bounds.

In modern times, a similar situation developed in modern times within the scientific community regarding questions of meaning. Wolfgang Pauli, in his "The Piano Lesson," which was an active imagination presented to his analyst, Marie-Louise von Franz, as a gift, wrote about the scientific and academic police who do not allow people to speak of their "dreams" and of transcendent meaning. Such topics are excluded from discussions because they are not scientific. Knowledge and meaning have parted company in modernity, and Pauli seeks to bring them together in his active imagination. Pauli compares the scientific culture police to the Inquisitors and to the KGB.

What these large historical movements have done on a massive cultural scale, families and tribes do on a smaller scale. Within tightly knit family units, the individual's quest for personal meaning is severely held in check by the biases of the group and its rules. The same dynamic can be observed in work groups, therapy groups, and groups of all sorts. The group's attitudes become locked into a particular frame of reference, and this restricts the possibilities for exploring non-orthodox thoughts and methods. The same holds true within the various schools of psychoanalysis. These too have become orthodoxies, with creeds, rituals, and taboos.

Psychotherapy aims to gain insight into how and why the repression of the human tendency to discover and to assign personal meaning to experience (which Jung called the instinct for reflection) takes place. It asks, like Freud did about dreams, about the source of the censor within the intrapsychic matrix. This is made up of the structure of complexes that have foreclosed openness to original meaning. Psychotherapy seeks to undo this repression in order to widen the horizon of possible meaning for the individual. In order to do this, it opens the doors to imagination and dream. The goal of psychotherapy is to open consciousness to the deeper psyche and to build up a sense of meaning that grows out of the experience of the individual and is not dependent on collective approval and validation. Personal meanings will, of course, always partake of the times to an extent, but they will be based on images and dreams and fantasies that arise from the individual's own experience and are not given ready-made by external sources.

Questions of finding personal meaning in life generally or in particular life experiences such as loss, death, disappointment confront the practicing psychotherapist every day. What is the therapist's approach to such questions? Certainly it is not to help the patient to create rationalizations and to defend them. Nor can the therapist provide meaning from off a shelf or out of a bag of shopworn meanings. The therapist's theories and general life experience or religious convictions are of not much help. They will only result in hollow platitudes and in a kind of "cliche therapy." The only feasable approach is to lookinto the possibilities for meaning in the patient's own material, which is composed of images, dreams, fantasies, intuitions, and occasionally full-blown visions that appear in the course of the therapeutic experience. More useful than any knowledge the therapist may have is faith that meaning will appear from within the patient's own psyche. However, the search for meaning without access to the unconscious results in sterile ruminations, circles of obsessive thinking that lead nowhere and remain locked in to the sequence of thoughts and possibilities currently available to consciousness. The precision of a particular and satisfying answer to the question of meaning is impossible to fashion from the offerings of a mere ruminative consciousness.

The search for personal meaning quickly brings one up against the problem of repression. The form the repression takes may not be only that the products of unconscious process are excluded from consciousness. They may enter in the form of dreams or intuitions, but their value is discounted. They are considered to be mere dreams and nothing but fantasies that have little of value to offer. The endless repetitions of values and meanings by the agencies of collective life - by church, national figures, various political, educational and social networks - creates a collective attitude in the individual that adheres to the givens of consensual reality and has the power to persuade the individual that authentic meaning can be discovered only by learning and integrating the given perspectives. Cultures do indeed hold and contain important guidelines to meaning, and these can form the starting point for the individual's quest for personal meaning. But culture also turns out to be a fierce guardian of its own formations and meanings and thus contributes to the repression of personal, individual attempts at meaning.

According to Galimberti, again:

The truly repressed of our culture is not instinct, but rather tranendence, understood as an extension of meaning beyond codified meaning, which is understood as symbol and is, because of its inherent ambivalence, free from the dictatorship of signs. This is the real difference between Freud and Jung, namely the difference in the diagnosis of the identity of the repressed and a difference in therapy, which, instead of attempting the sublimation of instincts, brings into play the symbol as extension of meaning beyond codified under-standings.[3]

It is by means of symbols that an expansion of consciousness and an expression of personal meaning become possible. Symbols open to the unknown, the mysterious, the unconscious. They make truly creative thinking possible, and they suggest transcendence.

To grasp how a symbol can perform this function of releasing and sustaining meaning within consciousness, it is helpful to understand how a symbol performs the function of linking the known to the unknown or unfamiliar. It is well known that the word symbol, from the Greek *symbolon*, derives from a practice in antiquity of breaking a coin into two pieces and distributing these pieces between two contracting parties. When the two parties later came together and presented the pieces, linking up what had been previously broken in half, their contract was confirmed and recognized as valid and binding. The *symbolon* was an object that linked separated parts and validated authenticity. The one part is held in hand, hence is familiar; the other part is held in someone else's hand and is therefore unfamiliar and unknown.

A symbol, as we use the term in psychology, has a foot in two areas of the psyche and links them. Absent the symbol, they remain divided and apart, incapable of relating to each other. In the psychic realm, it is instinct (soma) and archetype (spirit) that need to be connected in order for meaningful living and "flow"[4] to take place. The archetype presents itself as a symbol that gives direction and meaning to the energy provided by instinct. Energy without image

---

[3] U. Galemberti, *op. cit.*, p. 92.
[4] A term that was made famous in psychology by M Csikszentmihalyi by his book, *Flow*, in which he discusses the experience of meaningful and creative activities.

lacks a purpose and instigates activity without a sense of meaning; images and ideas that derive from archetype without connection to the energy provided by instinct are without effect and go nowhere. When connected, they generate meaningful activity. The symbol unites them, and the result is a surplus of energy flowing in a meaningful direction toward a goal. The symbol represents the union of instinct and archetype and can be used by consciousness for guidance and direction. Here the symbol functions as a "representative" (*Vertreter*)[5] for the united pair and can kindle the energy and meaning of the combination. Religious symbols have functioned like this since time immemorial as we see in the rites and rituals of all the world's religions.

While Freud spoke mainly of one instinct (i.e., sexuality), and then later of a second (death, or agression), Jung proposed five "instinct groups": 1) nurturance, 2) sexuality, 3) activity (including "play"), 4) reflection, and 5) creativity.[6] Although one can speak of these instinct groups as drives, they are experienced by the individual as psychological impulses or instigators. By the time the instinctual impulses reach the experiencing subject (ego-consciousness), they have been linked to an archetypal pattern by a process that Jung calls psychization: "Instinct as an ectopsychic factor would play the role of a stimulus merely, while instinct as a psychic phenomenon would be an assimilation of this stimulus to a pre-existing psychic pattern. "[7] This type of mechanism that Jung calls psychization is required to link instincts as pure stimuli to pre-existing patterns, which are the images provided by the archetypal base of the psyche, and thereby to provide the basis for meaning of the actions taken.

---

[5] For a discussion of symbol as "representation," see author's essay "On Psychological Interpretation," *Collected Writings*, Vol. 2.

[6] C.G. Jung, "Psychological Factors Determining Human Behavior," *CW* 8.

[7] *Ibid.*, par. 234.

Can we say anything further about how this psychization of instinct takes place? We recognize the appearance of its positive functioning and of its misfunctioning: meaningful activity and behavior on the one hand, meaningless or random discharge of physical and mental energy on the other. But the exact nature of the mechanism that links ectopsychic stimuli (instincts) and archetypal patterns (images, concepts, thoughts) is still obscure. Bion traced it to the mother's reverie, which stimulates alpha functioning in the infant through the psychic bond created by projective identification. Projective identification is, in the first place, the means by which the nascent ego invests in the world and by which the mother responds by investing herself in the infant. This is the means by which the psyche invests reality (i.e., the object world) with personal significance.

Once the alpha function has been established in the child's psyche as an on-going psychic function, the child can create meaning intrapsychically and independently. The alpha function links, among other things, ectopsychic stimuli (such as the instincts) to the images and thoughts that can give them meaning in consciousness. This is, I believe, also what Jung meant by the term psychization but never spelled out clearly. The pre-existing psychic patterns of which Jung speaks are not memory traces, neither personal or inherited. Circles, squares, stars, gold, diamonds, heroes, wise old men and women, the child, the mother are all images of high or ultimate value that appear among many peoples at many times. They may well have a specific referent for a particular culture, mythic system, or individual, but they also refer beyond that to some vague, unspecified, transcendent, and otherwise unarticulated realm. These are images that float around in the collective unconscious seeking specific content in order to receive concrete expression and emerge into the conscious world. When a link is created between one or more of the pre-existing images and one or more of the instinct groups, meaningful conscious activity of some kind can and will ensue.

Psychotherapy is incapable of creating either the instincts or the pre-existent images. It can neither create energy nor meaning; it can only work with what is already available. Its task is to create an open mental space where archetypal images, which emerge in dreams, fantasies, images, and thoughts, can enter freely and seek links to the vaguely felt ectopsychic stimuli that impinge on the edges of the psychic realm. Therapy's "free and sheltered space," to use the fine phrase of Dora Kalff, is created and protected by therapists who are careful to provide a secure relationship and who are able to enter into a state of reverie and mutual projective processes with analysands.[8] This can occur only in the absence of collective judgment. Therapy's sheltered space brackets collective attitudes and receives and accepts whatever comes into it from the unconscious without bias or discrimination. It suspends collective and personal value judgments. It entertains the non-rational, the illogical, the unconventional, the frightening and grotesque. It allows for links between the images and fantasy figures and other mental contents on the one hand and ectopsychic stimuli (i.e., instinctual strivings and demands) on the other to form, dissolve, and reform.

The release of instinctual energy from a state of latency in the unconscious and the transfer of it over into ego-consciousness and activity depend upon its linking up with an archetypal image that can give it shape and significance. The instincts need what I call a "field of operations" in which to function and to discharge their quanta of psychic energy, and the archetypal images define these fields and provide the psychic lenses that makes recognition of suitable objects in the world possible. When instinct and archetype connect, "flow" as described by Csikszentmihalyi results. This is the experience of meaningful, satisfying activity. Its expression ranges from infants nursing to monks meditating and chanting. Human activities are meaningful when instinct and archetype are joined.

---

[8] See C.G. Jung, "The Psychology of the Transference," CW 16.

Once they are firmly united, with the result that a field of activity has been created and employed several times, a symbol appears quite spontaneously that serves as an ikon for this union. This can be a word, an image, a sound. When this symbol is evoked, it suggests the field of activity from which it is derived. The symbol then represents the union and instigates behavior that is meaningful to the individual. The symbol can be used to retrieve memory of this field of activity having been employed in the past. It can be used to communicate meanings that relate to or are derived from that field of activity. It can be "traded," like a coin, and used to exchange one thing for another, or to engage other types of related activity and meaning. Widely traded symbols link to other symbols and become fields of cultural discourse, attitude and activity.

Personal and individual symbols are more difficult to use in this way, because the field of meaningful activity in which they are grounded is often too obscure to others and the collective to see and to appreciate. These symbols become a language that may be shared with one or two intimate friends or a psychotherapist but not generally. A deep and longerm analysis will often produce this type of a limited culture. Two persons engage in the activity of analysis, and in this context they share a number of intimate experiences. Dreams, images, and fantasies are experienced by both persons within the interactional field of analysis. They may refer to the analysis itself, which is itself a product of the marriage of instinct ("reflection") and archetype (the "mother" or the "healer" or another form depending on the school of psychotherapy and on the individual psychotherapist). Thus a dream or fantasy image can become an ikon for the analysis itself. Or the image may refer to another area of life (work, family life or inner space). Through the course of analysis these ikons form a culture, a universe of discourse, that is shared by analysand and analyst and joins them together. The meaning and the form of this culture will be as unique and idiosyncratic as the two individuals involved. It is their alchemical lapis, the product of their unique interaction with one another.

Another important function of the symbol is to point beyond the concrete and literal to the transcendent. This is its function as Ikon, a link to the world of Divinity. Since the symbol has its basis in the archetypal world of the collective unconscious, it connects the conscious rendition of the symbol, which functions as a sign, to the archetypal background. This gives the living symbol its most important value as "revelation" or "display" (*Darstellung*)[9] of that diension of reality. And it is this function of the symbol tht is denied by the police of modernity, as described by Pauli in "The Piano Lesson" and written about by Galimberti in the article quote above. The free space of analysis allows for this dimension to suggest itself and to be honored as valid. It gives life its spiritual value and it gives the activities engenedered by the union of instinct and archetype their transcendent meaning. The symbol lifts the gaze of conscious-ness to the heavens and links our concrete being in the world to what Jung calls in *The Red Book* "higher meaning" ("*Übersinn*"). This is meaning grounded in the transcendent, which, while this is not grounds for metaphysical claims, gives an individual life its sense of ultimate meaning by connecting ego-consciousness to the self.

---

[9] See M. Stein, "On Psychological Interpretation," CW 2, for further discussion of *Darstellung, Vorstellung.*

Dante's *Divine Comedy*: A Journey of Transformation[1]

Prelude

Dante's *Divine Comedy* has been my constant companion for some time now. I'm finishing this essay in February 2021 at my home in Goldiwil, Switzerland where I have been sequestered during the coronavirus pandemic that has cast its shadow over much of the world for the past year. In this dark time, I've read Dante's poem in several English translations and with ever increasing wonder at the depth of psychological insight contained in it. Now more than ever I understand the immense dedication of the many distinguished scholars who have spent their entire professional lives studying this work. Once hooked by the magnificence of the *Divine Comedy,* one is never free of its power to charm and teach. Dante uniquely captures and recasts the entire known world of his time in his poem. It is a novel creation much like the biblical Lord's of the world in six days. Dante has here transformed the whole extent of classical and Christian cultures into a personal artefact with an inimitable signature. As a whole, it is beyond my comprehension, so deep and complex and all-embracing is its differentiated coverage of this world and the next.

---

[1] Originally written for a conference in Ravenna, Italy (2021) celebrating the 700th anniversary of Dante's death.

A point of meaningful coincidence at this specific time in history is that the problems Dante confronted in his world are so similar to ours. The hostile political and social divisions that afflicted Florence in his time are equally present in our contemporary world, where an unrestrained lust for power has extinguished the possibility for cooperative community life. We are as split in our politics as Florence was in the days of Guelfs and the Ghibellines 700 years ago. Where there is only power, love is absent: That was Dante's problem, and it is ours. Dante found his way to a brilliant solution for himself by taking an inner path through an imaginal world. I believe that if we carefully read his narrative we will discover suggestive ways for tackling our own dilemmas. We might even find a cause for hope. A deep reading may even instigate a psychologically transformative experience in the reader.

The *Divine Comedy* is a magnificent artistic expression of psychological and spiritual transformation as experienced within the specific context of Dante's medieval culture. His poem represents distinct stages of an individuation process in the form of a journey through three imaginal spaces called Inferno (Hell), Purgatorio (Purgatory), and Paradiso (Heaven). It is this psychological development in the narrative that I am interested in highlighting here. I am not a Dante scholar and have read this magnificent work of art only in translation. I am therefore sadly deaf to the musicality of its poetic language, even though some of it can be heard distantly in the excellent translations that are available in English. Moreover, I am acutely aware that the depth and precision of insight that this work offers are beyond my powers of description. In this sense, I feel much like Dante did when he confesses that his imaginal experiences are often beyond his ability to capture them in words. The poem takes us into feelings and shows us images that are indefinable and beyond our powers of description in language. It induces a kind of cognitive arrest.

It is for all these reasons that I must venture cautiously into an exploration of these deep waters, but I proceed with the hope that

I may catch some of the poem's most essential psychological developments in the net of the Jungian theory of individuation. Can the *Divine Comedy* teach us something significant and relevant today about the individuation process in the second half of life? And can the theory of individuation help us to understand the *Divine Comedy* more profoundly? I trust the answer to both questions will be affirmative. I would like to think of my endeavor here as a dialectical exchange between a literary work and psychological theory, each contributing something important to the discussion of individuation and each learning from the other.

Introduction

In his late work, *Mysterium Coniunctionis,* C. G. Jung describes three stages of psychological development that occur typically in the second half of life. It begins with a crisis at midlife, which shatters the previously honed persona with its finely attuned cultural attitudes and its dedicated orientation toward specific goals of social and professional achievement. Often this crisis is initiated by a dramatic loss - of a social or professional position, of a loved one, of an idealized person or a cherished belief system – after which a period of disorientation and disillusionment sets in. Jung experienced this crisis at the age of 37 following the break in relations with Sigmund Freud, and Dante experienced it at about the same age following his exile from his home in the city of Florence. Whereas Jung's individuation journey did not conclude until his death many years later at the age of 86, Dante's ended with his death at the age of 56 in Ravenna and shortly after completing *The Divine Comedy.*

What we find in Dante's masterpiece is a singular account of a strange journey through the lands of the dead that presents a remarkable story of individuation in the second half of life. It is a pilgrimage that clearly reveals increasing degrees of psychological and spiritual development as the protagonist advances. The main character in the story, i.e., the figure of the pilgrim Dante, experiences a journey of individuation, while at the same time Dante as poet transforms this process into a work of art. Like Jung crafting his Red Book over more than a decade, Dante composed *The Divine Comedy* over a similarly long period of time, from 1308 until 1321 as scholars have estimated. Although he claims that the experience he is writing about took place in only a few days while he was in Rome during Holy Week in 1300, he spent the next twenty years thinking and writing about it in order finally to create the poem as we have received it. Both Dante's exceptional psychological gift for visionary experience and his remarkable literary talent for poetic expression go into making the work of art that we know as *The Divine Comedy*.

The story is told as a recollection of an experience in the past that Dante is only later recounting in the poem. It is not impossible that the core experience he is writing about took place in a short space of time. The account of it, however, took much longer to compose. It is a brilliantly burnished jewel of a poem that displays the strictest control of form – exactly 100 Cantos equally divided into three Canticles (*Inferno*, *Purgatorio*, *Paradiso*), the first with an extra Canto that serves as the introduction, and all of it written in "the preternaturally strong Italian terza rima,"[2] a poetic form that Dante invented specifically for this work. The story contains a complex mixture of events and personalities from Dante's life and times, plus many classical Greek and Roman figures, plus biblical and religious characters, as well as images and stories offered often with shock value and surprise by his imagination. The result is one of the greatest works in all of world literature; the psychological result of the journey is what I will speak of as transformation in the course of individuation.

As a Jungian psychoanalyst, I am looking at *The Divine Comedy* not primarily as a work of art but as a record of psychological

---

[2] I borrow the phrase from Harold Bloom in *The Western Canon*, p. 82.

transformation achieved through what we today call active imagination. The poem is a record of an individuation process that begins at midlife in a state of confusion and darkness (a *nigredo* state, in the language of alchemy), then moves through a long series of imaginal confrontations with shadow figures and themes and advances by rigorous reflection and analysis to reach an *albedo* state (in alchemy known as "the whitening"). Finally, it arrives at *rubedo*, the brilliant "reddening" in the alchemical opus, which signals that alchemical "gold" has emerged from the transformed *prima materia* that was placed in the vessel at the beginning of the process. This transformation in the alchemical vessel mirrors the simultaneous psychological transformation of the alchemist, in the poem of the poet. Dante is not only writing *about* a process that he is observing; he is all the while participating *in* the process he is writing about.

These stages of alchemical transformation correspond to the phases of individuation described by Jung in the final chapter of *Mysterium Coniunctionis*, "The Conjunction," where he explicates the psychological meaning of the alchemical process as described by the alchemist Gerhard Dorn. Dorn describes three stages of alchemical union, or *coniunctio*, as: 1) the separation of soul from body (a state of *unio naturalis*) and the subsequent union of soul and spirit (a state called *"unio mentalis"*) with the body left behind and out of the picture (this is the *nigredo* phase); 2) the (re)union of *unio mentalis* with body, which marks a transformation of body (the *albedo* phase); and 3) the union of this synthesis of body, soul and spirit with *unus mundus*, a transcendent reality (the *rubedo* phase). I will argue that the pilgrim Dante as portrayed in *The Divine Comedy* achieves the state of *unio mentalis* in the the second Canticle, P*urgatorio* (stage 1). He proceeds from there with Beatrice, who leads him through the fires and waters out of Purgatory and into Heaven, where his body becomes a subtle body, which represents a union of *unio mentalis* and body in a new synthesis (stage 2). In his new body, Dante is not subject to gravity, and he casts no shadow. In Heaven, he receives spiritual instruction from various illustrious teachers and undergoes a series of strict examinations that qualify him for the final numinous visions of the Celestial Rose and the Holy Trinity. It is beyond these that an electrifying moment of transformation occurs, which creates a permanent union with *unus mundus* (stage 3). The net result of his imaginal journey is individuation in the highest degree. This is the psychological lens through which I am reading *The Divine Comedy*.

Did the man, Dante Alighieri, really have the profound transformative experiences that he describes so convincingly in his work? If so, did he have them before he wrote about them, or did he have them while he was composing the poem? As the poet tells the story, he is looking back in faltering memory to experiences that took place in Rome during and shortly after Holy Week in 1300. *The Divine Comedy* could well be based on a series of intense visionary experiences that Dante had during that brief period of time, which supplied him with the *prima materia* for the later carefully structured and intellectually worked out literary masterpiece. To the original experience, he would have added material that amplified it and gave it further body and detail. In the completed work, then, Dante would be giving an account of a core visionary episode that occurred in a short span of time, like a week, which took years of reflection and imaginative elaboration to render in the full amplitude of breadth and meaning that it implied. The final product is clearly the result of a long process of cognitive digestion, which may well be based on an overwhelming numinous experience that occurred during those spiritually charged days of Easter weekend during the Jubilee Year that had been called for by Pope Boniface VIII for 1300.

The multitude of details in poem are far too numerous to consider here. The selection of scenes and characters that I have chosen to focus on are what I see as some of the critical turning points of significance in the individuation journey depicted in the poem. I do not intend this to be primarily a psycho-biographical study of Dante's personal psychological and spiritual development, but rather to consider the poem as a deeply considered expression of a process that has archetypal sources of energy and whose movement is driven and directed ultimately by the Self. Without question, Dante's psychological development and his work as a poet were deeply intertwined, as was the case with alchemists and the transformational processes that they were attending in the laboratory. *The Divine Comedy* is a testament to psychological transformation as an archetypal process, but doubtless it is the story of Dante Alighieri's personal transformation as well.

Act 1: The Journey through Hell - *Nigredo*

In the alchemical understanding of human nature as expressed by Gerhard Dorn, there are three basic aspects: body, soul, and spirit. Initially, the soul has a strong inclination to fuse with the body, and at the conception of a human being it does so and thereafter clings to it compulsively. This is called *unio naturalis*. This union is ordained by nature. The term "body," however, also has a broader meaning in that it includes the entire phenomenal world. The soul's attachment extends beyond the physical body to the mother in the first place and later to all of material and physical existence. This includes the person's entire social, economic, professional and political life. The "body" to which the soul is attached becomes the whole horizontal dimension of life in the world. The soul becomes totally absorbed in all of this, and for a time knows of nothing else.

This is Dante's condition before his crisis at midlife and his subsequent imaginal journey through the three regions of the afterlife. His consciousness was totally immersed in his life as a physical man, as a prominent member of an important family in Florence, as a political figure in his community, and as a courtly love poet of increasingly great renown. He was intensely attached and committed to his immediate world, and his energy was engaged to full capacity in a multitude of meaningful daily activities. Body and soul, in the alchemical sense, were wed in a tight embrace. This does not mean that he did not experience some minor traumas and setbacks in love and work, but on the whole his life showed a successful progression on the levels appropriate to the first half of life.

What remains left out of this close union of body and soul, according to Dorn, is the third element, "spirit." Spirit is Logos in the high sense of the word. It connotes Truth and ultimate Meaning as opposed to social or temporal meaning. Attachment of soul to body brings a sense of meaning on the mundane and horizontal plane through being active in worldly affairs, but it does not offer meaning on the spiritual plane. The world of spirit hovers above the soul/body couple and is alien to it.

The Self in the Jungian sense of the word demands greater consciousness than is offered on the horizontal plane. Psychological identification with one's time, place, practical tasks, persona and so forth is the natural result of development in the first half of life, and this is succeeded by further stages of individuation in the second half of life. It is this further development that the alchemist Gerhard Dorn refers to as the creation of *unio mentalis*, which is a union of soul and spirit, now with body left behind. This stage of develop-ment requires, first of all, the separation of soul from body, pictured as death in alchemical imagery. This brings about the *nigredo* phase of the process, the beginning of second of half of life individuation. The movement toward *unio mentalis* is initiated when the soul's habits of investment in life are frustrated and thwarted by events on the horizontal plane – failures, illness, death of loved ones. The individuation journey begins with a rupture in the established patterns of life, which results in a plunge into a mental state of confusion and radical psychological alienation from what has been a familiar world of persona identity and activity.

The *Divine Comedy* opens dramatically precisely at this moment of crisis. The poet wakes up in a dark wood, lost, and finds his way blocked by dangerous animals. He cannot get past them in order to return to his home and the familiar surroundings where his identity has been forged and located. In the opening lines of *The Divine Comedy*, Dante retrospectively recalls this terrifying moment:

> Midway in our life's journey, I went astray
>> from the straight road and woke to find myself
>> alone in a dark wood. How shall I say
> what wood that was! I never saw so drear,
>> so rank, so arduous a wilderness!
>> Its very memory gives a shape to fear.
> Death could scarce be more bitter than that place![3]

Jung would speak, albeit somewhat reluctantly, of this critical moment in life to his young students at the Swiss Federal Institute of Technology (ETH) in Zurich, as one familiar with its psychological challenges:

> I really should not stress this turning point in front of so many young people, it does not concern them and yet perhaps it is as well that they should know it. A point exists at about the thirty-fifth year when things begin to change; it is the first moment of the shadow side of life, of the going down to death. It is clear that Dante found this point... When this turning point comes people meet it in several ways: some turn away from it, others plunge into it, and something important happens to yet others from the outside. If we do not see a thing Fate does it to us.[4]

Dante plunged into it, as did Jung when he went through the experiences depicted in his *Liber Novus*.

Fortunately for Dante, a guide appears as he grows ever more desperate: the poet Virgil emerges from the shadows. He has been sent as an emissary by Dante's archetypal anima, his soul, the beloved Beatrice, who has observed his fearful condition from afar

---

[3] Dante, *The Divine Comedy: Inferno* 1:1-6.
[4] C.G. Jung, *Modern Psychology*, p. 223.

in her place in the transcendent realm of Heaven. She begs Virgil to go to Dante's assistance in the sweet tones of a beloved:

"O gracious Mantuan whose melodies
    live in earth's memory and shall live on
    till the last motion ceases in the skies,
my dearest friend, and fortune's foe, has strayed
    onto a friendless shore and stands beset
    by such distresses that he turns afraid
from the True Way, and news of him in Heaven
    rumors my dread he is already lost.
    I come, afraid that I am too-late risen."
Fly to him and with your high counsel, pity,
    and with whatever need be fore his good
    and soul's salvation, help him, and solace me.
It is I, Beatrice, who send you to him.
    I come from the blessed height for which I yearn.
    Love called me here.[5]

The intervention by Beatrice and the guidance of Virgil will prove decisive in Dante's journey. Without their help, Dante would have been consumed spiritually in a hopeless standoff with powerful instinctual forces that block his progress: three threatening beasts who block his way to the summit. One is a lion, a symbol of pride, presumably Dante's own and also that of his opponents in Florence; the second is a leopard, a symbol of lust and hopeless attachment to the pleasures of the flesh, to which Dante was especially prone; and the worst of all is an insatiably hungry she-wolf sent from Hell by Envy, a symbol of avarice. The she-wolf is never satiated, and in fact she becomes hungrier the more she eats.

Dante is helpless and knows of no way to get past these primitive forces in his nature, which would keep his soul locked in place and hopelessly entangled in futile conflicts within himself and with others interminably. He is baffled on how to proceed in life, but

---

[5] Dante, *Inferno* 2:58-72.

Virgil makes a suggestion: "He must go by another way who would escape/ this wilderness."[6] This other road will lead to a descent into the darkest shadows of the underworld and from there ascend to realms of transcendence beyond the limits of rational knowledge. This is what we would today call an individuation journey of psychological transformation through the realms of the unconscious to the Self.

Virgil will guide him onto path that will take them into and through the underworld. This descent follows the classical pattern of the hero's journey as described in Homer's *Odyssey* and Virgil's *Aeneid*. It is also the path into the unconscious that Jung writes of in *Liber Novus*.

At the outset, Virgil gives Dante a preparatory description of the journey ahead. First, he tells him, they will pass through the shadow world of Hell where he will "see the ancient spirits tried/in endless pain, and hear their lamentation/as each bemoans the second death of souls."[7] The people in Hell are there forever and their torment is eternal. They wait without hope for the "second death," which will take place on the Day of Judgment. From Hell, the poets will make their way to Purgatory, where he will "see upon a burning mountain/souls in fire and yet content in fire,/knowing that whensoever it may be/they yet will mount to the blessed choir."[8] This journey through the realms of shadow where souls are forever locked in place (Hell) and where other souls who are undergoing purification (Purgatory) will bring them to the entrance of Heaven where "a worthier spirit shall be sent to guide you,"[9] says Virgil, namely Beatrice, the transcendent anima.

In the journey through Hell, Dante discovers what happens when individuation is rejected as an option in life. The scenes show

---

[6] Dante, *Inferno* 1: 89-90.
[7] *Ibid.*, I: 108-110.
[8] *Ibid.*, I: 111-114.
[9] *Ibid.*, I: 116.

the consequences of compulsive and unrepentant (unreflected) attachment of soul to body. These are people who in life refuse to let go of the objects of their wanton passions, or even to attempt to free themselves from the force of their desires. They represent the psyche that resists the development from *unio naturalis* to *unio mentalis*. Dante frequently feels sympathy for them. Who wouldn't? Isn't it natural to refuse the invitation to greater consciousness? This is the lamentable human condition, as everyone knows. Dante is also horrified at what he sees. Were it not for Beatrice and Virgil, he might well be stuck here too, forever blocked by pride and lust and devoured by the she-wolf of avarice.

It must be acknowledged that the separation of soul from body is emotionally wrenching, an *opus contra naturam*, as Jung writes about it when he describes the challenges facing the person who attempts it:

> Since the soul animates the body... she tends to favour the body and everything bodily, sensuous, and emotional. She lies caught in "the chains" of Physis, and she desires "beyond physical necessity." ... the separation means withdrawing the soul and her projections from the bodily sphere and from all environmental conditions relating to the body... the disciple will have every opportunity to discover the dark side of his personality, his inferior wishes and motives, childish fantasies and resentments... in short, all those traits he habitually hides from himself. He will be confronted with his shadow... He will learn to know his soul, that is, his anima and Shakti who conjures up a delusory world for him.[10]

Separation of the soul from the body precedes a later union and is the precondition of further individuation. This is a tall order, and as humans we are naturally lazy and prefer to retain our habits of feeling and acting.

---

[10] C.G. Jung, *Mysterium Coniunctionis*, para. 673.

Among the most poignant scenes that Dante encounters as he travels through this dark world occurs in the Second Circle of Hell where he comes upon the adulterous lovers, Francesca and Paolo. Francesca is a sympathetic image of the soul's passionate attachment to the object of her desire. She reminds Dante of his own sensuality and love of life the body. In sharp contrast to Beatrice who also died young and was taken directly to the highest realm of Heaven, Francesca is consigned forever to the dark chambers of Hell because she refused to separate from her lover, the brother of her husband. Even in Hell she retains the image of a beautiful young woman, and she shows no remorse for her adulterous love for Paolo, laying the blame for the affair on romantic poets. Love seized Paulo first, she says, and she responded powerfully: "Love, which permits no loved one not to love,/took me so strongly with delight in him/that we are one in Hell, as we were above."[11] Sensual love is a folly hard for Dante to condemn. In much of his previous poetry, he too had sung the praises of courtly love, which celebrated precisely this type of amour. Francesca tells him in graphic detail the touching story of how it happened that she and Paulo became lovers while reading a poetic account of Lancelot's guilty love for Guinevere, and then she cries out: "That book, and he who wrote it, was a pander."[12] Meanwhile Dante hears Paulo quietly weeping nearby and is overcome with emotion: "I felt my senses reel/and faint away with anguish. I was swept/by such a swoon as death is, and I fell,/as a corpse might fall, to the dead floor of Hell."[13] Dante is overcome both by guilt for himself being such a pander and by feverish identification with the passion of the lovers.

After this it is hard for Dante to move on, yet he does so, albeit with obvious anguish. His steady guide, Virgil, who is traditionally taken to represent reason, presses him to continue the journey. The

---

[11] Dante, *Inferno* V: 100-103.
[12] Ibid., V: 134.
[13] *Ibid.*, V: 137-140.

transformation from *unio naturalis* to *unio mentalis* is assisted by, in Jung's words,"... the help of the spirit, by which are meant all the higher mental faculties such as reason, insight, and moral discrimination."[14] This is Virgil. And, beyond that, Virgil will lead Dante to figures who represent "...a 'window into eternity' and... convey to the soul a certain 'divine influx' and the knowledge of higher things,"[15] as we shall see in the figures of Beatrice and St. Bernard in the third Canticle, *Paradiso*.

I am reluctant to draw a parallel to psychoanalytic work, but the temptation is great to observe that Virgil functions much like an analyst who accompanies a client through retrospective shadow realizations. In studying *The Divine Comedy,* I have been fascinated by the figure of Virgil. As an analyst, I feel a sense of kinship with the part he plays in serving Dante as a witness, a guide, and a voice of encouragement when the anguish of guilt and shame mount like the furies Dante feels all about him as he passes through the awesome gate into Hell:

> Here sighs and cries and wails coiled and recoiled
>> on the starless air, spilling my soul to tears.
> A confusion of tongues and monstrous accents toiled
> In pain and anger. Voices hoarse and shrill
>> and sounds of blows, all intermingled, raised
>> tumult and pandemonium that still
> whirls on the air forever dirty with it
>> As if a whirlwind sucked at sand.[16]

This resembles moments in analysis when the prospect of encountering shadow material in its full reality is more than a little frightening, and the reassurance of the analyst, who knows this territory, has a soothing effect that allows the journey to go on. Similarly, Virgil explains the source of the voices crying out and urges

---

[14] C.G. Jung, *op. cit.*, par. 673.
[15] Ibid.
[16] Dante, *op. cit.*, III: 22-29.

Dante to continue on the way through Hell and then into and through Purgatory. It is a long and necessary journey through all the shades of shadow realization that precedes the eventual crossing over into the next stage of transformation.

Why is this necessary? Why can't Virgil just find an easy way to bypass all this misery, to take Dante straight up to Heaven, and once there to turn him over to Beatrice for a pleasant flight into his beatitude? The truth is that there are no shortcuts to individuation. In the now many years of working as a Jungian psychoanalyst, I have occasionally seen the unhappy consequences of this attempted leap over the shadow into what was claimed to be "liberation" or "enlightenment" or "true self" and "higher consciousness." It is an aged person's sad story. The denial and avoidance of shadow does not eliminate it. Looking away from the problems presented by a threatening confrontation with the shadow looks like an easy solution in the short distance, but the person will later arrive right back at the starting point of the journey. In fact, time may run out and they will remain stuck in the shadowland of hopeless suffering and despair, like the souls Dante observes in the circles of Hell. The separation of soul and body must be faced and worked through - deeply, painfully, patiently - in order to prepare the soul for its union with spirit in *unio mentalis*. That is the work shown to the poet and his guide in *Purgatorio*.

Act 2: The Journey through Purgatory - *Albedo*

In the alchemist Dorn's depiction of the achievement of *unio mentalis*, there is first an imperative to separate soul from body, which is followed by the union of soul and spirit. The first is a moral achievement; the second is a commitment. In Dante's *Divine Comedy*, the first step takes place by observing carefully the shadow figures in Hell and registering their suffering and the reasons for their placement there. They show the consequences of keeping the soul attached to the body to the very end of life. This leg of the journey is followed by the passage through Purgatory, where Dante witnesses and himself experiences the process of separation of soul from body, step by step.

The exit from the shadow realm of Hell requires facing ultimately what Jung named "absolute evil."[17] This confrontation is depicted in the descent to its frozen bottom where a three-headed Satan, the shadow of the Holy Trinity whom Dante will encounter in Heaven, is sealed solidly in ice. It means looking absolute evil in the face, which is, as Jung writes in his late work, *Aion*, "a shattering experience" (*"erschütterende Erfahrung"*).[18] When Virgil shows Dante the figure of Satan and tells him, "Now see the face of Diss! This is the place/where you must arm your soul against all dread," Dante stammers: "Do not ask, Reader, how my blood ran cold/and my voice choked up with fear. I cannot write it."[19] Some commentators have speculated that Dante nearly went mad at this stage. Virgil, the steady guide and emissary of the divine Beatrice, takes Dante close to himself and slips down the frigid body of the "Emperor of the Universe of Pain" whose "upper chest [jutted] above the ice."[20] When they reach the level of Satan's thighs, their direction suddenly reverses and the way down becomes the way upward. This rather dizzying turn at first disorients Dante, for now suddenly they are ascending and making their way upward through a narrow passage where they find themselves at the top of the world. Hell is now forever beneath them, and the rest of the journey is an ascent into the light. We now enter the stage of the alchemical *albedo*.

Until now Dante has been a mostly passive witness of the shadow figures who are locked in place forever in Hell. He engages in conversations with the damned, but he is not required to take a

---

[17] Jung, *Aion*, para. 19.
[18] *Ibid.*
[19] Dante, *Inferno* XXXIV 20-23.
[20] *Ibid.*, XXXIV: 31.

more active part in the journey. Entry into Purgatory, however, calls for his participation, for active commitment with consequence. At the entrance to Purgatory, they meet Cato, the archetype of the moral hero from Roman times, who instructs them on how to proceed. After that, they come upon three large, colored steps at the gate to Purgatory, which call for heartfelt contrition (white), confession (black), and ardor for good works (red).

Unlike Hell, which is static, Purgatory is dedicated to change. As in Hell, there is suffering, but here there is the promise of advancing from level to level, culminating in access to Heaven. The shadow traits that must be confronted in Purgatory are represented by figures who are being slowly and meticulously transformed. Whereas the passage through Hell showed Dante the consequences of soul clinging compulsively to body, the journey through Purgatory becomes a master class in shadow confrontation and separation of soul from body. And Dante actively participates in this class.

In the ante-chamber to Purgatory, they find the lesser sinners: The Excommunicate, The Lethargic, The Unabsolved, and Negligent Rulers. In Purgatory proper, they find seven levels of more serious but still hopeful sinners: The Proud, The Envious, The Wrathful, The Slothful, The Avaricious, The Gluttonous, and The Lascivious. Each type of moral turpitude must be transformed through the purgatorial process and replaced by the corresponding virtues: humility, mercy, peace, solicitude, generosity, abstinence, and chastity. Each of these successive processes calls for an additional degree of separation of soul from body and a deeper union of soul with spirit, thus moving the individual along toward *unio mentalis*. In diagnostic terms, this involves transformation of shadow aspects and features of character disorders such as pathological narcissism and borderline tendencies. This is a statement of an ideal outcome. As anyone who has been in long-term analysis knows, this process of encounter with the shadow is an ongoing work and takes immense stamina and commitment. The ego's self-protective defenses resist violently. Purgatory is a place of salutary and meaningful suffering, unlike the suffering that we see in *Inferno*.

As the angel of God who stands on the red stair at the top of the staircase makes ready to allow the poets entry to Purgatory, Dante is surprised: "Seven *P's*, the seven scars of sin/his sword point cut into my brow. He said: 'Scrub off these wounds when you have passed within. '"[21] These marks will be expunged as he ascends through the levels of Purgatory, and their removal will serve as certification that he has achieved the corresponding virtues. This will be evidence that he has achieved a high level of *unio mentalis*. Dante is now fully engaged in the process of transformation.

Accompanied by Virgil, Dante climbs successively through all seven levels of Purgatory. Along the way, he speaks at each circle with one or more of the souls located there who are being slowly and painfully purged of their sins. For them, it takes incredibly long periods of time – years or centuries. For Dante, it moves much more quickly. As the wounds on his forehead are washed away one by one, he can advance. The treatment is swift and effective in Dante's case. He seems to get the message at each level and thus finds himself released from the attachment that would hold him there.

Finally, Heaven is practically in sight, and the two pilgrims hear the angels singing in the near distance. But before Dante can pass over into that ultimate destination, he must undergo the test by fire. An angel announces: '"Blessed ones, till by flame purified/no soul may pass this point. Enter the fire/and heed the singing from the other side.'"[22] Dante shivers with dread and is understandably reluctant to go forward as he vividly remembers a scene he had once witnessed of burned bodies. But Virgil reassures him ('"Within that flame/there may be torment, but there is no death'"[23]), so hesitantly he finally steps into the flames:

---

[21] Dante, *Purgatorio*, IX: 112-114.
[22] *Ibid.,* XXVII 10-12.
[23] *Ibid.,* XXVII: 20-21.

"Once in the flame, I gladly would have cast
my body into boiling glass to cool it
against the measureless fury of the blast.
My gentle father, ever kind and wise,
strengthened me in my dread with talk of Beatrice,
saying: 'I seem already to see her eyes.'"[24]

The ordeal in the refiner's fire is the final stage in the forging of *unio mentalis* as a stable state of consciousness. It is a critical moment in the process of transformation. The alchemists would have called this operation *calcinatio*, the treatment by fire that burns away the metal's dross and impurities.

Following this point, Virgil will take his leave:

"Expect no more of me in word or deed:
here your will is upright, free, and whole,
and you would be in error not to heed
whatever your own impulse prompts you to:
Lord of yourself I crown and mitre you."[25]

Virgil's leave-taking from the pilgrim Dante is for me one of the most touching scenes in *The Divine Comedy*. It is a moving blessing given by the archetypal father poet to the younger. Dante has now arrived at a stage of development that frees him from the need for Virgil's further guidance. He is now free and on his own. No longer confused as he was when Virgil first approached him in the dark wood, he can now fully trust himself and his impulses. The union of soul and spirit has been accomplished, and Dante is now prepared to take the step into the final leg of his journey to fulfillment.

Act 3: The Journey through Heaven - *Rubedo*

When Dante leaves the realm of unresolved shadow as depicted in the *Inferno*, he enters into Purgatory, where light again prevails as

---

[24] *Ibid.*, XXVII 49-54.
[25] *Ibid.*, XXVII 139-143.

it does at dawn. Whereas Hell represents the psychological state of resistance to becoming conscious, Purgatory is equivalent to *albedo* in the alchemical process, a realm of increasing movement toward consciousness and transformation. As Dante is about to leave Purgatory, he is met by the transcendent anima figure of Beatrice. The anima's role is to link ego-consciousness to the Self. She has performed this role so far through her emessary, Virgil, and now she will take Dante into Heaven. This is the *rubedo* stage in the alchemical transformation process. where base materials (*prima materia*) transform into alchemical gold.

Who is Beatrice? Dante's Beatrice was a young girl in Florence whom he fell in love with when he was nine years old, and after that he saw her only occasionally and mourned her death when she passed away in her 20's. From the first moment she was a symbol of his anima. How and why she was taken up to Heaven straightaway upon her death and installed among the highest saints in the Mystic Rose in close proximity to the Virgin Mary herself is unexplained and a mystery. This elevation is a unique creation of the Dante's imagination. Harold Bloom writes of Dante's bold creation in his inimitable fashion: "Nothing else in Western literature... is as sublimely outrageous as Dante's exaltation of Beatrice, sublimated from being an image of desire to angelic status. . ."[26] Sublimation (*sublimatio*) is a familiar process in alchemy, referring to the transformation: of base materials (*prima materia*) to the *lapis philosophorum*, alchemical "gold." This is what has happened to the human figure of Beatrice. She has become an exalted symbolic representation of the anima archetype. On the base level, the anima is a spinner of illusions through the psychological mechanism of projection, but at another stage of development she is the go-between the ego and the self. This is the anima as we see her in the figure of Beatrice in *Paradiso*. For Bloom, a literary critic, this transformation is "sublimely outrageous," but for a Jungian

---

[26] H. Bloom, *The Western Canon*, p. 72.

psychoanalyst it is not so strange. Beatrice, once human, has in death become archetypal, and now in the inner world of the psyche she takes the form of a subtle body and inhabits the realm of symbolic reality. As anima in this sense, Beatrice now becomes Dante's guide and will take him over the threshold to the center of the Self, which is represented in *The Divine Comedy* as the Godhead.

In order to join Beatrice in her transcendent world, the pilgrim Dante must himself undergo a process of sublimation and also become a subtle body. This occurs toward the end of *Purgatorio* when he is immersed in the river Lethe, which purges him of his past, and then drinks deeply of the waters of the river Eunoë, which restores him to his original primal essence. Here Dante achieves full *unio mentalis*: his body, which until now has cast a shadow, changes into a subtle body that is transparent and is no longer subject to gravity. His soul is now united with the spirit, and this unity is represented in a new transfigured body. When soul commits absolutely to spirit, consciousness is transformed. It participates in life as a subtle body and participates in a "fifth dimension," as it is sometimes called by contemporary philosophers of religion.[27] The celestial figures Dante encounters in *Paradiso* are quite different from the physically vivid figures portrayed in *Inferno* and *Purgatorio*. They are visible but more ephemeral. Jung quotes the alchemist Dorn concerning this transformation of the body:

> At length the body is compelled to resign itself to, and obey, the union of the two that are united [soul and spirit]. That is the wondrous transformation of the Philosophers, of body into spirit, and of the latter into body, of which there has been left to us by the sages the saying, Make the fixed volatile and the volatile fixed, and in this you have our Magistery. Understand this after the following manner: Make the unyielding body tractable, so that by the excellence of the spirit coming together with

---

[27] J. Hick, *The Fifth Dimension: An Exploration of the Spiritual Realm.*

the soul it becomes a most stable body ready to endure all trials. For gold is tried in the fire.[28]

Dante still has some trials ahead of him.

Although Beatrice is a symbol of Eros in the highest sense of the meaning of Love, she speaks surprisingly in the exalted language of Logos as she instructs Dante and shows him the sublime architecture of the universe. At this stage of the journey, the poet Dante goes beyond memory and poetic mastery (as expressed by the presence of Virgil) and employs visionary imagination that reveals the primal forms and structures of Being, in short, the foundations of the collective psyche. This is the world of archetype, entry into which is assisted, as Jung writes, by "... the spirit [which] is also a 'window into eternity' and... conveys to the soul a certain 'divine influx' and the knowledge of higher things..."[29] This visionary state of mind is mediated by Beatrice. Dante's imagination here is of the type that Henry Corbin describes in the writings of Sufi mystic, Ibn 'Arabi. Corbin argues that this type of imagination reveals, objectively, the invisible spiritual world:

This manifestation [of God] is neither perceptible nor verifiable by the sensory faculties; discursive reason rejects it. It is perceptible only by the Active Imagination ... at times when it dominates man's sense perceptions, in dreams or better still in the waking state.... The "place" of this encounter is not outside the Creator-Creature totality, but is the area within it which corresponds specifically to the Active Imagination, in the manner of a bridge joining the two banks of a river. The crossing itself is essentially ... a method of understanding which transmutes sensory data and rational concepts into symbols by making them effect this crossing.[30]

---

[28] Quoted by C.G. Jung, *Mysterium Coniunctionis*, par. 685.

[29] C.G. Jung, *Mysterium Coniunctionis*, par. 673.

[30] H. Corbin, *Alone with the Alone*, pp. 188-89.

In *Paradiso*, Dante engages this type of Active Imagination, which goes beyond metaphor, transgresses the limits of conscious mental capacities, and "shows" (*darstellen* = to represent, to display, to reveal) an ultimate mystery. Jung writes in this mode about the numinous visions he experienced while recovering from illness in his later years:

I would never have imagined that any such experience was possible. It was not a product of imagination. The visions and experiences were utterly real; there was nothing subjective about them; they all had a quality of absolute objectivity...

The objectivity which I experienced in ... the visions is part of a completed individuation. It signifies detachment from valuations and from what we call emotional ties.[31]

What Dante describes in *Paradiso* is a revelation of the subtle structure of the cosmos and its fundamental energic organization. Beatrice's lectures are geometric and have a degree of mathematical clarity and exactness. They resemble a university course in astronomy or physics, but they are delivered with a profound feeling of soulfulness, of love. In this, she symbolizes the sublime reality of *unio mentalis*, the union of soul and spirit, Eros and Logos, within the feminine form of a subtle body. Dante speaks of becoming "trans-human" ("*Transumanar*")[32] in this realm. In a sense, he and Beatrice are bodiless, but more precisely they occupy an imaginal or subtle body, for they still have distinct form. They are figures of Active Imagination in Henry Corbin's sense of the term.

The Cantos of *Paradiso* that lead up to the final supreme revelation describe in careful order the various realms of all creation. There is an ascent from a space named Earthly Paradise through the circles of planets and stars and on to the exalted

---

[31] C.G. Jung, *Memories, Dreams, Reflections*, pp. 295-96.
[32] Dante, *Paradiso*. I: 70.

Empyrean. Once there, Beatrice shows Dante the wondrous Mystic Rose, crowned by the Virgin Mary and in which Beatrice holds a prominent rank. Suddenly Beatrice vanishes and Dante has a new guide, the famous medieval mystic and devotee of the Virgin Mary, St. Bernard. It remains now only to experience the ultimate vision of the Godhead. Dante's educational lessons in *Paradiso*, as delivered by Beatrice, the Apostles, and St. Bernard are all aimed at preparing him for this *ne plus ultra*, which is described in the 100th and final Canto of *The Divine Comedy*. This is the scene in which the third stage of the *mysterium coniunctionis* as outlined by Gerard Dorn and expounded by Jung is accomplished: the union of the body transformed by *unio mentalis* with the *unus mundus*. In Jung's view, "this would consist, psychologically speaking, in a synthesis of the conscious with the unconscious."[33]

Initially, St. Bernard signals to Dante that he should follow "the aura/of the high lamp which in Itself is true."[34] As the poet turns there and gazes steadily into that light, he has a glimpse of total Unity (the Self, in Jung's terminology):

I see within Its depth how It conceives
all things in a single volume bound by Love,
of which the universe is the scattered leaves;
substance, accident, and their relation
so fused that all I say could do no more
than yield a glimpse of that bright revelation.
I think I saw the universal form
that binds these things, for as I speak these words
I feel my joy swell and my spirits warm.[35]

It is a vision of totality that takes in at once all of history and its energic essence of love. As Dante gazes steadily into the light, some details emerge:

---

[33] C.G. Jung, *Mysterium Coniunctionis*, par. 770.
[34] Dante, Paradiso, XXXIII 53-54.
[35] Ibid., XXXIII 85-93.

> Within the depthless deep and clear existence
>> of that abyss of light three circles shone –
>> three in color, one in circumference:
> the second from the first, rainbow from rainbow;
>> the third, an exhalation of pure fire
>> equally breathed forth by the other two.[36]

This vision of three circling spheres then further differentiates, and Dante sees a human form vaguely represented in one of them. As he gazes into this mystery, he hits the limit of his capacities and confesses: "...but mine were not the wings for such a flight," and then suddenly "the truth I wished for came/cleaving my mind in a great flash of light."[37] This sudden flash of visionary insight marks the final and supreme point of Dante's spiritual and psychological transformation - union with the *unus mundus*. The result is expressed in simple words because it exceeds the sublime language that even a master poet can inscribe in verse:

> Here my powers rest from their high fantasy,
>> but already I could feel my being turned –
>> instinct and intellect balanced equally
> as in a wheel whose motion nothing jars –
> by the Love that moves the Sun and the other stars.[38]

The poet cannot describe what he saw in this vision. It is beyond his imagination and verbal capacities. My impression is that he gazed into the very bottom of the collective unconscious, into the Self, where All is made One. But even more importantly, he experiences union with the Self and becomes invested with Love, its fundamental energy. Individuation has here reached its ultimate goal and is now complete to the extent that this is humanly possible.

---

[36] *Ibid.*, XXXIII 115-120.
[37] *Ibid.*, XXXIII 139-141.
[38] *Ibid.*, XXXIII 142-146.

Dante died on "the night of September 13 (1321), having just finished the final cantos of the Paradiso."[39] "Legend tells us that Dante was pointed out in the streets as the man who had somehow returned from a voyage to Hell, as though he were a kind of shaman."[40] One may add that in his poetic account of the journey through Hell, Purgatory and Heaven, Dante shows the readers of his poem just how far the process of individuation can extend. It begins in loss, confusion and fear; then passes through penitence, reflection and transformation; and finally attains the highest reaches of spiritual and psychological integration. This would make of Dante a true prophet and in the style of a master poet.

Postlude

The outcome of the three-stage process of transformation as described by Dorn and interpreted by Jung is a transformed personality, as the *Divine Comedy* so movingly depicts. As psychotherapists, we might wonder, given our experience in working with clients who are in the process of individuation, to what extent is this a real possibility? Or is this a fantasy – granted, on a high level, but fiction nevertheless? Does numinous experience in Active Imagination such as we find described in the *Divine Comedy* make a real difference in how people ultimately feel about life and themselves, in how they behave toward others, in how they formulate the meaning of life in the final analysis? Does the effect last or is it only a momentary highpoint?

We do not know much about how the imaginal journey through the underworld and the afterlife (i.e., the unconscious) changed Dante Alighieri, the man. Did he become what he claims for the pilgrim in the poem? From my experience as Jungian psychoanalysts, I can testify that deep engagement with dreams and active imagination over a period of time does make a lasting impact

---

[39] T. Bergin, *Dante*, p. 44.
[40] H. Bloom, *The Western Canon*, p. 83.

on the lives of our clients. We also know that this process in analysis does not entirely remove the effects of early traumas and the consequent complexes, although it does assist a person in outgrowing them and relativizing their effects on consciousness. The creation of an ego-self axis on the inner level shifts the locus of control from persona concerns about prestige and power to a type of selfhood that brings with it a considerable degree of loving acceptance of self and others. And beyond that, there are inner experiences that give one a perspective on life that frames personal experience in a more objective concept. In some cases, this makes the difference between choosing life over death. This would testify to the veracity of Dante's claim that one's being can be brought into harmony with the "Love that moves the sun and the other stars."

I prefer to understand the journey as described in *The Divine Comedy* in its totality – *Inferno, Purgatorio* and *Paradiso* – as a mandala that describes human wholeness. There are parts of the personality that are forever frozen in place and will never change (the figures depicted in *The Inferno*). These are intransigent complexes that continue to exist even in advanced stages of individuation. There are other parts that can be transformed like the figures in *The Purgatorio*. These are amenable to change and are capable of undergoing transformation. And there are numinous parts of the Self in the archetypal realm of the psyche that are glimpsed from time to time in dreams and visionary experiences. These are the figures depicted in the exalted realm of Heaven, in The *Paradiso*. Ego consciousness can locate itself principally in any of these realms, and may travel through all of them many times in the course of a long individuation process. It is possible that in later life, if a state of wisdom is achieved as described in Dante's poem, the predominant position will be fixed more or less steadily by the achievement of a union with *unus mundus,* and love and generosity will predominate in the conscious attitude.

In a conversation with the Zen Master Shin'ichi Hisamatsu, Jung, who was then in his mid-80's, was asked a sharp question after they had spent a good deal of time comparing the goal of Zen

Buddhism, i.e., liberation from all suffering, with the goal of analysis, i.e., psychological wholeness. They had agreed that freeing a person from the suffering caused by the complexes, personal and cultural, and even from archetypal influences, was a common goal. The conversation then comes to a climax with this exchange:

> **SH**: From what you have said about the collective un-conscious, might I infer that one can be liberated from it?
>
> **CGJ**: Yes! [41]

This produced a gasp of surprise among the people present. It was an astonishing response, given Jung's usually more modest estimations of human potential for individuation. What makes this important for our present reflection is that it suggests Jung's agreement that transformation of the type Dante describes in the *Divine Comedy* is psychologically possible, even if only for a moment. One can step out of personal history with its accumulation of complexes and cultural conditioning (by bathing in the river Lethe), attain to a transformed sense of self (by drinking the waters of Eunoë), and even go beyond the most sublime archetypal images imaginable (Beatrice, the Mystic Rose, the Holy Trinity) and be struck suddenly by lightning (the satori experience in Zen Buddhism, the ultimate numinous experience in *The Divine Comedy*), which transforms consciousness to such a profound degree that only the transcendent Self (God) and its Energy (Love) rule over it. This is a tall order, but no doubt other mystical traditions such as Cabbala, Sufism, and Kundalini Yoga would concur.

Even if not often seen in the outcomes of the individuation processes unleashed and fostered by Jungian psychoanalysis, the vision offered in Dante's poem can serve as an inspirational image for the goal of individuation.

---

[41] Muramoto, S. (tran.) (1998). "The Jung-Hisamatsu Conversation." p. 46.

References

Adler, G. and Jaffé, A. (1973-75). *Letters*, 2 vols. Princeton, NJ: Princeton University Press.

Apuleius. (1995). *The Golden Ass*. Oxford: Oxford University Press.

Beebe, J. (1992). *Integrity in Depth*. College Station, TX: Texas A&M University Press.

Benjamin, J. (1995). *Like Subjects, Love Objects*. New Haven, CT: Yale University Press.

Bergin, T. G. (1965). *Dante*. Westport, CT: Greenwood Press.

_____. (1971). *Dante's Divine Comedy*. Englewood Cliffs, NJ: Prentice-Hall.

Bion, W. R. (1977). *Learning from Experience*. In *Seven Servants*, New York: Jason Aronson.

Bloom, H. (1995). The Western Canon. New York: Riverhead Books.

_____. (2000). *How to Read and Why*. New York, Simon & Shuster.

Bollas, C. (1987). *The Shadow of the Object*. New York: Columbia University Press.

Bonafoux, P. (1990). *Rembrandt: Master of the Portrait*. New York: Harry N. Abrams.

Brown, N.O. (1966). *Love's Body*. New York: Vintage Books.

Carotenuto, A. (1983). *Secret Symmetry: Sabina Spielrein Between Freud and Jung*. New York: Pantheon.

_____. (1986). *Tagebuch einer heimlichen Symmetrie: Sabina Spielrein zwischen Jung und Freud*. Freiburg im Breisgau, Germany: Kore.

Chapman, H. P. (1990). *Rembrandt's Self-Portraits.* Princeton, NJ: Princeton University Press.

Chevalier, J. and Gheerbrant, A. (1994). *A Dictionary of Symbols*. Oxford: Blackwell Publisher, 1994·

Corbin, H. (1969). *Alone with the Alone: Creative Imagination in the Sūfism of Ibn 'Arabi*. Princeton, NJ: Princeton University Press.

Cornford, F. M. (1950). *The Unwritten Philosophy and Other Essays*. Cambridge: Cambridge University Press.

Csikszentmihalyi, M. (1990). *Flow*. New York: Harper & Row.

Dante Alighieri. (2003). *The Divine Comedy*. Translated by John Chiardi. New American Library.

Dallett, J. (1988). *The Not Yet Transformed God*. York Beach, ME: Nicolas-Hayes.

Edinger, E. (1992). *Transformation of the God Image: An Elucidation of Jung's Answer to Job*. Toronto: Inner City Books.

_____. (1996). *The New God Image*. Wilmette, IL: Chiron Publications.

Erikson, E. (1968). *Identity: Youth and Crisis*. New York: W. W. Norton.

_____. (1998). *The Life Cycle Completed*. New York: WW Norton.

Fordham, M. (1978). *Jungian Psychotherapy*. New York: John Wiley & Sons.

_____. (1985). *Explorations into the Self.* London: Academic Press.

Freedman, R. (1996). *Life of a Poet: Rainer Maria Rilke.* New York: Farrar, Straus and Giroux.

Freud, S. (1927/1964). *The Future of an Illusion.* New York: Anchor Books.

Galimberti, U. (1989). "Die Analytische Psychologie in Zeitalter der Technik." *Zeitschrift fur analytische Psychologie und ihre Grenzgebiete* 20.

Gill, M. (1994). *Psychoanalysis in Transition.* Hillsdale, N.J.: Analytic Press.

Guggenbtihl-Craig, A. (1975). *Marriage: Dead or Alive.* Dallas, TX: Spring Publications.

Harnack, A. (1961). *History of Dogma.* New York: Dover Publications.

Hayman, Ronald. (1982). *Kafka.* New York: Oxford University Press.

Hick, J. (1999). *The Fifth Dimension: An Exploration of the Spiritual Realm.* Oxford: Oneworld.

Holland, W. J. (1949). *The Butterfly Book.* Garden City, NY: Doubleday.

James, W. (1902). *The Varieties of Religious Experience.* New York: Longmans, Green, and Co.

Jung, C.G. (1953-1983). *Collected Works,* ed. Sir H. Read, M. Fordham, G. Adler, and W. McGuire, 20 vols, Princeton, NJ: Princeton University Press.

_____. (1896-1898/1983). *The Zofingia Lectures.* In *Collected Works,* Supplementary vol. A.

_____. (1909/1949/1961). "The Significance of the Father in the Destiny of the Individual." In *Collected Works,* vol. 4.

_____. (1912). *Wandlungen und Symbole der Libido.* Leipzig and Vienna: Franz Deuticke.

_____. (1912/1961). "The Theory of Psychoanalysis." In *Collected Works*, vol. 4.

_____. (1916/1991). *Psychology of the Unconscious.* Princeton, NJ.: Princeton University Press.

_____. (1925/1989). *Analytical Psychology. Notes of the Seminar Given in 1925.* Princeton, N.J.: Princeton University Press.

_____. (1925/1931/1964). "Marriage as a Psychological Relationship." In *Collected Works,* vol. 17.

_____. (1928/1967). "Commentary on *The Secret of the Golden Flower.*" In *Collected Works,* vol. 13.

_____. (1928-1930/1984). *Dream Analysis.* Notes of the Seminar. Princeton: Princeton University Press.

_____. (1931/1966). "Problems of Modern Psychotherapy." In *Collected Works,* vol. 16.

_____. (1932/1934/1966). "Picasso." In *Collected Works,* vol. 15.

_____. (1933/2005). *Modern Man in Search of a Soul.* London and New York: Routledge.

_____. (1935/1958). *Modern Psychology.* Lectures given at the ETH Zurich, edited by Barbara Hannah. Privately published.

_____. (1936/1937/1960). "Psychological Factors Determining Human Behavior." In *Collected Works*, vol. 8.

_____. (1940/41/1954/1969). "Transformation Symbolism in the Mass." In *Collected Works,* vol. 11.

_____. (1944/1968). *Psychology and Alchemy.* In *Collected Works.* vol. 12.

_____. (1946/1966). "The Psychology of the Transference." In *Collected Works*, vol. 16.

_____. (1951/1968). *Aion.* In *Collected Works,* vol. 9ii.

_____. (1952/1969). *Answer to Job.* In *Collected Works,* vol. 11.

_____. (1952/1970). *Symbols of Transformation.* In *Collected Works,* vol. 5.

_____. (1953/1966). *Two Essays in Analytical Psychology.* In *Collected Works,* vol. 7.

_____. (1955-6/1970). *Mysterium Coniunctionis.* In *Collected Works*, vol. 14.

_____. (1961). *Memories, Dreams, Reflections.* Recorded and edited by Aniela Jaffe. New York: Vintage Books.

_____. (2009). *The Red Book: Liber Novus.* Edited by Sonu Shamdasani. New York: W. W. Norton & Company.

Kalff, D. (1981). *Sandplay.* Los Angeles: Sigo Press.

Kerr, J. (1993). *A Most Dangerous Method : The Story of Jung, Freud, and Sabina Spielrein.* New York: Knopf.

Klots, A. B. (1950). *The World of Butterflies and Moths.* New York: McGraw-Hill.

Kohut, H. (1971). *The Analysis of the Self.* New York: International Universities Press.

Lakoff, G., and M. Johnson. (1980). *Metaphors We Live By.* Chicago: University of Chicago Press.

Leppmann, W. (1984). *Rilke: A Life.* New York: Fromm International.

Lewis, A. (2001). "A Meeting with Jung." *The San Francisco Jung Institute Library Journal*, Vol. 20. No. 1.

Lifton, R. J. (1993). *The Protean Self.* New York: Basic Books.

McCormick, F. (1962). *Carl Gustav Jung, 1875-1961, A Memorial Meeting*. New York: The Analytical Psychology Club.

McGuire, W. (1974). *The Freud-Jung Letters.* Princeton, N.J.: Princeton University Press.

Meier, C. A. (ed.) (2001). *Atom and Archetype*: *The Pauli/Jung Letters 1932-1953*. Princeton: Princeton University Press.

Muramoto, S. (trans.). (1998). "The Jung-Hisamatsu Conversation (1958)." In *The Couch and the Tree,* edited by Anthony Molino. London: Open Gate Press.

Nietzsche, F. (1954). *Thus Spake Zarathustra*. In *The Portable Nietzsche*. New York: Viking.

_____. (1956). *The Birth of Tragedy*. New York: Doubleday.

Pauli, W. (1953/1998). "The Piano Lesson: An Active Imagination," translated by H. van Erkelens & F. W. Wiegel, in *Psychological Perspectives*, 38:1.

Portmann, A. (1964). "Metamorphosis in Animals: The Transformations of the Individual and the Type." In *Man and Transformation*, edited by J. Campbell. New York: Bollingen Foundation.

Prater, D. (1986). *A Ringing Glass: The Life of Rainer Maria Rilke*. Oxford: Clarendon Press.

Richardson, J. (1991 and 1996). *A Life of Picasso*. 2 vols. New York: Random House.

Rilke, R. M. (1982). *The Selected Poetry of Rainer Maria Rilke.* Translated by Stephen Mitchell. New York: Random House.

_____. (1992). *Duino Elegies*. Translated by David Oswald. Einsiedeln, Switzerland: Daimon Verlag.

Shorter Oxford English Dictionary. (1973 -) Oxford: Clarendon Press.

Stein, M. (1973/2020). "The Devouring Father." *Collected Writings*, Vol. 2. Asheville, NC: Chiron Publications.

_____. (1983/2020). *In MidLife*. In *Collected Writings*, vol. 2. Asheville, NC: Chiron Publications.

_____. (1978/2020). "On Psychological Interpretation." *Collected Writings*, vol. 2. Asheville: Chiron Publications.

_____. (1985). *Jung's Treatment of Christianity*. Wilmette, IL: Chiron Publications.

_____. (1987). "Jung's Green Christ," in *Jung's Challenge to Contemporary Religion*. Wilmette, IL: Chiron Publications.

_____. (2011). "Faith and the Practicing Analyst." Journal of Analytical Psychology 56:3.

The Holy Bible, Revised Standard Version. (1989). Oxford and New York: Oxford University Press.

Varnedoe, K. (1996). "Picasso's Self-Portraits." In *Picasso and Portraiture: Representation and Transformation*. Edited by William Rubin. New York: Museum of Modern Art.

Weisstub, E. (1993). "Questions to Jung on 'Answer to Job.'" *Journal of Analytical Psychology*.

White, C. (1984). *Rembrandt*. London: Thames and Hudson.

White, V. (1955). "Jung on Job." *Blackfriars* 36, pp. 52-60.

Index

CPSIA information can be obtained
at www.ICGtesting.com
Printed in the USA
BVHW080848060521
606646BV00004B/256